Eating Disorder. What springs to mind? Anorexia. A p
grow out of it. Grow. Ha.

But I was 27 years old, a FULLY FLEDGED ADULT (I
under the Mental Health Act and admitted to hospital for urgent medical stabilisation. I
had an Eating Disorder. But I wasn't a teenage girl. I had also had eating disorders for
over ten years of my life and was yet to grow out of them.

Contents

SECTION ONE: THE BENDING ERA 5
   1. MY TIPPING POINT 6
   2. DESCRIBE SOMEONE WITH AN EATING DISORDER TO ME 10
   3. THIS BOOK IS FOR YOU. AND FOR ME. 22
   4. MY EATING DISORDER HELLSCAPE 27
   5. WHY DO I HAVE AN EATING DISORDER? WHY DO YOU? WHY DOES THE MAN OVER THE STREET NOT HAVE ONE? 39

SECTION TWO: THE MENDING ERA 51
   6. ASK YOURSELF THE DIFFICULT QUESTION: THE ONE YOU DON'T WANT TO KNOW THE ANSWER TO 52
   7. THE PLAN OF ACTION: FOOD 71
   8. THE PLAN OF ACTION: COPING 76
   9. DOING IT: KNOWLEDGE IS POWER 87
   10. DOING IT: THREE MEALS AND THREE SNACKS A DAY. 90
   11. DOING IT: PROTEIN, CARBS AND FATS. 95
   12. DOING IT: NO RESTRICTION 106
   13. DOING IT: EATING IT NOT YEETING IT. 117
   14. DOING IT: FACING THE GOBLIN. REFRAMING THE THOUGHTS. 121

SECTION THREE: THE NEVER-ENDING ERA 125
   15. REFRAMING: CALORIES 127
   16. REFRAMING: I NEED TO BE SKINNY FOR OTHER PEOPLE TO CARE ABOUT ME 130
   17. REFRAMING: FOOD 135
   18. REFRAMING: SOCIAL EVENTS 146
   19. REFRAMING: COMPARISON 155
   20. REFRAMING: RESTING 162
   21. REFRAMING: MY BODY 166
   22. REFRAMING: SICK ENOUGH 173
   23. REFRAMING MY LIFE 182

24. THE (LITTLE) THINGS THAT MADE ALL THE DIFFERENCE 222

SECTION FOUR: YOUR BENDING MENDING AND NEVER-ENDING ERA 242

DISCLAIMER: **I'm just some random gal**

Eating disorders are complicated. They are serious mental illnesses which have physical manifestations. The mental illness side is dangerous. The physical risks are dangerous.

You can be at great physical risk regardless of whether you are underweight or not: the risk comes with the behaviours of the disorder and with the associated malnutrition. You can be malnourished at any weight. Your physical health can be compromised by disordered behaviours at any weight. And you are probably MORE at risk at a higher weight because people *assume* that as long as you are not visibly underweight, that means you MUST be physically fine. Not the case. I know someone who died from their eating disorder when she was slap bang in the middle of the BMI scale: to the outside world, gloriously healthy. To her malnourished body: dying quickly.

This is why I would always encourage you, wherever possible, to seek the advice of genuine medical professionals first and foremost to help you with your unique disorder, your unique body and your unique needs. Every SINGLE body is different: you have a different background to me; you will have had different behaviours to me, for different severities and different amounts of time; and you have different genetics to me. This means that your body will physically be different to mine and therefore will act differently to mine. Listening to people tell you how they healed THEIR body might not work for you. Medical professionals will be able to pick up on things that you may not be aware of yourself, and identify any underlying health conditions that may be related, or unrelated, to your eating disorder. They will be able to guide your recovery from a point of view that takes into account where you personally are in your physical and mental recovery process. Regular blood tests can be vital in picking up deficiencies and imbalances caused by the disorder that you may be unaware of. Your heart rate, blood pressure and oxygen levels are important physical observations that can need monitoring to give insight into possible risk. Working with a dietician or a nutritionist can be key in nutritional rehabilitation to make sure you are getting the right balance of everything and identifying what foods and nutrients you need to add into your diet. Medication may be helpful to manage your symptoms.

HOWEVER. Big *however.*

I recognise that this advice is simply not possible for everyone. Not everyone has the privilege of being able or ready to access medical support. There are so many barriers. Weight thresholds mean people get turned away even though they have the exact same behaviours that someone at a lower weight would get treated for (I know, ridiculous). Some countries don't have free healthcare. Some do but the waiting list is far too long and the treatment, when you get it, insufficient. Some people have *had* treatment, endless cycles of it and found that it has done nothing. Equally, not everyone is in the place, mentally, where they are able to ask for help yet or willing to stick their head out of the dark and admit to the world what's going on. I certainly wasn't ready to do this for over a decade. I was physically and mentally very unwell for about eight solid years before I even *thought* about speaking to a doctor. In the end, I sent a blank self-referral form and then didn't follow up on it for over a year.

I'm not a doctor, a nurse, a mental health professional or a dietician. My degree is in English Literature. But I'm willing to bet that you already listen to many other people on the Internet who aren't professionals anyway, and they're giving *much* more harmful advice than me (like intermittent fasting and making cheesecake out of ground up nuts instead of cheese) so I suppose there's no harm in throwing my unsolicited hat into the ring. Anyway, I do have *one* qualification that I *did* spend over ten years getting: Real Life Experience.

At the end of the day, I'm a mentally ill gal who goes out in public wearing pyjama leggings as trousers, strawberry earrings, oversized pastel clothing from the men's department, and neon yellow crocs. Should you listen to me? Probably not. But. ***I have over a decade of lived experience. I have gathered a lot of data about what works for me. Well. Mostly I've gathered data about what doesn't work for me.*** But this has formed the basis of my recovery. Anyway. Over a decade of lived experience. Lots of thoughts. So for those of you unable to access medical care right now; for those of you that *are* accessing it and still struggling; for those of you who have accessed it in the past and are still unwell; for those of you who are on waiting lists, or *thinking* about reaching out one day: I wanted to write down all my unprofessional, unsolicited opinions in the hope that it helps someone, somewhere, even just a tiny little bit.

Eating disorders are ridiculously difficult to shake loose from and I know personally that it is likely that no amount of medical care is ever going to be enough to help you kick it alone. That can be some consolation at least for those of you who cannot access treatment: it is no golden bullet, most people do not recover simply due to the medical care they receive. They have to do the hard stuff themselves, outside of treatment. **You need to work at it yourself, every single minute of every single day.** Gross, I know. But worth it. And this book is my process of doing that and hopefully even one thing in here can help you in your own gruelling daily battle against the absolute GREMLIN that is an eating disorder.

SECTION ONE: THE BENDING ERA

These pages loosely focus on my own eating disorder(s) in order to lay out the context for my recovery. I discuss my tipping point for deciding to recover; outline what it looks like to have an eating disorder; explain my reasons for writing this book; and attempt to simplify and explain the causes of my eating disorder. As someone who has been sick for well over a decade, but in denial for much of that time, I felt like this background context is vital. It sets the scene for my recovery because, without the years and years of tangled, messy pain, *I wouldn't know what I know now*. I wouldn't have learnt these lessons: tough lessons, heartbreaking lessons but *useful* lessons.

I want to be very clear, here, though - this is MY story. Yours will look different. I was not more sick than you; you were not more sick than me. **Anyone with an eating disorder is TOO SICK**. I am not telling my story to invite comparison. I am telling my story to show how I've reached the place I have in recovery and because I firmly believe that all rivers flow from the same source. Therefore, the lessons I have learnt may benefit someone else even though the roads we have walked will be varied and different.

I call this **my bending era**. It would be very easy for me to call this my breaking era. But. I do not want to think of myself as broken. I do not want you to think of yourself as broken, either. If you go there, that's a place so dark you'll get lost for years. If you think that there's something fundamentally wrong with you and that you are "just broken", you absolve yourself of the need to try. You absolve yourself of the duty to fight. **If you are broken, it's not your fault that you aren't getting better.** How could the world expect anything from a broken thing? The most important thing I have learnt is that if you lay down and accept that you are broken, it's over. If you give the eating disorder that kind of fuel, it will set it ablaze and dance on your broken body. *Believing yourself to be broken, helpless, hopeless is dangerous: those are the very things the eating disorder needs you to believe in order to keep you there forever.*

So, although it looked otherwise for many years, I did not break. I bent. A willow in the rough storms of a mental illness I was not prepared for but still managed to weather. A messy tangle of bent and weeping branches. But not broken. Ready to stand up and fight one day. Ready to slowly unbend, unfurl, and grow again. Ready to begin the mending of the bending.

This section is important because it details my descent into madness. It describes my rock bottom. **And then it pulls together the process I followed when I started to rise back up. It shows the thoughts that I had, in all their mangled, disorganised glory, as I began to feel my way back towards the light. As I began to open the curtains in my brain and let the sanity seep back in, slowly, slowly, slowly but *surely*.** You don't have to follow the same processes as me but I do think it can be useful to see it set out on paper. Because I did the one thing that, in all the years of sickness, I had stubbornly refused to do before: <u>**I actually sat down and tried to work through my thoughts and feelings.**</u> I know. Revolutionary. But I bet there's a good chance you haven't done this either, and reading my experience might help you begin your own self-reflection. Look at your own bending. Then join me in the mending.

1. MY TIPPING POINT

<u>I ***do not recommend*** getting so unwell that you have to spend a month of your adult life locked up in a hospital.</u> I'm not being dramatic. I *was* locked up. Nothing, and I mean NOTHING (not even a decade long battle with my ED; a childhood full of addiction, divorce and attachment issues; my father's death; my traumatic relationships; SA; my battle with SH; depression; BDD) challenged my mental health and made me want to leave this planet more than those days in that hospital.

Those endless days. Those dragging days. 24 hours in the same room. Over. And over. Screaming patients. No sleep. Constant beeping. A window looking out into a world I was forbidden from. A window that wouldn't open. Stagnant, heavy air. Nurses coming in and touching my body like it was nothing. Never checking for consent. Medical staff with no knowledge of eating disorders. Triggering comments constantly. Poking and prodding. Blood tests bruising my arms. Daily. ECGs. Breasts out in front of strangers. Constant 1:1 supervision. Watched. Never alone. Overstimulation. Groundhog day. Over. And over. Nobody telling me when I would be able to leave. Psychiatrists coming and giving me half truths. Whole days where I waited to be seen to discuss my care and discharge but nobody came. Showering at the speed of light because the door was always open. Feeling dirty. Always. Elderly dementia patients bursting into my room. Other patients whispering about me. Nurses on the night shift stealing my food from the fridge. Being asked about my bowel movements. Friends and family coming in. Staying for a couple of hours. But then leaving. Walking out. Feeling the air on their skin. Me, watching them from the window. A window that wouldn't open. Friends posting pictures on Facebook of the parties I was missing. Me, doing crosswords. Reading books. Wanting to scream. Being treated like a child by people barely older than me.

I **_do not recommend_** getting so unwell that you have to spend a month of your adult life locked up in a hospital. BUT. It changed my life forever. It changed everything. Because being sectioned and DETAINED in a hospital really makes you think: HOW DID THIS HAPPEN? HOW DID I END UP *HERE*? *How did that little girl with all those big plans end up HERE?* There's this trend that circulates sometimes on social media with an inspirational tagline along the lines of: "if your younger self could see you now, they'd be so proud". It was like the opposite of that, I remember thinking. If my younger self had seen me there, in the hospital, weak, malnourished, crying over her body, not allowed to work, not allowed to *walk around*, she would have refused to believe it was her. It wasn't her.

I had never in my life confronted HOW ILL I actually was. I had not often THOUGHT about my illness as an illness. I had not faced up to it. It had always just been a part of my life, it had always just been my "normal". I don't think I wanted to think about it. If I had thought about it, I may have had to do something about it. And I wasn't ready.

Hospital did two important things for me.

1. **It made me realise the final destination of an eating disorder would only ever be death.**

I had been ill, properly, for about ten years. But I had struggled with eating and body image since I was ten years old so, all in all, by the time I sat in that hospital bed: seventeen years. **Seventeen years of a life spent destroying my body slowly but surely**.

Until I asked myself, in the hospital bed, what my end goal was. What was the *point*? What was I *aiming* for? To be thin enough? Thin enough for *what*? Because by the time I was hospitalised, I was THIN. Thin enough to be diagnosed with severe anorexia. Was that the end goal? Because it didn't feel like it. It didn't feel like I had won. *I felt like I could be thinner.* My personal weight loss goal had been attained many pounds heavier. And it wasn't enough. So I had gone below my goal weight. It was never enough. I reached the goal weight. I went lower than the goal weight. **And the promised happiness didn't come. In fact, any happiness I had left had receded so far I didn't see myself ever feeling joy again.**

And that's when I realised. I would never be thin enough. The end goal didn't exist. My eating disorder would drive me to continue to try to get thinner and thinner, endlessly, until my body could survive it no longer. And I would die. It sounds dramatic, right? But think about it logically just for one second. If you never feel thin enough, you will never stop trying to lose weight. You will never stop putting strain on your body, and engaging in behaviours that make you malnourished and cause your organs to begin to fail. It doesn't matter if you never become "underweight" by the silly BMI scale. The more you starve yourself, the more you overexercise, the more you purge or use laxatives…the weaker and closer to death your body becomes. **A leading cause of death in eating disorders is heart failure: this can, and does, happen at any weight, due to the strain sufferers place on their body.**

The end goal may not be *death* but that's the end destination either way.

2. **It gave me all the time in the world to think.**

I had never in my life done very much deep thinking. Like many of us, I am sure, I avoided it like the plague. **Look inside? At the sludge? Try and do difficult mental work? Think about my trauma? Think about my feelings? NO THANK YOU.**

Anyway, I was TOO BUSY. Adult life is busy. Work, bills, hobbies, social life, family, existential stress, researching mortgages, trying to decide if you want kids, MOTs, booking your own dentist appointments, cleaning…the eating disorder had just become part of my life, all entangled in everything that I was rushing around and doing. I was constantly on the go. I didn't have *time* to sit down and unpick what I was doing with food and my body.

Or, maybe, I didn't want to. Because I could have found the time. Especially when COVID hit and we were suddenly locked in our houses. But I had puzzles to do then. I was still working. We were all on ZOOM quizzes every night.

You can only hide from your thoughts for so long in a hospital though.

The hospital took everything away from me. Work, friends, hobbies. I had endless hours. At first, I obviously tried to distract myself still. Crosswords. Reading. I watched whole series of old Married at First Sight, supersetting episodes until my eyes felt square. I racked up an insane amount of screen time. I spent whole days on Reddit.

And then. I ran out of things to do. My brain became TOO BORED. And I finally had to do it. I finally had to sit and face myself. Who I had become. What I had done. I finally had to actually sit down and think about my disorder. To sit with myself for hours a day and unpick the past to try and understand *how* things had gone so wrong, to try and understand *how* I had ended up here so that I could make sure it NEVER. HAPPENED. AGAIN.

Now, listen.

You do not need to be locked up in a hospital yourself to have the above two epiphanies because I have had them for you.

1. **The end point of an eating disorder is death. So you need to recover, basically.**
2. **To recover, you need to sit down with yourself, face yourself and THINK. Think for hours. Think for days. Think until your brain hurts.**

I do not want anyone else to waste as much time as me. I do not want anyone else to have to go through what I went through in that hospital. So. I'm going to walk you through my recovery in the hopes that you can choose to walk with me. I am writing this book in the hope that reading it can be your tipping point: **the moment where you realise that the only real choice left to any of us is to recover or die.** And the moment where you see that recovery *can* be done. It just takes work. So. Much. Work.

This book is going to be a wild ride. It's going to have a bit of everything. Me facing myself. Me asking myself the big, nasty questions. Me exposing myself. Me asking *you* to face yourself. Me asking *you* to ask yourself the big, nasty questions. Me asking you to expose yourself. HA. No, I can't write that. Can I? That sounds creepy. I don't want you to expose yourself to me. Just to yourself.

This book is going to be a cesspit of unprofessional, unsolicited advice and opinions. It's going to be everything that I have learnt over the decade (or more) of my illness. **It's going to be everything that I knew, deep down, all along, but chose to ignore.** I am choosing to explore my mess out here in the open because I cannot bear the idea of other people making my mistakes. I cannot bear the idea of other people waking up in their late 20s, or 30s, or 40s, and realising, as I did, that they wasted all that time, all that life, for NOTHING. My biggest mistake was refusing to do the work that I needed to do because I was scared. If me sharing my story can do *anything at all,* I hope that it shows you a) how to start doing the work and b) that it will be worth it.

I wasted ten whole years of my life. Nothing changed. Nothing got better. This proves that eating disorders do not, and cannot, make your life better. They do not, and cannot, make you happy. If I can prevent even one person from walking with their ED for as long as I walked with mine, I will feel like those ten years were not a waste.

2. DESCRIBE SOMEONE WITH AN EATING DISORDER TO ME

What would you say if a researcher on the street said to you, "**describe someone with an eating disorder to me?**" I mean, apart from the FIRST really important question of "**why are you asking me that?**". It's hypothetical okay. Because, in reality, if someone DID ask you that, you really should question **why** in order to ascertain whether you think whatever research they were doing is likely to be harmful research rather than useful research. There is already too much stigma and misinformation about eating disorders floating around in the world without more researchers sticking their insensitive, ill-informed oars in.

ANYWAY. I imagine if you are reading this book, you *might* know that this is an impossible question. Impossible because **we are all different.** There *is* no 'someone with an eating disorder'. If someone said "*describe a human being to me*" you would struggle to be very specific, right? Because who are you describing? Male, transgender, female, non-binary, pangender? Tall, short? What is the colour of their skin? Where were they born? Do they have big feet? What clothes do they wear? What colour are their eyes? What colour is their hair? Curly hair or straight or frizzy? Do they have freckles? Do they use a wheelchair? Do they like to eat lemon drizzle cake?

It's the exact same concept. **Because 'someone with an eating disorder' is just another human being.** *Male*, tall, born in South Africa but raised in Birmingham, brown skinned, blue eyes. Bald. Jeans and jumpers. Sometimes a nice pink shirt, for dates. No freckles, apart from in the summer. Prosthetic left leg so only one size 11 foot. Loves lemon drizzle. *Non-binary*, not sure if they are tall or short, really, olive skinned, born in London, raised in Sheffield, living in Japan, really small feet - bonus as they can buy children's shoes. Dungarees and leggings and oversized hoodies, but also sometimes skirts and crop tops. Green eyes, dyed hair - lilac at the moment - freckles. Ambivalent to lemon drizzle. *Female*, short for her age. White as snow. Born in the Welsh valleys, still there. Small feet but still growing. Shorts. Always. Even to school. Even when the boys tease her. Brown eyes, blonde hair, no freckles. Straight hair but it's a wig. Alopecia. Lemon drizzle? No way. Chocolate.

All of the above could be 'someone with an eating disorder'. **You probably walked past 'someone with an eating disorder' on your way to work this morning.** You probably cut 'someone with an eating disorder' up on a roundabout last week. You'll probably get in the way of 'someone with an eating disorder' at the supermarket on your next weekly shop.

You can't describe us unless you describe us all.

But for those who haven't been here, for those who do not **understand**, I can tell you what they might say. Because over the years I have heard the same murmurings over and over again, seen the same myths plastered and perpetuated all over social media, seen the same images and stereotypes and tropes over and over again. Over the years I have seen the single supposed image of 'someone with an eating disorder' and been *viscerally aware that this is not an image that I matched.*

<u>I felt myself to be entirely alone, encompassing a space that I shouldn't exist in.</u> I am sure that many of us feel this way. Those of us that are *older*. Those of us that are in *the wrong kind of body.* Those of us that are the *wrong gender.* Those of us that have *the wrong disorder.* Those of us that are *undiagnosed*.

But also, I have a confession. **I felt alone, and like I shouldn't exist in the eating disorder space of the world because, I, also, deep down, had the stereotype living in my head.** Well. Maybe not even deep down at all. If someone had asked me to describe someone with an eating disorder, despite ALL of my LIVED EXPERIENCE, despite BEING SOMEONE WITH AN EATING DISORDER, the first thing that springs to my mind would be some young, boney girl, white as a ghost, maybe wearing a ballet leotard. We all have a stereotyped image in our heads. The FIRST thing that my silly, stereotyped little brain conjures up is your cookie cutter anorexic. **And this is DAMAGING because it means that so many of us spend so much longer than we could being unwell and suffering in silence a) because we feel we cannot seek help until we fit the bill and b) because we gaslight ourselves into thinking we can't have a *real* eating disorder because we do not fill the bill.**

Why? Because society only represents one version of an eating disorder. Society only talks about one version of an eating disorder.

So. Let's do it.

> Someone with an eating disorder is anorexic. They hate food. They are scared of food. They never eat. They drift around, looking pale and bony and sick. They never laugh or smile or join in with life. They definitely don't eat birthday cakes. Maybe they smoke as an appetite suppressant. They look cool, though. They

dress in oversized hoodies and leggings and big boots and they're probably wearing eyeliner. Oh, and they're a teenage girl.

She had to take some time off school to go to hospital because she was so skinny. Her parents, delightful middle-class John and Jane, have no idea why their daughter has chosen to starve herself. "Honey, can't you just eat?" they beg her as she weeps silently into her pasta. Or her bread. Or her rice. It's always the carbs that she cries into. She just wants to eat her steamed broccoli. She just wants to suck on her ice cubes. She'll weigh herself once she's finished eating her five pieces of pasta to check what her weight is. Then she will look in the mirror to check her thigh gap. She'll stroke her protruding bones.

It's okay though because she's sixteen at the moment. It's just a body image thing – it's tricky being a teenage girl with all the hormonal changes and pressure of exams. Soon, she will snap out of it. She will put on a few pounds and she will be fixed and recovered in a lovely slim body. Life will move on again. Her teenage girl disease will be forgotten about, only whispered about by her parents' acquaintances at church. *"She looks so much better now,"* they'll say. *"Now she's finished with that silly business of starving herself. All the girls are doing it I hear!"*

Let me offer you an alternative someone.

She is ten years old. She isn't anorexic. Not at all. She loves food. She isn't particularly skinny or particularly large. She likes to eat a lot though. Her mum is a very good cook - when Mum is having a good day, she makes spaghetti bolognese and roast dinners and meatballs and pasta.

Sometimes the girl takes food from the cupboards when her mum isn't looking. Biscuits and chocolates. Her brother does it too. They sneak down like little mice and eat the chocolate because they're only allowed it once a week and that's boring. She thinks this is normal, to sneak down and eat chocolate. It must be because her brother does it too.

But also sometimes she REALLY wants to eat MORE. And weird things. It doesn't really matter WHAT. She just wants FOOD. Like spoonfuls of coleslaw straight out of the tub. Or bits of cheese. Or pork pies. Or dry pieces of bread. It's like she JUST HAS TO eat it immediately. Right there. Right then. Normally it happens when things are bad in the house. Things at home aren't great most days to be fair. There's lots of shouting and screaming and stuff but she thinks that's quite normal. It's hard to adjust to a new baby. But that's when she gets the

SUDDEN URGE TO EAT FOOD. Any food. All food. When the baby has been crying a lot and things are tense. The food is yummy and distracting from the tension. When she's eating it, it's like, for a moment, she's not there. She's not there in the house. She's not there in the stress pit. She's just at peace.

She is sitting on the stairs with her Christmas Advent Calendar. She has eaten the whole thing. All 25 chocolates. Normal, right? Except it's the 2nd of December. And the evening. It's not morning, either, so why was she even opening the calendar? Because she's a ten year old child! And children love chocolate. But also, something just DROVE her to do it. She didn't even think about it. She just sort of…zombie walked over to it and before she knew it she was opening the doors, scraping aside the tin foil, shoving the sweet chocolates in, one by one, and swallowing the big goopy mess. She didn't even really check them to see what shape they were. Snowman, Santa, Robin? Who knows. They were all in her mouth before she had time to process it.

But now she's going to have to pretend that she hasn't eaten it all or her parents will be cross. Her step dad says that sugar is addictive and poisonous. He bought her mum a gym membership for her birthday. Her mum agrees about the sugar. She said, "Darling, you need to stop choosing a Yorkie bar for your weekly Friday chocolate bar or you might get fat. Maybe choose a smaller one, like a Dairy Milk?"

A boy at school said that to her once, too. He said there was too much ham in her sandwich. He said, "My mum said if you eat too much, you get fat. You don't want to get fat." She didn't really know what to say to that, so she just put the rest of her sandwich back in her lunchbox. Then her mum shouted at her for not finishing her lunch. She remembered thinking: **it's so hard to know what you're meant to do with food.**

The next morning, after the Great Advent Eating, her stomach is sticking out a bit, she thinks. She prods it as she pulls at the waistband of her school skirt. Is the skirt tighter? Has she got fat now? Being fat is bad. She goes downstairs to get breakfast and picks up the loaf of bread. She turns it over and reads the label on the back.

Calories. What are those?

She reaches up into the cupboard and takes a little white box from the top shelf. It has a pink label on it. She's a tall child. A "big girl". She's taller than her mother *already. So she can reach the top shelf. The white box says "ADIOS. Maximum Strength. Can help speed up weight loss naturally". She takes some. That'll solve the advent calendar problem.*

How about another alternative someone?

*She IS a teenage girl. She hasn't taken any time off school to go to the hospital, though. She's not anorexic. Definitely not, that would be incredibly impossible. Because she's NOT skinny. Quite the opposite, in fact. She's not the fattest girl in her year but she is the **second** fattest. She knows this because the boys have told her, many times. She's the fifth fattest in the whole school. She worked this out herself.*

Her mum, a single mother, twice divorced, is currently on A BRANDED DIET PLAN and so she thought it would be a nice thing for them to do together, as a family, you know? But not Brother and Sister. Brother and Sister don't need A BRANDED DIET PLAN. Brother and Sister can eat what they like. This is not an eating disorder, of course. It is a diet. Those things are different. Diets are good for you. She needs to lose weight, she knows she does. She hates the expanse of her body. The folds of pale, rolling fat. Getting changed for PE is hell. All the other girls are so small and toned and smooth. They don't have rolls. They run around the field without breaking a sweat whilst she lumbers along, clammy and panting. So she does try to stick to the diet.

But the salad she has for lunch just isn't enough. She's so hungry that she eats it during break time every day and then by lunchtime she's ravenous. So she goes to the canteen with her friends and buys another lunch. Pasta from the salad bar. Jacket potato and beans. Cheese salad rolls. And she gets a cookie with it too, because it comes as part of the deal. The cookie is only £1! And everyone else has the £1 cookies too. And BRANDED DIET PLAN chocolate muffins taste like sadness.

She doesn't know why she does it, but when she gets off the school bus, she goes into Tesco and she buys a multipack of chocolate bars. Every day. Some days, it's Mars bars. Some days, it's Double Deckers. Dairy Milk bars. Snickers. KitKat Chunky. Crunchies. It's only a ten minute walk home but she eats them all by the time she arrives, one bite after the other, shoving them in so quickly she can barely taste them at all. But it makes the walk more enjoyable. She finds walking boring, but eating? That's not boring. That makes her feel happiness, for a brief ten minutes at least. It fills something in her. And then she gets in, sits down at the table and eats a full meal with her family even though she's not even slightly hungry.

She just doesn't have self control. That's how she got so fat, right? You don't get to being the second fattest girl in the year by having self-control. But it doesn't seem fair. She sees the other girls, the skinny ones, eating chocolate bars and THEY don't swell up into big white whales. Plus, she's five foot eleven at this point, towering over most of the boys, even, and the other girls are all small and dainty and pretty. People call her Hagrid, sometimes, because she's got the hair to match the stature.

For a few moments, the chocolate bars distract her from the way she hates herself. From the fact that she's walking home to a house where there will, no doubt, be screaming and shouting and door slamming. From the world. She's free for ten minutes as she chomps chocolate and walks slowly down the road.

As time goes on, it does get worse though. The control isn't there. She finds herself eating two multipacks. Sometimes a whole tube of Pringles, too. She doesn't have much money of her own so sometimes she steals it out of blazer pockets in the changing rooms or purses that people have left in their bags during PE. She just NEEDS to. She just needs the food. She never really intends for any of it to happen until the moment it does: the stealing or the eating. It's like it just…happens. Something takes over her, like she's possessed, and she can't actually stop herself. She tries not to think about what she's actually doing too much. If she doesn't think about it, she won't feel the shame. The shame of stealing money. The shame of spending it on food that she doesn't need. Food that is just making her fatter and fatter, and more and more out of control. The shame of this person that she's become. A thief. A greedy, fat thief.

The worst is at Easter. Her siblings and her always get loads and loads and loads of eggs and, to save space, her mum gives them each a tupperware box. They smash up their eggs into the box and that's their chocolate for the next few weeks. But because the eggs are smashed, you can't tell exactly how much is in them, really. So she steals her siblings' chocolate. How bad is that? Stealing chocolate from her brother and sister. But she can't stop herself. She just keeps finding herself there, standing in the pantry, eating the chocolate from their boxes, shaking it around to make it look like it's not going down.

Sometimes, when there's nothing nice in the pantry, she eats weird things. Dry crackers. Raisins. Cold baked beans out of the tin.

She doesn't have an eating disorder though, she knows that so it's not like she can ask anyone for help. What would she even say? Sometimes I eat too much. People would say yeah, we can tell. They would say yeah, join the club. They would say, try OTHER BRANDED DIET PLAN if BRANDED DIET PLAN didn't work. Or slimming pills. Or exercise. Try going for a run. Take better care of yourself. Stop eating so many treats and eat some fruits and vegetables.

There's a girl at school that **does** *have an eating disorder. A pale, skinny ghost who never eats. She already went to the hospital once. Her mum comes in at lunchtime to sit with her and make sure she eats. She would never eat eight Mars bars on the walk home! She's the one with the eating disorder. She doesn't love food. She's the one that needs help! It doesn't make any sense, why anyone would starve themselves when food is just TOO GOOD to stay away from.*

What about another someone?

She is 22 years old. She is a primary school teacher. And she's very good at her job. She's a success story, really. The kids love her, the parents love her, and she's just been made Head of Maths at her school even though she's only just in her second year of teaching – a role that comes with a pay rise. She lives in a cute little flat by herself, has a loving family who she visits every Sunday for a roast dinner, and she plays netball a few times a week. She does yoga and she lifts weights, too. On the weekends, she goes out drinking with friends, or goes to pub quizzes, or sometimes they go on hikes. Sometimes she goes on dates.

Her life looks pretty wholesome. The kind of life that you would watch a vlogging channel about on YouTube. It looks balanced and healthy and happy.

When she finished university, she used to weigh XXX pounds. Now she weighs XXX pounds. She lost XXX pounds in the space of six months. She did Couch to 5K and started off on a little diet. It was sensible at first. People congratulated her. They told her how good she looked and how healthy she was now. They were impressed by her transformation. Told her they were thrilled for her, for taking control of her health and wellbeing. They asked her for tips. "Oh you know," she would say. "Just healthy eating and exercise. I was really unhealthy at university with all the binge drinking and noodles. I guess I've just found the balance now. You know - 80:20!"

Eventually, people did start to tell her she should probably stop now. That she'd lost enough. But it took a while. At first, her shrinking was a good thing. At first, they were impressed that she was becoming less of the thing they thought was dreadful: being fat. "You're slim and healthy now," they would say. "Go on, have a piece of cake. I can't afford to have one - " they would pat their stomach - "but you can!"

She started eating more, eventually. Because it had reached the point where she was starting to feel faint and where she would be driving down the road and nearly pass out. She was too hungry to focus at work and was snappy with the kids, which wasn't good. She was starting to get slower at netball, which she didn't like, and couldn't lift properly at the gym. She lost her period, too, which was weird.

So now she eats three meals a day, and they're healthy. Porridge and fruit for breakfast; roasted vegetable pasta salad or couscous for lunch; salmon and veggies, or curry, or stir fry for dinner. She snacks on fruit, peppers, pickles and cucumbers. She goes to the gym 4-5 days a week, and she still plays netball and does yoga whenever she can fit it in. She's HEALTHY again. She's found the balance.

But. Every so often, she finds herself in the kitchen, eating. But. It's not really eating. Because she chews it up, the food, and then she spits it out into the bin. She's aware that this is NOT a normal thing to do. But. She's not actually hungry, right? She just wants to TASTE the bread and the chocolate and the sweets. So this is how she can do that. There's no point EATING them because she's NOT HUNGRY so why would she waste calories eating food she doesn't need in her body? Anyway, it's harmless. A little odd, for sure, but harmless.

Another one?

She is 25 years old. She is a Master's student, studying a conversion degree in psychology. Alongside this, she works as a support worker for adults with learning disabilities and she's very good at it. Next year, she is going to apply to do a PhD. Everyone always says how clever she is. She's not convinced, though. It's all a lot of luck and hard work that has got her to where she is now. She's nothing special.

People comment often on her body and how they wish that they could eat as much as she does. "You wouldn't understand," they say, almost fondly, almost like she's stupid. "You're naturally skinny. A beanpole. Your metabolism is so high you could probably eat anything whereas I just have to look at food and I gain weight." She does have a nice body. She's a size 10 and tall, so looks on the slimmer side of this, and has long legs and an hourglass figure. She looks incredibly healthy, actually. Toned, but not too toned. Slim, but not too slim. The kind of person who is just effortlessly healthy. The kind of person people wish that they were like.

Appearances can be deceptive.

She does eat a lot. In front of people. She can eat a whole packet of biscuits in one go. When they go out to restaurants, she eats a starter and a main and a dessert and finishes off other people's food. For lunch, she brings huge tupperware boxes of pasta or stir fry or couscous. She's vegan, though, so OBVIOUSLY she needs to eat more to stay full. Everyone knows that. And, as others say, she's got a high metabolism, right? That's what she says, when people comment on how much she can eat and still stay slim.

What people don't know, though, is that she doesn't keep the food inside. Any of it. The packet of biscuits, the three course meals, the giant lunches. She eats that much because she has no intention of digesting it. If anyone watched her closely, they would notice that she always goes to the toilet about ten minutes after eating. Always. Without fail. She drinks a lot of water and diet cola and tea and energy drinks, so people just think she's got an overactive bladder - which she does to be fair. It's a good excuse. It's a good reason to slip off to the toilet without raising suspicion.

She throws up the food easily. She's had lots of practice. Years of practice. Years of vomiting every day. She doesn't need to use her fingers. She just bends over the toilet and it all comes out. Easy. Job done. She gets to eat what she wants and stay slim. Sometimes, she wishes that she didn't throw up easily, though. She knows that for lots of people, making themselves sick is hard. She thinks if that were the case with her, maybe she wouldn't be in so deep. Maybe she wouldn't be losing more and more of herself every day.

On weekends, it's not just normal meals that she throws up. Oh no. She goes out to buy whole feasts. Multipacks of chocolate bars, sharer bags of crisps, whole loaves of bread to make into sandwiches, packets of biscuits, pork pies, sausage rolls, pizza, pasta bake, garlic bread, flapjacks, whole cakes, croissants, crumpets, bacon, eggs, sausages, mashed potatoes. Anything, really. Any food.

The vegan thing takes a break when the bingeing and purging takes over. She spends £50 each time, around about. Goes home. Over the course of a few hours, eats it all. Stops in between to throw up as she gets too full. Empties out. Eats more.

Some days she will go to the shops more than once. Some days she will order food. Around £100 of takeaway. Fish and chips, or pizza, or pasta. If it's early enough in the day, breakfast cafe food or sausage rolls and cakes and pastries from bakeries. Enough food for several people. "Hungry?" the delivery men often joke. They think it's funny because she's a slim young woman answering the door to five large pizzas, three garlic breads, three calzones, onion rings, garlic mushrooms, fries and wings. They think there's no way it's for her. "All for me," she says and they laugh. She gets a sick kick out of the joke that's not a joke. Some days she orders more than one takeaway so she does one from BRANDED DELIVERY SITE and one from other BRANDED DELIVERY SITE so nobody gets suspicious.

She knows she has an eating disorder. She's not silly. She knows it's not normal to eat ridiculous amounts of food and vomit it back up. Jesus, of course she knows.

She also knows that nobody would think she has an eating disorder, because she's not sickly skinny and she eats a lot in front of people and because she's an adult, and too sensible and successful for that. She looks healthy - people tell her all the time. Fit and strong and slim. She also knows that she can never tell anyone about her eating disorder. She knows the name of it, of course. She's bulimic. Go figure that she would get the disgusting eating disorder. She sometimes imagines telling people. Seeing the disgust on their face. The confusion. How could anyone do that? Eat that much food, vomit it back up? Every single day? For years?

The worst part of it is that it hasn't even made her skinny. She's stayed the same weight, kind of, for the past five years. She gains and loses the same ten pounds. Up and down. Up and down. It's not fair. She's wasting all the money, wasting all that time, for nothing.

But she can't stop. She's tried. Obviously. Over and over again. But nothing works. She always finds herself in the supermarket or on BRANDED DELIVERY SITE, a compulsion stronger than she has the willpower to ignore. At this point, she's kind of given up. It's just a part of her day. It's just something she does.

Like a deranged hobby. Something to do. Knitting or glass blowing or bulimia, you know?

If I asked you to describe someone with an eating disorder, which one would you have been closest too? Probably none of them. Because they're all so different. Like each individual. Like each eating disorder. **But the average joe on the street? They would have described the first girl. They may have gotten close to the others eventually, but not FIRST.** The first thing that usually springs to mind, <u>*including my mind,*</u> is that teenage girl with anorexia.

When, in reality, she's not that common.

Anorexia? Only around 10% of people diagnosed with an eating disorder are diagnosed with anorexia. That means the other 90% are diagnosed with something else.

Less than 6% of people with eating disorders are underweight. **That's probably not even an accurate statistic, either, because there are so many people living with eating disorders who have never, and may never, tell anyone.** So they're not included in those numbers. I wasn't underweight for many years and nobody knew I had an eating disorder, so I wasn't in that 'less than 6%' statistic. But I definitely DID have an eating disorder.

Oh and those girls above? You might have guessed it. Not including Girl Number One, who is so obviously fictional in her caricature? **They're all the same girl. They're all me.** Confusing, right? Because they seem to describe different disorders. And they seem to describe a different person from the 27 year old in the hospital bed.

But.

An eating disorder is not just a nice, small, contained package. It's not just a single little diagnosis and behaviour (anorexia, starving yourself to be skinny). It's not just a case of you get it when you're a teenager, have a bit of treatment, and then go on to live your life as a healthy, paleo-eating, yoga-going woman with a BMI that's on the lower side of healthy.

It's enduring. It evolves. Behaviour after behaviour. Year after year. Denial. Starvation. Bingeing. Purging. Anorexic? Body dysmorphia. Ankle weights. Atypical? Hyperfocus on food. Yoga. Too much food. Bulimic? Run. Too little food. Puke. Weight lift. Binge Eating Disorder? Go vegan. Yoga. Whole foods only. Pilates. Not Otherwise Specified?

NO OIL. Otherwise specified? Train your core. Eat a whole loaf of bread with butter. YouTube workout videos. Fucked in the head? Throw up Christmas dinner.

A child. Into a teenager. Into an adult. Into a lifetime?

Nobody ever knowing. Hiding in the dark. Just a fat kid. She eats too much. Puppy fat. It'll go away. Just a fat teenager. She eats too much, she's lazy, she spends too much time sitting down and studying. Just a slim 22 year old. Pretty normal. Went away to uni, lost loads of weight, doesn't she look great? She's so healthy. She did it through healthy eating and running. She stopped eating all that junk. How inspiring. Her bones are sticking out a bit now though so she should stop. Just a slim 25 year old. Gained a few pounds back, looks healthier now. She can eat whatever she wants. She's naturally slim. Naturally athletic. She's so healthy.

What disorder am I diagnosed with? What disorders have I been diagnosed with in the past?

Binge eating disorder? Bulimia? Anorexia? Atypical Anorexia? OSFED? EDNOS?

Does it matter?

I have, and have had, eating disorders for most of my life. My behaviours have changed and evolved and crossed over, gone back on themselves, repeated, looped around, got better, got worse, been added to, sometimes even faded away for a few blessed moments of silence. **But they've always been there.** Underlying. **They've always been there, ignoring the tick sheets that would try and place me in boxes, entangling themselves into one thing that I refuse to define with an NHS label.**

Yes, I do have a diagnosis. And yes, in the past, I have had other diagnoses. I have been diagnosed with five different eating disorders and this is why I think the labels are ridiculous. <u>**So I say what I have: I have an Eating Disorder. Which one? An Eating Disorder.**</u> I will not give it a name other than that because it does not need one. They all come out the same in the wash.

Anyway, this has turned into a very long answer to a supposedly simple question: describe someone with an eating disorder. It's not a simple question, though, is it? We all know that.

The NHS website, for all the over-complication of the actual diagnosis system, actually puts it quite well:

> *An eating disorder is a mental health condition where you use the control of food to cope.*

Does that not prove my point? That description could be about any of the people I have described above. If we focussed more on talking about EATING DISORDERS in the media rather than ANOREXIA, we may not be where we are now. With you reading my book. **Which I wrote. Because I'm an adult. With an Eating Disorder.** Not a pale teenage girl with anorexia.

3. THIS BOOK IS FOR YOU. AND FOR ME.

So this is why I am here now, writing this book. There are many books and films out there about eating disorders. Most of them, as you can imagine, are disappointingly stereotypical. You probably don't *need* to imagine it - I am sure you have probably read or seen some of them and know exactly which I am referring to. **If there's one thing about those of us with eating disorders, it's that we don't know what content we should be staying away from.** Or, rather, we *do* know but *who would want to resist the urge to be delightfully triggered*? That Eating Disorder needs fuel to burn! Books and novels? Perfect.

Anyway, the eating disorder depicted? Anorexia. The sufferer? A young female who was always thin and just became even thinner. I have read the books. Watched the films. I think they are always meant to be inspiring tales of hope but I never found inspiration or hope in them because I never saw myself in those depictions. **They did nothing for me other than make me feel invalid, and odd, and out of place, and like none of the healing shown was possible for me because my sickness was so far removed from the fictional representations.**

It is hard to believe that you can heal when the only people you have seen heal (in books, films and online) are people who have been sick for a lot less time than you; people who are much younger than you; people that have been sick in a very different way to you; people who have not been enmeshed in a hundred different, complex behaviours; and people who seem to recover almost overnight after a sudden revelation that they want to be strong not skinny.

So I am writing this book to you. Whoever you are. Whatever "someone with an eating disorder" you are. And I am writing it to myself. All those past versions of me. I am writing it to us all. I am writing to tell you: you *can* heal from an eating disorder even if you're not a teenage girl and even if you're not anorexic. You *can* heal if you are both of those things, too. You *can* heal even if it doesn't happen overnight. You *can* heal even if it's been years of entangled, enmeshed and deeply rooted behaviours. You can. I can. We can.

I want to tell you: you are not alone. If you do not fit that stereotype, you are not alone. If you are an adult. If you are a male. If you are undiagnosed. If you are diagnosed with the wrong thing. If you are bulimic, or anorexic, or have EDNOS or ARFID or OSFED or orthorexia or BED or whatever new label they come up with to slap on you and fit you in a box. If you know, deep down, that none of those labels fit you and you would prefer, like me, to just say 'Eating Disorder'. If you don't *have* an eating disorder yet. If you feel like you are at risk of developing one. If you feel like you have a bad relationship with food and your body.

You are not alone.

In fact, there's SWARMS of us. Hundreds of thousands of us. Suffering in silence and shame because our illness does not fit the popular media image. Because we don't meet certain criteria in a medical manual. Because we don't look the way we "should" if we have an eating disorder. **There's no "shock factor" to a middle aged woman walking around in a size 12 body; there's no sick fascination when looking at a man in his twenties who wears size medium; there's always something else stereotypical to assume about a morbidly obese person.** The media don't portray a wide range of people with eating disorders because the media only care about what they can sell. And that stuff doesn't sell. <u>**Real suffering, unsensationalised, doesn't sell.**</u> Suffering only sells if there's a shocking bag of bones to go with it and capture attention. Suffering only sells if it's marketable: young and skinny people are marketable.

So there is a whole generation of adults, and teenagers, and children, who do not fit the prototype, lost and silent and hurting.

Suffering in silence and shame because our behaviours are not talked about enough so we feel like we cannot talk about them. We feel like we shouldn't talk about them. We feel like nobody else in the world is acting in the utterly deranged way that we are. Because our behaviours are stigmatised and seen as unacceptable whereas, in a diet obsessed society, anorexia and self-starvation is just quite normal. People wouldn't act horrified if you told them you stopped eating; if you told them you were eating and yeeting, though, that's a different story.

A whole generation of people in larger bodies, feeling unable to say I HAVE AN EATING DISORDER because we know what people will say. Even if they don't say it to your face. You'll see it behind their eyes. *You don't have an eating disorder. You're not thin. Fat people can't have anorexia. You clearly don't have a problem with eating. Eating too much, maybe!* A whole generation of people WHO DO HAVE ANOREXIA but because they do not exist in underweight bodies, they *know* nobody will believe them. They *know* if they say they don't eat, people will think it's just a diet. It CAN'T be an eating disorder, right, because they're not underweight!

A whole generation of men, feeling unable to say a word because they know what people will say. *What is he, a woman? Does he want to be skinny like a girl? Men don't have eating disorders. Boys don't cry. He should go to the gym and lift weights.*

A whole generation of adults, suffering in silence and shame because we think we are alone, the only ones, freaks, weirdos - how can you be a GROWN UP and not able to eat properly? How can you be a GROWN UP and spend all this time obsessing over food and movement and your body? How can you be a GROWN UP and throw up your food? Grown ups don't do stuff like that. That's teenage girl stuff. That's anorexic stuff. Grown ups go to work in their suits and their polished shoes. They eat their vegetables, and salads, and drink plenty of water. They pay the mortgage, mow the lawn, water the plants, watch TV. Get married and have kids. Host dinner parties. Iron their clothes, make the bed, vacuum the house. Do tax returns. Take the car for its MOT. Grown ups don't starve themselves. They don't throw up. They don't go running at 3am after eating three large pizzas. They don't [INSERT A CACOPHONY OF BEHAVIOURS HERE]. Grown ups don't have eating disorders.

But I do. I do. I do. We do. We do. We do. I see us. I see you.

And we keep doing the other grown up stuff as long as we can. Because what choice is there? Going to work. Polishing our shoes. Eating, vomiting. Body crumbling. Making the bed. Vacuuming. Running. Running. Grumpy. Paying the bills. Meeting friends and family. Starving. Stuffing. Keeping up a charade. Cold. Exhaustion. Taking the car to the garage. Getting a new tyre. Sad. Struggling to breathe. Having friends over for dinner. Numb. Going to the supermarket. Cleaning the fridge. Dizzy.

How can we recover, if we are hiding? How can we recover if we put the disorder away in a box whilst we go to work, do the food shopping, go for dinner with colleagues, then get it out whenever we are alone? **How can we recover in silence and shame? We keep going because we can't tell anyone because this DOESN'T HAPPEN to adults.** *Somehow, somewhere, something went really wrong in our genetic code and we brought the TEENAGE GIRL disease into adulthood*. But a much less neatly packaged, socially acceptable version of it. A much messier, more deranged, larger, less boney version. We can't get help though because we can't tell anyone. This doesn't happen to adults. We know it doesn't happen, because nobody else around us has an eating disorder. We know it doesn't happen because we've never met another adult with an eating disorder. Right?

Wrong.

I'm not much of a gambling gal but I would stake my LIFE on the fact that you know AT LEAST one other person who has an eating disorder. And one is me being optimistic for your friends and family and acquaintances. When a video of mine unexpectedly went viral on TikTok, I started to get messages from people who had seen me there. And I panicked, at first. And then I realised. *I wouldn't be showing up on their pages if they hadn't been accessing content related, in some way, to eating problems.* And then, slowly, slowly, they came out of the woodwork.

Around 30 people that I know PERSONALLY messaged me to say they also had disordered eating. They had also been struggling for years. They had also thought they were alone. THIRTY PEOPLE. Let that sink in. THIRTY. I had sat at dinner with some of these people. Worked with them for years. Grown up with them. **And me, who HAD an eating disorder, who KNEW what it could look like, never saw it either**. And they never saw it in me. *Because when you're not "obviously" ill - a pale little skeleton who refuses to eat in public - it's so easy to fly under the radar.* And as we all fly under the radar, we all think we are alone, and we swirl there, in our vortex of pain and shame and hunger and suffering. Needless.

If you DO fit the stereotype, though, this book is still for you. If you ARE a teenage girl. If you ARE underweight. If you've ONLY EVER been anorexic in a "typical" way. **Because the chances are, even though you DO get more representation in the media, you probably still feel completely, entirely, utterly alone.** That's what eating disorders do. They pull you away from life. They WANT you to feel alone because then you WON'T tell anyone. Then you WON'T get help. Then they get to stay. And they want to stay, so badly.

This book is for us all, because no matter who we are, and how we are sick, we are sick. We have an eating disorder. And we deserve to get better. I lost my entire teenage years and have nearly lost my 20s to my disorder. I don't want you to lose yours too, if you haven't already. I don't want you to lose your thirties, or your forties, or maybe even the chance to live at all. Heck, if you're still 12, maybe YOU might want to miss out on those teenage years of pure hell, spots and teenage love but I don't want you to. They're a key part of life. ***I'm sad that I spent more time hating my body than I did hating boys. I'm sad that I spent more time trying to fix my weight than I did trying to fix some hopeless, sad teenage boy who smoked around the back of school. I'm sad that I spent more time breaking my own heart than letting others break it.*** I'm sad that my 20s were spent losing and gaining weight, rather than losing and gaining memories. I'm sad that they were spent eating, and not eating, in a deranged manner, rather than eating with friends, family, and dates. I'm sad that they were spent exercising in ways I hated, focussed on maximum burn and aesthetics, and hating every minute of it, rather than finding joyful forms of movement that I loved and made my body feel balanced and calm. I'm sad that they were spent browsing the Internet for hours, researching food and calories and weight loss instead of swiping left and right on men instead. **<u>I'm now watching all of my friends buy houses, get married and start building real adult lives whilst I, rootless and alone, have vomited my savings down the toilet and never invested time into finding a partner.</u>**

That's why I'm writing this book.

Because I, having lost all of that, am now solidly in recovery. **And I, whilst losing all of that, and in the process of beginning my recovery, have learnt an awful lot.** I've ruminated a lot. I've had some deep thoughts (and many shallow ones). I wanted to share them all with you because I wish I could go back to my younger self and tell her what I know now. I wish I could go back and squirt all this knowledge into her head, to stop her, to stop her, to stop her. Then, she may have had her heart broken by a teenage boy, danced with another one at prom, become a yoga instructor, found a boyfriend, bought a house. Or another, completely different life. But. If she had known, if she had stopped, she would *have had a life*. She wouldn't have lost more than a decade.

So. Here. Have my unprofessional and unsolicited opinions. Digest them (ha). Sit with them. Maybe decide they don't apply to you. Maybe decide they do but that you're not ready to recover. Come back when you're ready. Come back when you're sick of the ED. I'll be here.
And, I'm going to be really honest. This book is for all of the future versions of me, too. This book is mostly for me, to be honest. So that when I hear the siren call of the eating disorder, I can turn back here. I can read these pages over and over again. I can remind

myself of why I said goodbye. Why I turned my back. Why I walked away. **This book will remind me of all that I lost with my disorder; all that I gained with recovery; and all that I stand to lose or gain in the future depending on the decisions that I make every time my eating disorder voice tells me not to eat, or tries to persuade me to throw up.**

4. MY EATING DISORDER HELLSCAPE

I won't title this 'my eating disorder story' because 'story' really feels like the wrong word. 'Story' feels too soft. Too sweet. It conjures up images of a child being tucked in at night. It makes you think of fiction. Something not real. **But there is nothing soft, sweet or fictional about life with an eating disorder.** Well…actually…I suppose all the lies you tell to the people around you when you're sick are DEFINITELY fiction. And the lies you tell yourself. And the lies that the eating disorder tells you.

But 'story' also suggests a linear pathway. A neatly packaged narrative of beginning, middle and end with a lesson learnt along the way. You see it online quite a bit. People say: 'My eating disorder started like this. It was bad for a bit. Then it ended like this. I recovered and lived happily ever after'. They say: 'The moral of the story is that you just shouldn't care what other people think about your body'. It's all so neat. It started and it was over, often within a couple of years. The middle bit can be a little messy, but even then it's following an even trajectory of steady decline in physical and mental health, followed by the RISING FROM THE ASHES glory moment of gaining it all back.

This was not my experience. In fact, I struggle to pinpoint a start. It could have been at numerous different points. It could have been there all along. I don't know where the middle is. There was no even trajectory, no steady decline. **It was a constant rollercoaster, an incessant UP - DOWN - UP - DOWN - DOWN - DOWN - UP - UP - LOOP THE LOOP - WHAT THE FUCK I'VE FALLEN OUT.** My 'story' never seemed to be going anywhere. It was like one of those adventure books - 'choose option B and turn to page 42' - where you end up going in circles back to the same pages over and over again and you can't figure your way out of the pages. And I'm not too convinced there will ever be an end. Not a real one anyway. Not a conclusive one. Not a neat one, not a 'happy ever after'. At times, I may have thought I had reached an ending. And then I turned around and realised I had been reading a prequel all along and it was about to get SO MUCH WORSE. **No literary agent would publish my eating disorder 'story' because they would say *this makes no sense, it's so disjointed, it jumps all over the place, who is the main character? Where is the beginning, where is the end?***

This is not my 'EATING DISORDER STORY' because it isn't a story. It's got no plotline. *It's a twisting, turning mindmangle of thoughts and feelings and actions and behaviours spreading out over years and years of my life.* It's not a story. It's just a life. A life lived in immense torment. A life full of waste: wasted time, wasted moments, wasted money, wasted muscles, wasted potential. A life that I would never wish on another human being. A life that I thought would be mine for the rest of time. But now, sometimes, a life that I believe I can leave behind. **It's not a story. Oh no. This is something else: this is my eating disorder hellscape.**

It's very important that we don't romanticise anything. Any kind of softness, any kind of gentle treatment of eating disorders, gives them room to wiggle in your brain. And if they have room to wiggle in your brain, they have room to wriggle. And wriggle they will. Back into your life like the stupid little parasites they are. So be clear. No stories. No beginnings, middles and ends. No happy ever afters. **It. Is. A. Hellscape.** A hellscape, a mindmangle, a battle to the end. Pure non-fiction: ugly, hard, messy, plotless, painful truth.

So. What is my eating disorder hellscape, then? People ask me about it a lot. I don't want to go TOO much into my own actual eating disorders, diagnoses and behaviours. And there's a few reasons for that.

Aside from the reasons I will list below, you have to remember that unlike lots of the content we see online, eating disorders are often not short. Many of us have not been unwell for just a couple of years. Many of us have been unwell for decades. As such, if I gave my full story, this would be an incredibly long, incredibly depressing, incredibly repetitive book. If I were to type out my whole story from wherever the hell the true beginning was until the present day, we would be looking at a saga. People would stop reading in the first few hundred chapters because it would be endless drudgery. *The same cycles, over and over again, spanning out, year after year after year.* The same plotlines, rehashed, over and over - like a TV soap. Over a decade of my eating disorder life is just not worth reading. It was, to be honest, incredibly boring. An eating disorder may seem like it has dramatic appeal from the outside, and it may do when people are saying I STARVED MYSELF FOR THREE MONTHS, HAD A HEART ATTACK, WAS TAKEN TO HOSPITAL IN AN AMBULANCE, THE POLICE HAD TO COME AND BRING ME BACK BECAUSE I ABSCONDED, I WAS ON A DRIP, I WAS ON A HEART MONITOR. **But mostly, an eating disorder is boring. Every single day is the same.** Every single day is spent endlessly calculating. Every single day is spent thinking about food. Every single day you wake up and feel immense dread at the number of hours you have to get through with the thoughts and the hunger and the urges. Every single day you go to bed feeling you didn't do enough. Knowing that you have to wake up tomorrow and go all over again. See. It sounds boring already, right? Imagine that multiplied by 365. Then by 10. Maybe 15. Maybe 20. Can you see where I'm going with this? **Eating disorders are, at their core, incredibly dull.**

But there are also, aside from pragmatic, literary reasons, some deeper disorder related reasons that mean I won't delve too deep into the icky sticky wounds of my past and present struggles.

Firstly, eating disorders are competitive. I know it. As much as I hate to admit this about myself, there were many times in the past where I would find myself on social media, on Reddit, or just looking at people in the world and thinking *aha I am sicker than them* or, worse, *they are sicker than me, I need to be sicker.* The waiting room at my eating disorder clinic was the worst place in the world. You would walk through the doors and a bunch of malnourished people would be sitting there. Their eyes were all on you, judging if you were sicker than them. Your eyes were on them, trying to work out if they were sicker than you. A group of people with eating disorders, weighing themselves against each other, trying to figure out what diagnosis each person had and who was the best at it. Now I am healing, I am a little embarrassed about that. But that's the disorder, isn't it? It does what it wants. And what it wants is to WIN. It wants to be the BEST. It doesn't want someone else to be sicker.

If I went fully into detail, someone's ED would be happy. It would smugly think: *I am worse than that. Let's keep going so we can keep being the sickest.* If I went fully into detail, someone else's ED would be angry. It would think: *I am not that sick. I need to get sicker.*

Secondly, I don't want anyone to pick up any ideas they don't already have. I have done a lot of things during my disorder. The main behaviours we all already know, unfortunately - restriction and bingeing and purging and overexercising. However, there are a thousand horrible ways that you can try to control your body and your weight that are less well known - thank GOD. I know most of them, though. Many of my habits and disordered behaviours, unfortunately, I picked up from others - online and from reading books. It was deliberate. I went out seeking advice on how to GET MORE SICK. Of course, at the time, in my head, I was just looking for advice on how to lose weight. But really, if you're reading anything on those dark spaces on the Internet, you know you're deeply, deeply unwell.

Ironically, the most dangerous behaviour I learnt that was 100% the one that led me to the hospital, was actually found in a self-help recovery book written by *actual medical* _professionals_ and GIVEN TO ME BY AN EATING DISORDER CLINICIAN. In fact, that reminds me…I still need to write a letter of complaint to someone about that because there is **genuinely** a book out there in circulation that gives a ***detailed description of an incredibly harmful eating disorder behaviour***. (NOTE TO SELF - ADD TO OVERFLOWING TO-DO LIST) Anyway. That's another reason I don't want to delve too deep into THE SPECIFICS of what I did and how much I did it and how long I did it for. I don't want anyone else to start doing it too. And as much as people would be like "that wouldn't happen", most of us here know that it absolutely _would_ happen because that's the disorder. Someone's eating disorder would go _hmm well she did this and she got really sick so maybe…just maybe…we just need to get a little sicker before we recover so we could try it?_ And before you know it, you're entrenched. I know. I copied people's behaviours and now look at me, nearly 30 and trying to rip the claws free from where they're lodged deep inside me.

So if you picked up this book looking for a manual of how to get sicker - you can bog off. This book won't help you with that. I'm joking. Don't bog off. Read the book. It might help. And next time you try and find content to deliberately trigger yourself, don't buy the book written by the adult who wears strawberry print pyjama leggings and blue crocs in public. She's probably not toxic in the way you want her to be.

Thirdly, I don't want anyone to feel invalid. Again, eating disorders have a fantastic way of making your brain think and do things that afterwards you can barely believe you thought and did. Feeling invalid is one of them. _Looking at others and thinking "oh well they spent seven thousand years in inpatient with eight tubes down their nose and had to be restrained by fifty two registered mental health nurses but I only passed out in class a couple of times from MY eating disorder", for example._ If someone else's story is WORSE, it can persuade us that we were NEVER SICK. That we are INVALID. That we are FAKING. And then what does the eating disorder do in response to those claims? Well, it wants to GET WORSE of course because it wants the world to see it in all its sick little validity. So me going too deep into the specifics of my journey COULD make someone else feel invalid, and think that until they get "that bad", their eating disorder doesn't count. But it does. **If your life has been impacted negatively in ANY WAY by your relationship with food and your body, it counts. It matters. And you are valid to me**. And that's all that counts, right, because I'm the author here. This is my hellscape I've invited you into, and I'm giving you a cup of tea and a slice of lemon drizzle cake and a hug NO MATTER WHAT your own hellscape looks like. It's still a hellscape.

Finally, everyone's story is going to be wildly different. For that reason I don't think it's particularly helpful to have the specifics of my story. You see these stories online (often, again, the typical young anorexic girl!) and you think *"well I can't relate to that story because it's nothing like mine"*. You think *"that wasn't how it happened for me"*. So then you disregard the fact that this person is saying you can recover. You decide it only worked for them because they had a different experience. Their disorder was different. Not as bad. Not as entrenched. Not caused by the same triggers. My story will be different to yours. And to the girl over the road. And to the man in the Tesco car park. And to the old woman in the hospital.

You may wonder, with the above point, why I am even bothering to write this book at all. And here's why: despite every single experience being different, I do believe that they all have **key similarities.** I genuinely believe that many eating disorders are, at the core, incredibly similar.

Many people will say this isn't true. If you have BED, for example, and exist in a "larger" body, you may look at someone with AN and say that it's ridiculous to suggest you are similar. You will tell me that I don't understand. They are *skinny* and you are *not*. They have *self-control around food* and you *do not*. They are DIFFERENT ISSUES. There is NO WAY you can RELATE or BE SIMILAR to an anorexic.

But. I have had BED. I have had BN. I have had AN. I had been "normal"; "overweight"; "obese; and "underweight". With each of those diagnoses, and at each of those weights, I FELT THE EXACT SAME WAY ABOUT MY BODY, FOOD AND EATING. I exhibited the same behaviours and had the exact same thoughts, feelings, highs and lows. Some behaviours were more prevalent at certain times. Some receded, came back stronger. Some stuck through the years. Some went. Others lurked in the background. When I had BED, I would look at people with BN and AN and EDNOS and think we were completely different. Different issues. I thought I was messed up in ways that they would never understand. I yearned to be able to do what they did, to exist in bodies smaller than mine, to exert some control - any control - over food and body. But then when my BED turned into BN and my BN looped into AN and then I swang wildly between them all on some deranged merry go round ride for years, I realised: **I was the same person the whole time. When I had BED. When I had AN. I was the same me. The same hurting, disordered me.**

Whatever people are doing - bingeing, purging, restricting, overexercising - it comes from the main road. They may be on different sideroads at the moment, but they all came from the same place. It all comes from the same place and it all ends in the same place. That's why I wanted to write this book. Because the tips and the tricks and the ways in which I have been learning to recover, I believe are relevant to most of us. Regardless of our behaviours, regardless of our own diagnoses.

That's why I am so convinced that the things I have learnt about recovery will, in some way, be relevant to us all. Because they were relevant to me at every point in this journey - at every diagnosis, at every weight. At every miserable moment in my hellscape.

For the context of things that may come up within the book, I will give you a TL DR version of my hellscape. That way **you may be able to trust me, a little bit, when I say that I kind of know what I'm on about here**. But it won't be specific. A Cliff Notes version.

And if you think even this, even a dry account of the most boring years of my life, might be triggering - rip these pages out of the book and throw them away. Then read the rest of the book. Because this bit isn't that important in comparison to the rest of it. This bit is just setting the context. You don't need the context of MY LIFE to recover from YOUR HELLSCAPE.

SO STOP HERE.

Sit with yourself. Ask yourself right now: <u>am I in the right space to read this section?</u> Is reading someone else's TL DR eating disorder hellscape going to make me feel invalidated, or not sick enough? Is reading someone else's TL DR eating disorder hellscape going to make my ED react in any way, positive or negative? If the answers are yes - yeet these pages in the bin. Please.

33

My Personal Eating Disorder Hellscape: TL DR

1. **Ten years old.** Healthy weight. Normal child. Difficult home life. Loves chocolate.

2. **Eleven years old.** Healthy weight. Not particularly active. Difficult home life. Has started stealing chocolate when nobody's looking. Nothing drastic. Just two or three bars, or some extra biscuits, or a whole advent calendar.

3. **Eleven years old.** Still a healthy weight but feels fat. Hates her body. And her newly developing breasts that adults point out. *Oh she's an early bloomer.* Difficult home life. Puffy from the food she eats when nobody's looking. Starts taking diet pills. Stops eating lunch at school. Throws up sometimes, but only once or twice. Loses weight again.

4. **Twelve years old - Eighteen years old.** Loses control. Gains weight steadily. Healthy weight to overweight to obese. Hates exercise. Hates her body. Home life has gotten worse following a bereavement. At thirteen, mother divorces step dad and they move house. Home life gets even worse. Mother puts her on diets. None of them work because she gets off the bus and eats a four pack of chocolate bars. And eats two lunches at school. Pieces of bread out the packet. Whole tubes of crisps. Sometimes just slices of ham out the fridge. Anything she can get her hands on. Sometimes she loses some weight after she commits to a diet for a while. Salad. No breakfast. But then she can't keep it up and it comes back. It's an endless cycle. She doesn't feel particularly sad. She feels quite numb. Sometimes she's sad. But mostly numb. She hates her body, though.

5. **Eighteen - Twenty One.** The University Years. Went on a diet after A-Levels before university, but not a crash one. Just walked more, ate better. Lost a few pounds. Now technically overweight still, but feels better. Doesn't think about food or body too much at university at all. Lives life. Is happy. Binge eating has pretty much stopped - other than on nights out but EVERYONE does it then. In a tricky relationship. As it progresses and things get trickier, there are days of binges here and there. She eats more than she's hungry for, too, so does gain weight. But she doesn't mind too much. She doesn't love her body but doesn't hate it as much as she used to. She's also too busy living to try and change it. She exercises sometimes - she plays hockey once a week and walks in to uni. She has a bike. She doesn't feel too unhealthy. Not like she used to at school. Her boyfriend is a bit of a feeder which doesn't help. But oh well.

6. **Twenty One.** She knows it's the right thing to do. She ends the relationship. She's sad. Very sad. Then, at a party, something earth shattering happens to her. Not the worst thing in the world, not at all. There are worse things. So many worse things. But pretty bad. She looks in the mirror. Sees a body that has had THINGS done to it that she didn't want. Sees a body that no longer feels like her own. Sees a body that her ex, who she still loves, and will always love, used to adore. She doesn't want to live in this body anymore. She needs a new body. A body that nobody else has touched yet: a new body for nobody to touch without her permission, a new body that her lost love has never kissed. She needs to seize control. So she goes on a diet. It starts off relatively sane. Rice, chicken, veg. She starts running. Religiously. Love Island is on at the time. The bodies on there make her determined to see the number drop more. She starts eating less so that she can have a snack in the evening. Then she stops eating the snack. Now she's eating tomatoes for lunch. Now she's not eating lunch. Weight is dropping. People have stopped saying she looks great and are now a bit concerned. She is shrinking in front of them. She moves back home for the summer. Now she is barely eating. She's not hungry though. But. She's stopped losing weight. How is that possible? She's not underweight, no way near, so why is her body betraying her?

7. **Twenty Two.** She has moved into her own flat. Got her first job as a teacher. She is vegetarian now. Takes big boxes of salad and vegetables to work for lunch, doesn't eat the rest of the time. It's what everyone else around her is doing too so it seems normal. Starts going to the gym. Lifting weights. Doesn't gain muscle. Doesn't lose weight. Is sad. Realises she has to eat very little now because if she isn't losing weight eating this, she will gain weight eating more.

8. **Twenty Three.** She moves back in with her mum temporarily because the man in the flat above her threatens to kill her. No, really. He was an alcoholic and thought she was banging on the ceiling one night. It wasn't her but she doesn't feel safe anyway. Now there's this BIG ISSUE. She cannot eat more food because she will gain weight. But. She cannot starve herself because she has a teenage sister. Her sister is sixteen and has a history of NOT EATING. When she was 12, she went through a phase of hiding her lunch. She got very skinny. She's doing better now. But. If she sees her big sister modelling self-starvation? It'll put her at risk. So what to do? Eat. But eating = gaining weight. What to do? Get rid of the food. How? Can't hide it. Too obvious. Can't exercise it off because no time for extra exercise and no idea how many calories in mother's dinners. Too many, probably. What to do?

9. **Twenty Four.** She lives on her own. She's a healthy weight. She's been stuck in a cycle since she lived at her mum's and vomited for the first time. Vomiting is dangerous because you think it's only once. But when you've done it once, you think, I'll just do it once more. And then again. And then every time you eat too much. And then, one day, she realised that it didn't even have to be just when she ate a bit too much. She could eat EVERYTHING she wanted and didn't let herself have and then GET RID OF IT. She could FEAST. So she did. Once a week. Went to the supermarket. Bought boatloads of food. Feasted. Got rid of it. Maintained her weight. True, the rest of the time she was still not eating much. Still over exercising. Still stressed and worried about food. But sometimes she got to eat all the foods she wanted. It was great. It was so great. Until it started to increase. Until it wasn't once a week. But 2-3 times a week. Spare evenings and weekends.

10. **Twenty Six.** And now it's every day. Every single day. Without fail. It's been every day for nearly a year and a half. On really bad days, like the weekends, it can be two, three, four times a day. Spending £50, £60 in the supermarket. £100 on Takeaway. Enough food that could feed a family for a week. Eat for hours. Vomit in between. Flushed down the toilet. Everyday. No time for anything else. Life becomes: work, study, gym, eat, vomit. It's endless. Bleak. Her social life suffers. Her weight is healthy. But it goes up and down, up and down, up and down, gaining and losing the same pounds over and over again. Her skin is awful. Dry and spotty. Her hair is dry and falling out. Her face is constantly puffy.

11. **Twenty Seven.** The holy grail. She looks like the stereotype now. She's lying in a hospital bed, hooked up to an IV. Sunken face. Jutting bones. But she's not a teenager. She's an adult. Signed off from work. How embarrassing. Sectioned under the mental health act. Watched by a 1:1 nurse 24 hours a day. Sick in all the same ways she was sick before. But now her body has given out. Years of abuse culminating in this: a sad, shrunken grown woman in a hospital bed, unable to leave, unable to make her own decisions. Staring down the barrel of what she has lost: all of her 20s. And for what? For this? *This* was the end goal? It doesn't seem worth it. It doesn't seem like a goal.

12. **Twenty Seven.** She walks out of the hospital. She can walk. She's still a little breathless but three weeks ago she had to sit down in between walking around the room. Now she can walk out of the hospital. She feels the sun on her face. She decides. This is it. No more lost time

But it's helpful, at the end. To open your eyes and look at it. The shortened version helps. Because you can begin to see the patterns. **You can begin to look at what happened from a zoomed out place, and see what should have been obvious all along. It was all the same. And it was all coming from the same toxic root.**

Go and get a notebook. I bought a mustard yellow journal with narrow lined pages. I *love* narrow lines. It had cream paper too. I stuck stickers all over the front of it. It was my recovery journal. Much of this book was written using pages from that journal. Importantly, it doesn't have to be neat. The content of this journal isn't going to be pretty, right, so there's no need for it to look pretty either. Just scrawl it all out. Spill your pain onto the pages.

Go to the first page.

Have a go at your own TLDR. Maximum of one paragraph per 'phase' of your hellscape. You might need to take several goes. Put it down. Come back to it. Thoughts will come to you throughout the day. You'll be washing up, and go…OH BUT WHEN I WAS EIGHT I DID XYZ. You'll be driving down the motorway and…BAM. REMEMBER THAT PARTY WHEN YOU WERE FIFTEEN AND YOU HAD THAT THOUGHT? Pretending you're listening in a work meeting and…OH MY GOSH YOU WERE SO DISORDERED DURING THAT YEAR YOU SPENT IN ARGENTINA!

Don't rush it. Do it slowly. It's heavy work. Sad work. Cry. Sit with yourself. Grieve for those past versions of you. Be thankful that you're not there now - even if where you are now feels even worse. It's still somewhere else. Be gentle. Keep going.

And when it's done, look at it. Closely. Think about it. Look for patterns.

5. WHY DO I HAVE AN EATING DISORDER? WHY DO YOU? WHY DOES THE MAN OVER THE STREET NOT HAVE ONE?

Before you read this chapter, bear in mind what I told you earlier: I am not a medical professional. This is all conjecture. This is all stuff I have made up based on my own life experiences. *But, ultimately, this is all stuff that lead to my recovery.* The causes and risk factors of eating disorders are still, largely, unknown. There are several theories floating around. There's the added complication that - as with everything - for different people there may be different causes. There's the added compilation that it's a mental health condition and governments love to underfund research into mental health.

Some people believe that eating disorders are caused by growing up living in a fatphobic society, embedded in diet culture, surrounded by adults who model bad relationships to food and their bodies. But. We all grow up embedded in diet culture. Too many of us grow up surrounded by adults who model bad relationships with food and bodies. Too many of us are called fat by family members or kids at school or random strangers on the street. But only some of us end up with an eating disorder.

Once I had written it all out in my TLDR, in black and white simplicity, it became hard to ignore that **there was a simple pattern** in the mindmangle that I had always, for years, seen as an entirely random and uncontrollable disorder. Yes, it's more complicated than it looks on paper. Yes, there are a thousand more details to the hellscape, a thousand more twists and turns; a thousand more moments of pain and shame and suffering. But. Looking at it, *really seeing myself for the first time in years,* I began to understand.

I began to understand WHY I had developed an eating disorder. I had always wondered *why me?* What *specifically* about me made me too weak to eat like a normal person? Why did *other people* not have this problem?

I thought there was something weak and wrong with me, compared to other people, that meant that I couldn't resist the pulls of diet culture. I thought that I was too vain. Too self-obsessed. No willpower, no strength of character. But. It was never that simple, see. If I had looked at the REAL beginning sooner, I would have seen that. Because I used to think that my story started when I was twenty one and went on **that final diet.** But it didn't. It started when I was a child, compulsively overeating food with no understanding of why. The blame was never on me in the way that I thought it was. And I didn't find my capacity to begin healing until I held a lifetime of disorder up to the light and really looked at it.

I looked at the start. The binge eating. Stealing food. Buying extra food. Eating when I wasn't hungry. Eating for no reason. The kid who loved food a little bit more than most kids loved food.

I will not tear my parents down. **My parents are human beings and they were doing the best that they could with what they had.** Poor mental health, addiction, postnatal depression, money struggles, grief. My parents were in dark places. And because of that, life was sometimes very dark for us all. I have forgiven them for it all. I loved them then and I love them now, endlessly. When I was in the hospital, and afterwards, they were all that I needed them to be and more. Even in the darkest times, my siblings and I have always known that, no matter what we need, they will put everything aside to do what they can.

But.

Growing up with struggling parents is damaging. It's damaging because you don't UNDERSTAND. I had no concept of why they were acting the way they were acting, or doing the things they were doing. The only logical conclusion I could draw, therefore, was that it was *me*. I was the problem. I was bad. I was flawed. I was horrible. It didn't help that my birth father had absconded when I was a baby. *I was an abandoned, unlovable child and none of my family wanted me very much.* <u>I was DEEPLY SAD.</u>

As I have made clear, I am not a medical professional. Anything and everything that I say here is based on Internet research; other people's experiences that they shared with me; and my own life story. And as we *should* know, that means there is **a fair chance it's not all true!** But I have drawn from multiple sources and fact-checked anything that sounded dodgy, so you can be faintly convinced that it may be factual information. Maybe. When I decided that I was ready to face my eating disorder head on (or, rather, when I had no choice left to me, anyway, let's not give me too much credit here) I turned to the internet. I wanted to understand as much as I possibly could about WHY. And I needed to start at the start. Which was *not* the diet I went on in my 20s, but the binge eating when I was an eleven year old girl.

Researching the science behind binge eating led me to the following understanding: *Eating is a pleasurable experience. Food tastes nice. We enjoy it. And this can trigger the release of dopamine in the brain. Dopamine is a reward chemical in the brain that makes you feel good. So, your brain makes a link that goes* **<u>FOOD = NICE = HAPPY.</u>**

And I was sad. I was a sad child. I spent a lot of time alone, or being shouted at, or feeling hopeless and helpless and unlovable. There was lots of shouting in the house.

Banging doors. Tense silences. Instability. We walked on eggshells. I lived in a constant state of fight of flight, my young body flooded with cortisol and adrenaline every hour that I was awake. **So of COURSE my brain latched on to the one thing that did seem to bring happiness. Food. Dopamine. Feel sad. Eat. Happy for a bit.**

It began to make a lot more sense, then. The furtive trips to the fridge. The rummaging through cupboards. Why sometimes I would go weeks without doing it. And other times, it was several times a day. Why, when I did it, I *needed* to do it. Why it became so much worse when I was a teenager and things were even harder. Why it stopped at university. And why it came back again afterwards. My brain *needed* me to do it: it wanted that dopamine and it knew how to get it. And when the brain is in control of the body? It can drive a person to the fridge: compel them to spoon coleslaw into their mouth uncontrollably.

Eating disorders are WILDLY complex and COMPLETELY UNIQUE in their actual triggers and beginnings. It might be that yours WAS caused by diet culture and toxic models - in which case, you can work to unpick that and address that. But first, sit with yourself and go back to the start. Look at your hellscape again. Ask yourself: Could it be more? *Could it be more complicated than just wanting to change your body?*

I wasted years of my life being drastically unwell BECAUSE I wasn't ready to sit with myself and think about it. I just kept telling myself that it was diet culture. That I needed more willpower. **That when I got a nice body, I would be able to stop**. *But it wasn't about my body so that was never going to work.* I think, deep down, that part of me just wasn't ready. I *think I always knew that there was a lot of trauma and pain and complexity beneath the surface that was causing and reinforcing my disorder, but I wasn't ready to do all of the incredibly hard work I would need to do to repair it.* It was easier to tell myself it was diet culture. It was easier to shift the focus away from me and my mangled brain.

When I was forced, by my endless days in hospital, to actually dive into those murky waters, I identified that *my eating disorder was significantly likely to be A COPING MECHANISM* that my brain had developed.

1. I was trying to fill the emotional holes in my heart from not being loved enough as a child.
2. I was using self-hatred and self-harm to numb the pain that I felt because feeling nothing was better than facing the trauma.
3. The dopamine response of my brain to eating food taught me that when I was sad and hurting, food could make me feel better.

4. Once it became a habit, I was, for want of a better word, FUCKED. There is no better word. I was FUCKED.

So, a key factor in *why* I had an eating disorder: I needed a coping mechanism to deal with the sadness I was experiencing and, in the absence of any healthy mechanisms, food and attempted body control became that mechanism.

And the other key factor? The other thing was too obvious and too simple for me to want to acknowledge it. And too scary.

Restriction.

When I was a sad, lonely, broken little child that nobody loved, I learnt that eating made me feel better. My parents, and the other adults around me, were deranged about food. They didn't let us eat too much sugar. They would comment on it when we did. Talk about getting fat and rotting our teeth and how we didn't eat enough vegetables. We were allowed one treat a day, and it had to be a small treat, and we were only allowed cake on weekends, and if we went out to a cafe, we could only get a hot chocolate OR a piece of cake, not both together. **I wasn't restricting myself at this stage: but I WAS being restricted. Food wasn't free.** *So my brain felt restricted.* And the more your brain thinks it isn't allowed something, the more it wants it.

This is something that can go unnoticed in childhood, I think. Adults think they are doing the right thing. They are helping children grow up healthy. Everyone knows the risks of sugar. Childhood obesity. Blah. Blah. Blah. I'm not going to sit here and say I know the answers to how this should be managed because I don't. I don't know the answers for making sure children can grow up nourished and healthy both physically and mentally. It's tough. ***But what I do want to say is this: please, if you have a child in your life think about whether or not you may, deliberately or not, be making them feel restricted around food.*** Because if you are, you could, unfortunately, be contributing to flawed brain patterns that could result in their poor little brain coming to view food as something to control and to yearn after and to hate.

So, we have my melting pot. **Sad, lonely, broken child that feels nobody loves her. Finds happiness in food. Is restricted from certain foods. What was my brain ever going to do, exactly, other than try and get the food?** It knew food made it happy. It knew it wasn't allowed as much as it wanted. And therefore, it wanted it more.

I was sad. I was restricted from food. So we cue it in. Start the music. Bring up the curtains. Shine the lights. I begin to eat the foods that were RESTRICTED. I begin to sneak chocolate and crisps and coleslaw and pork pies. All the little yummy things adults try to stop me eating "too much" of. Because those things are restricted in my diet and I WANT them more because that's just how the brain goes. Forbidden fruit and all that jazz. *And, when I'm eating them, I feel better. I feel better because I HAVE what I was being restricted of. And because of the dopamine ride I'm on.*

When I got older, the same similarities were there.

I was a sad teenager. I was a sad adult. I didn't have appropriate coping mechanisms. I didn't go to therapy because I was busy, like most people, pretending that I was totally okay. Although there is more open discussion and less stigma about mental health now than there was when I was growing up, it's still not something you feel 100% like you can shout from the rooftops about. So I was spinning in my sad little orbits, full of pain but unwilling to reach out for help that may have led to me developing better coping mechanisms.

And at the same time, I was restricting.

I wasn't "allowed" to eat certain foods. Either because my mother had put me on a BRANDED WEIGHT LOSS PLAN, or because I had put myself on my own starvation diet, or simply because society told me not to eat them. I'm not sure anyone ever explicitly told me not to eat oil but it was definitely a restriction that had buried itself deep in my swirling mangle of a brain.

Sometimes, I was restricting FOOD itself and other times I was just restricting ENERGY. Even if I was eating what I "wanted", I was meticulously calorie counting to keep myself in a deficit. Or I was over exercising and not replacing the energy throughout the day. Or I was eating "enough" to maintain my weight but it was all "clean" food. Restriction was always there, in some form, lurking like a boring person at a party dressed in beige, ready to spring out when you go near the snack table and say, "*I haven't eaten sugar in seven hundred and nine years because it's more addictive than cocaine, did you know?*"

Anyway, I believe that I developed an eating disorder largely due to those two key factors. And because those two key factors persisted throughout the years, so too did the disorder.

SADNESS (*with no healthy coping mechanisms*) + FOOD MAKING MY BRAIN HAPPY = AN EATING DISORDER

SADNESS (*with no healthy coping mechanisms*) + FOOD MAKING MY BRAIN HAPPY + ALWAYS RETURNING TO RESTRICTION = AN EATING DISORDER HAMSTER WHEEL

When I was in the hospital, I thought very deeply about the fact that I had been unwell for so long. I thought about why. And it wasn't because the world is fatphobic, *although it is*. It wasn't because of diet culture, *although it sucks and should get in the bin*. It wasn't because of the way I was raised, *although it was impossibly difficult*. It wasn't because of the Instagram fitness models, *although that is a toxic online world*. It wasn't because of my mother, *although it could have been*. It wasn't because I was genetically hard-wired to have an eating disorder, *although I believe I am*. All of those things are **RISK FACTORS**. They were things that were making it **HARDER** for me to break free. In combination, those things created a perfect storm and I was standing in the eye of that storm, unable to see my way out through the wind and the rain. But they weren't **THE** reason.

The reason was that I had not looked at the <u>root causes and</u> thought about <u>what I might need to do to address them</u>. Because I didn't want to. Because I knew the answers were somewhere deep within me but I DIDN'T LIKE THEM. I didn't like them. It was easier to blame diet culture, or my mother, or fat phobia, or Instagram, or genetics, because that got me off the hook. **If it was the fault of those things, there was nothing that could be done, right?** I was just doomed to the eating disorder, it wasn't my fault and there was nothing that I could do about it. *I was absolved from responsibility for my own healing.*

We need another metaphor.

Stop tending to the dying flowers and look at the rotten roots

Imagine you've got a lovely big plant. I know nothing about plants so if you know about plants, choose a plant that this could apply to. I'm just growing a hypothetical plant here. If you know about plants, and this is also not how plant health works...just ignore it. It's just a metaphor. Metaphors don't need to be scientifically accurate, right?

So I've been growing this plant for many years. I've not done much to the plant, to be fair, just kind of let it get on with things, given it some food and water here and there, but kind of ignored it. Left it in a corner. Never looked too closely at it. Definitely not pruned it. Definitely never read a guide or information on how to look after it.

Lovely big plant. It's dying. It's been dying for a while, but I never looked at it. Until one day, someone says something. *Are you sure that plant is okay? they ask. Yes, of course, I reply. Why wouldn't it be? It's fine.* I go on with my day but the thought is niggling me. The concern on the other person's face is swimming around in my head. The slightly haunted look in their eyes. The frown, like they thought I was lying, when I said everything was okay. The way I could tell they didn't believe me.

So I go up to the plant and I look at it. Some of the leaves are dead. Some are wilting. Some of the flowers have lost all their petals. I take off the dead bits and go away again. Sorted. I come back again. More dead leaves. More wilting. More lost petals. I take off the dead bits. Sorted. Come back. More dead leaves. Just dealing with the dead bits hasn't solved the problem. I'm just doing surface level work.

That's what my attempts at recovery were. One day, I would eat three meals. *I would be picking off some of the dead flowers, trying to fix the plant that way.* But they would still be restrictive meals. I would still be over-exercising. I would still be fixating on food and my body as a means to control my life and numb my emotions. *So the plant would continue to die.* I would rebound back into the cycle. Then, I would decide. This is it. EAT WHAT I WANT. *I would pick off more dead leaves and dead head some flowers.* But I wouldn't eat what I wanted for long. I would eat what I wanted and then I would think about how I was LOSING CONTROL and then I would go straight back into compensatory behaviours. *More dead bits.*

It was a constant cycle of tending to a dying plant by picking off the bits that were already dead, whilst doing nothing to stop any more of it from dying. That's what happens with eating disorders sometimes. You try to 'fix it' by changing behaviours suddenly and drastically, but without actually addressing why the behaviours are there in the first place. You can't kill off a behaviour just by 'getting rid of it' for a little bit, because, if the root is still damaged, it's going to happen again.

What I needed to do was stop looking at the flowers and the leaves of the plant. They were already dead. Where had they come from, and why were they dying? I needed to look at the roots. *Why* was this plant dying? What was it about the structural foundations of this plant that meant it was unable to sustain life? **I had known, all along, that I needed to look at the roots. But I didn't because I knew what it would mean. Hard work. Difficult work. Time consuming work. Starting from the beginning. Rebuilding.** Pulling off dead leaves was easy. It let me fool myself into thinking that I was doing **something**. I was **trying**. Even though I knew, of course, deep down, that it wasn't actually doing anything to fix the problem. I was just prolonging the survival of the plant, knowing that eventually it would die. Eventually, whatever was happening in the roots would lead to too much death and decay and the plant would shut down.

That was me in the hospital. My plant had reached the stage of just being the roots and a sad stem. The leaves and the flowers were long gone. But it hadn't happened overnight. It had taken years. A slow death. A death that, at any point, I could have prevented by looking at the roots. And if I had done it sooner, if I had looked at the roots sooner, I would have had a lot less work to do. I would still have had some leaves and flowers. I wouldn't have had to regrow entirely. And my stem? Damaged forever. Long lasting side effects. If I had stopped sooner, if I had looked at the roots, the stem could have stayed healthy. No long lasting side effects.

Listen. Wherever you are with your plant, stop now. Don't let it get to the stage of being roots and a sad stem. Because it will, one day. **With an eating disorder, there's no different end destination other than a body that is worn down, tired and crumbling.** You are killing yourself when you are engaging in behaviours. You just don't realise it because the rotting, the dying, happens slowly and subtly. It happens inside you. From the roots. And then one day it's too late. You wake up and nothing works right anymore. You are weak. Depleted.

And then what? The plant will die. Or. You'll have to regrow it. And if you've let it go that far, there's so much more regrowth to do. So much more to fix. So. Look at the roots now. Wherever you are on the journey. Stop before it all dies. Because I'm telling you. **It all ends the same.** So you may as well turn around before you get there because it's not a place worth going.

So. I finally took heed. I realised that I had wasted a decade trying to fix something by dealing with the surface wounds only. I realised that I had wasted a decade superficially pruning a plant, rather than trying to help it to heal. I had ignored the fact that the damage went incredibly deep and tried to pretend that it was all surface level.

I did the only thing left for me to do. The only thing left that might save that sad little dying stick that used to be a plant with so much potential. I dug around in the soil. Looked at the roots and figured out what they needed in order to repair.

My eating disorder. I went deep. **I stopped thinking about diets and my body size and Instagram and the things my mum had said about her body, and my body, and other people's bodies. I stopped thinking about fat rolls and defined abs and looking good in a bikini. I stopped thinking about whole foods and processed foods and health risks and diabetes.** Because ALL of that was too simple. If my eating disorder was a result of any of those things, I would have been able to beat it at some point in A DECADE. ***But it had to be deeper than that. Otherwise, everyone in the world would have lost a decade to an eating disorder - because everyone in the world was surrounded by the toxic sludge of diet culture.***

Using the TLDR from earlier, I was able to finally see that it DID go deeper.

The things making my roots sick were:
1. SADNESS (IN THE ABSENCE OF HEALTHY COPING MECHANISMS)
2. FOOD MAKING MY BRAIN HAPPY
3. A DESIRE TO LIVE IN A SMALLER BODY
4. ALWAYS RETURNING TO RESTRICTION

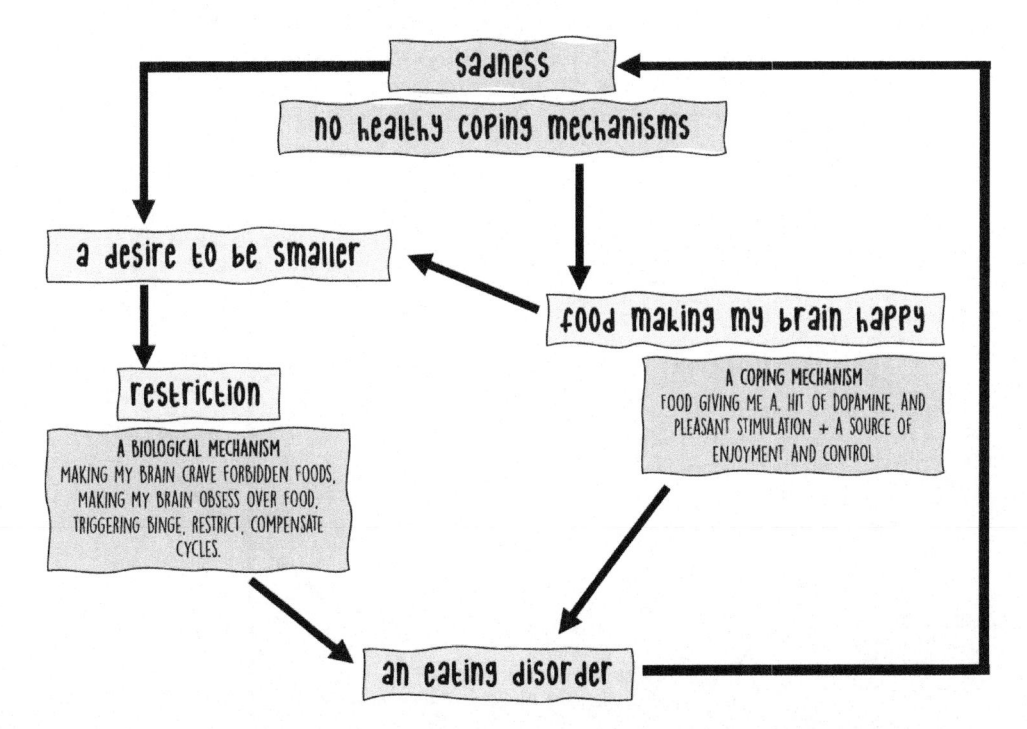

```
                    sadness
          no healthy coping mechanisms

  a desire to be smaller
                          food making my brain happy

      restriction              A COPING MECHANISM
   A BIOLOGICAL MECHANISM    FOOD GIVING ME A HIT OF DOPAMINE, AND
 MAKING MY BRAIN CRAVE       PLEASANT STIMULATION + A SOURCE OF
 FORBIDDEN FOODS,            ENJOYMENT AND CONTROL
 MAKING MY BRAIN OBSESS
 OVER FOOD, TRIGGERING
 BINGE, RESTRICT,
 COMPENSATE CYCLES.

              an eating disorder
```

I had bound myself up in a cycle. I was sad. I had no way of coping. **My brain had learnt that food made it happy so I would be driven to eat. I would eat all the things that I never allowed myself to eat. But then the desire to be smaller would sneak back in: the tentacles of diet culture wrapped around my brain. I would go right back to restricting. And then I would be sad again. The restriction added to that, of course, because it's quite hard for the brain to be rational and cope with**

life when it's malnourished. So we went on. Over and over again. Sad. Eat. Panic. Restrict. Sad. Eat. Panic. Restrict.

But.

Once I knew the *why* of my eating disorder, I could finally think about *how* I could start to fix it. I came to the answers embarrassingly quickly for someone that had spent a decade being ill. Because if the answers had been there all along, why had I wasted so much time?

1. THERAPY TO ADDRESS MY SADNESS AND LEARN HEALTHY COPING MECHANISMS
2. FINDING OTHER THINGS TO MAKE MY BRAIN HAPPY BESIDES FOOD
3. WORKING ON MY BODY IMAGE ISSUES THROUGH THERAPY / JOURNALING / FOLLOWING MORE POSITIVE SOCIAL MEDIA
4. NO. MORE. RESTRICTION.

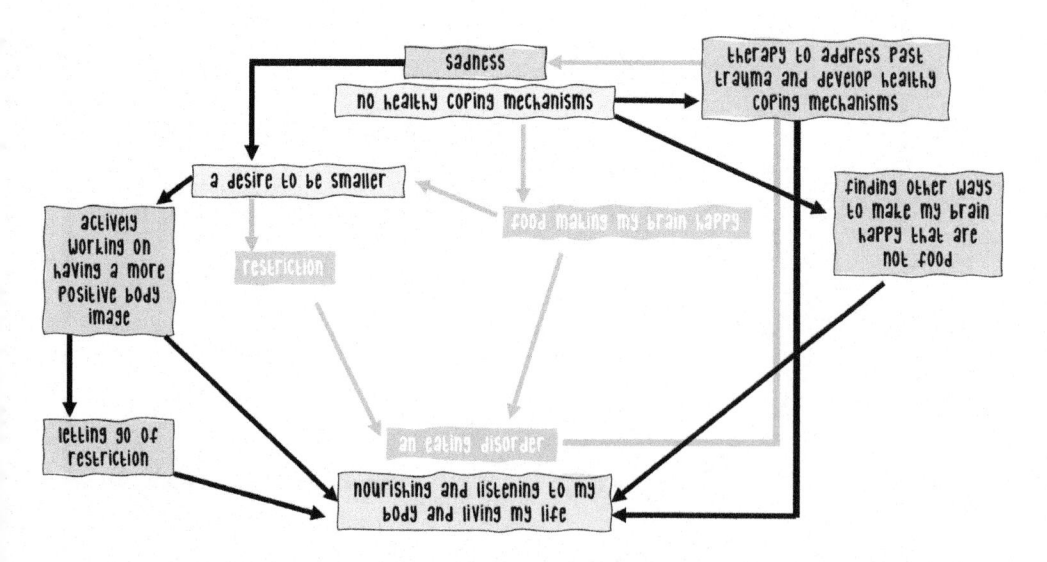

The sadness was the root *because* I had no healthy coping mechanisms. If I could learn to address my sadness and learn healthy coping mechanisms through therapy, I would no longer turn to food to make my brain happy. Simultaneously, I could seek new activities in my life besides eating that would also help make my brain happy so I could do those things instead when I was feeling low. I wouldn't need to turn to food for dopamine hits if I had healthy mechanisms and other things in my life that met those needs. I am realistic in knowing that the desire to be smaller is likely to remain with me for life. I live in a world where smaller bodies are valued more. *But just because society values smaller bodies, doesn't mean that I have to.* So rather than dealing with the desire to be smaller through restriction, which would lead to my eating disordered patterns, I could instead actively work on my body image and let go of restriction. **By removing restriction and by removing the need to use food as an unhealthy coping mechanism, I would be weakening the pathways that led to, and continually reinforced, my eating disorder.**

None of that was rocket science. But I hadn't done any of it in all of the time that I was sick. Why not? **Because those things, whilst not rocket science, are HARD. Therapy? Hard. Scary. Stigmatised. Long waiting lists if you need to access it for free. Very expensive otherwise.** And for what? I needed a lot of therapy for a lot of different things. How was I meant to choose?

Finding other things to make my brain happy? What? Not exercise because that was a risk factor for me. I already had friends and families and hobbies. My attention span was too short to find anything fun for very long. And food was just always there, waiting in the wings.

Working on my body image? No more restrictions? How? In a world of diet culture, in a world of bigger bodies being stigmatised, in a world where I had once been larger and been bullied for it? In a world where you constantly hear about how processed food is poison, and sugar will kill you? Where women aren't considered pretty unless they are thin? How was I meant to let it go?

But. **When you're nearly 28 and you realise that you have lost your 20s because of the above reasons, it suddenly seems a little bit silly.** *I realised that I COULD have spent the last eight years having therapy, learning about my brain, finding new ways to get dopamine, and unlearning everything that society had taught me about my body.* I could have, at 28, been in a very different position. **Not healed, maybe, but with healthy coping mechanisms and a better understanding of how to manage my thoughts and a stronger resolve against diet culture and weight related BS.** But I wasn't. Instead I had just wasted those years stuck in a cycle that had never actually made me happy.

So. Even if it takes eight more years. I'm doing it now. I would rather be 36 and healing than 36 and stuck. Or dead.

Why don't you give it a go? Grab your journal. I've got my mustard yellow old trusty notebook in front of me as I type. Look at your TLDR. Have a think about the things that could have led you here. **Because by understanding it, then you can isolate what you think you may need to heal the roots.** I'm going to take a punt, though, and suggest that they may be VERY SIMILAR to the things I need to do to heal my roots. Draw a table like the one below, if you like. It doesn't even matter if you cannot think of any possible solutions yet: you will have done the hardest part by trying to figure out the things making your roots sick.

Thing Making My Root Sick	Possible Solution
Sadness and trauma	Therapy to address the trauma. Process the past. Journal. Read books about trauma. Talk about it.
A desire to be smaller	Work on body image in therapy and through journaling. Think about your value outside of your body size. Unfollow social media accounts that make you feel bad about your body and follow more positive ones.
Restriction	Stop restricting. Allow yourself permission to eat what you want, when you want. Eat regularly. Eat all of the food groups.
Food as a source of joy	Find new sources of joy. New hobbies, new quick hits of happiness. Build new routines to replace the routines where food made you feel better.

The thing about all of the above, is that it has to be an ACTIVE and ONGOING process and that is often the part that people miss. I could very well say "I unfollowed these social media accounts and thought about the reasons why I value my body for what it can do rather than what it looks like" but if I do not *sustain* this, my eating disorder will slip back in. If I find new coping mechanisms, but do not actively focus on using and maintaining them, my eating disorder will slip back in. If I find new sources of happiness outside of food, but stop engaging with them, my eating disorder will slip back in. It's not a quick fix. It's an ongoing journey. It's an active and ongoing process of monitoring your thoughts, identifying your triggers and establishing new and healthy ways of dealing with them. **This may sound exhausting and like it is too much effort. But is it *really* more exhausting and more effort than life with an eating disorder?**

SECTION TWO: THE MENDING ERA

So. As you can see, things went a little bit wrong in my life. My eating disorder had subsumed me. It had taken over completely: initially, it may have started small, as something that I was living *with*, living *around*. Over the years, it gathered strength and grew stronger, like the parasite that it is. **And I woke up one day, with no real concept of quite how I had got there, and rather than living with the disorder, rather than living around it, I WAS the eating disorder.** The eating disorder was everything. Everywhere. Every action I took, every thought I had, every moment of every day - it was all driven by the eating disorder. I had lost so much. Time. Money. Friends. Memories. Health. Opportunities. My sanity.

I was at a crossroads. Go one way, continue to live in the eating disorder. Or. The other way. A longer road. A harder road, *at first*. But a road that had a light at the end, rather than a road that was shrouded in darkness from the beginning to the premature end. I decided that I had been walking on my dark road for long enough. It was time.

The willow. Unfurling.

This next section is probably just as messy and deranged as the previous one. I have attempted (*key word*) to capture the things that helped me in the process of *beginning* to unpick all of the tangled horror in my mind. This is the mending. Or, the beginning of the mending. The first stages. The slow mending. The almost imperceivable mending. Keyhole surgery, at times.

Picking through the mess. Picture me, a tired, angry woman, in the ruins and rubble of a building that has been burnt to the ground. Fragments of my life scattered among the ruins. Photos. Books. Smashed mugs. Torn pages of diaries. **I am angry because someone burnt down my home. I am tired because life is tiring. I pick through the mess.** Slowly. Turn over the stones; choke on the smoke in my lungs. And I begin to realise, as I piece together the clues I find in the rubble, that there was nobody else to blame. *I was the one that had burnt my home down. I was the one that had caused the rubble.* Someone else may have handed me the matches; I may have bought more myself. Match after match after match. I had lit them and burnt little bits of the house. Over and over again until there was nothing left. **And somehow, even though I had been burning my house down for years, I had only managed to see that it was all gone when there was nothing left.**

So I sob, for a little bit. Naturally. A burnt down house is sad stuff. But then I set about picking up the bricks that are the least damaged. Dusting them off. Looking at them.

Reshaping them. Mending them. Taking what was there, taking the ruins, and finding a way to make them whole again. Salvaging the things that should be salvaged. Leaving the things that shouldn't.

This is me, picking through my head. Finding the bent and mangled parts and unbending them. Noticing the bits that don't need to come with me, and finding ways to let them go. Creating Carla. The mending after the bending.

I mean, it's mostly just my thoughts. Because that's the thing, and the thing that kept me stuck for quite a while: when we want to heal, we often think that we need to *do* things. We need to take ACTION. We need to seize the day. A new diet, a new exercise plan, a new regime. Go, go, go. Hustle. **But actually, a lot of the work of eating disorder recovery happens where the eating disorder lives: in your head.** Because, despite the media stereotype, eating disorders are mental illnesses. *So the only way to really begin to get better must be to go where they are, meet them there and work on it there: inside your head.*

<u>*"How did you heal from your eating disorder?"*</u>
<u>*"Oh, I just did a lot of thinking."*</u>

Sounds stupid. But I think it might be, months or years down the line, the answer that I give.

I'm not healed yet. Nowhere near. But. For the first time ever, I'm *thinking*. And, for the first time ever, I'm *healing*. Seems like a little bit of a coincidence to me. So come with me. You don't have to decide, right now, that you're ready to recover. But come with me through the journey I took. You don't even need to move an inch. I did all of this work whilst sitting on my sofa. Or lying in my bed. Or spread eagled on the floor. Or driving. There's a lot of time for thinking whilst driving. Just make sure you pull over when the crying starts.

6. ASK YOURSELF THE DIFFICULT QUESTION: THE ONE YOU DON'T WANT TO KNOW THE ANSWER TO

The process has to start somewhere. If nothing changes, nothing changes. I had spent YEARS wondering why I wasn't able to get better. I was baffled, honestly. I just KEPT TRYING and didn't see why TRYING wasn't working. I would wake up EVERY DAY and decide that THIS WAS IT. This was the FIRST DAY of the REST OF MY LIFE. **It probably didn't help that I was expecting it to be instant and to require no actual**

work on my part. I thought I could just WILL myself into being better. I genuinely believed, every day, that I could just decide that I was done with it and that be that.

I would always start with a watertight plan of HOW I was going to live without my eating disorder.

I would wake up and I would eat HEALTHY, BALANCED MEALS throughout the day. I would NOT eat snacks. I would NOT eat the staffroom biscuits. Because I was a BINGE EATER. I knew that. If I ate one, I would EAT THEM ALL. I knew this to be true as I had done it before, a hundred times. So NO SNACKS. Just nice, healthy balanced meals. Then, after work, I would go to the GYM where I would follow an EXERCISE PLAN that I had purchased from some lean, perfect influencer. I would BUILD MUSCLE because everyone knows MUSCLE WEIGHS MORE THAN FAT and everyone knows that if you have MORE MUSCLE YOU CAN EAT MORE FOOD. Everyone knows that you can RECOMPOSITION YOUR BODY to have A FLAT STOMACH AND A ROUND BOOTY AND A SNATCHED WAIST if you just EAT CLEAN and LIFT HEAVY.

Sometimes, instead of the weightlifting programme, I would decide to do a DAILY REGIME OF YOGA to help TONE AND LENGTHEN AND LIFT MY BODY because all of the yoga influencers online were all so slim and toned so a YOGA BODY MUST BE THE ANSWER.

Sometimes, there would be fat burner pills in there too. Appetite suppressants.

A strong focus on PROTEIN. RESISTANCE BANDS. Running, sometimes, too. Pilates. *I never quite got deranged enough to try CrossFit.*

I was going to get 10,000 STEPS A DAY because that's GOOD FOR YOU and NOT ACTUALLY JUST A RANDOM NUMBER THAT MEANS NOTHING FOR OVERALL HEALTH AND WELLNESS. 10,000 STEPS is how the PILATES PRINCESSES GET THEIR SNATCHED WAISTS, not just a number that came from a Japanese pedometer in the 90s.

I was going to CUT OUT SUGAR and ARTIFICIAL SWEETENERS and PROCESSED FOODS because EVERYONE KNOWS that they MESS WITH YOUR GUT HEALTH and CAUSE INFLAMMATION and this then makes you STRUGGLE TO LOSE WEIGHT.

It would be easy because *IT WASN'T A DIET, IT WAS A LIFESTYLE CHANGE. IT WAS HEALTHY.*

I ate fruit and vegetables and very few carbs. I was a cauliflower rice girly, an edamame bean noodle gal, a "I prefer rice cakes to bread, no really I do" chick. I was a "I can't imagine not going to the gym everyday I love it so much" girl. The Instagram stories were rife with bowls of watery porridge; roasted vegetables; and painfully posed gym selfies. Or worse, videos I had taken of MYSELF working out, pretending someone else had been videoing me. Embarrassing.

I am sure you can imagine how each and every day went. I woke up with these resolutions to "just" live that life, like it was an easy, balanced and healthy thing to do. I think it's obvious that the above is not a balanced way to live. But it IS the way that we see people online telling us to live, right? They seem happy and healthy and they have perfect bodies and perfect lives. Surely all I had to do was live like them, and I would also be happy and healthy and have a perfect body? **Surely my food issues would just GO AWAY if I forced myself to eat healthy? Surely my body issues would just GO AWAY if I could build a lean, toned body?**

It didn't work. I managed it for two, three days sometimes. Mostly less. Mostly I never even lasted a day. By lunchtime, I would have eaten a whole packet of biscuits in the staff room. Resolved to start again tomorrow. Or, I would make it through to dinner, eat my vegetables and eggs and still be hungry. And then, instead of just eating a bigger meal, I would go and binge and purge because at least that way I would be getting the calories out. I would find myself in the gym, hating every second of the lifting programme, sucking at it because I didn't have the energy to do it properly. Or I would be running through the park, red and puffy, hating it because I hated running. And lightheaded and dizzy because I was hungry. After exercise, I would be ravenous. I might try and eat a small snack. But the hunger would still be there. Growling away. Gnawing away. So I would just eat a handful of crisps. I would tell myself THIS is balance. 80/20 rule. Let yourself have SOME things you love and the more you do, the less you crave them.

Right? For me, apparently, wrong. A handful became the whole bag. Which became me going out to the supermarket and buying £50 worth of food.

Then I would wake up the next day. This was it. This was the FIRST DAY of the REST OF MY LIFE. And so on.

So. I thought about the lifestyle I had lived all those years. And I thought about the tricky questions and the reasons why the way I was living was PROBABLY the EXACT REASON I was unable to get better. I reasoned that it must be. Because I had not changed anything. I had just kept doing the same things, over and over, and not getting better. So, if I wasn't getting better doing those things...the problem must be hidden somewhere within those things, right?

And after I had sat down and drawn out my TLDR, and identified the roots of my disorder, I had to accept the fact that I *had* been restricting. Not just when I was on a diet. Not just when it was obvious. But the whole goddamn time.
The MILLION DOLLAR QUESTION: Are you restricting?

This is the first question you need to ask yourself. Your first instinct is going to be to say NO. The eating disorder is defensive. Restriction is insidious. Sly. Hard to see. It doesn't help that we live in a society that normalises restriction. Every Tom, Dick and Harry is probably restricting under the genuine belief that they are being **balanced and healthy.**

I'm not going to make you tell me the answer. I didn't want to tell myself the answer for a very long time. If you know the answer, that means you have to change something. That means you are, in some way, responsible. So. Read through this. See if you can see yourself.

Calorie-controlled diets
For some, the answer will be a really obvious yes. I was, at times, deliberately and obviously restricting. If you are on any form of calorie controlled diet, you are restricting your intake. If you have downloaded a calorie counting app, or are adding numbers up in your head and eating less than you know you need to maintain your weight, you are restricting. I'm guessing you know that, though, right? That's why you are doing it. Calorie counting can involve eating "whatever you want" but LESS in an "if it fits your macros" approach, or it can involve eating "healthy foods only" as you can generally eat more volume if your diet is based on vegetables rather than chocolate bars and lemon cheesecake. However, any diet where you eat FEWER calories than your maintenance is restriction.

ARE YOU RESTRICTING? Yes.

Looking back, it wasn't therefore THAT surprising to me that, when I was on deliberate diets where I ate less than my body needed, I was having struggles with a binge, restrict, compensate cycle. My body was doing the totally logical, sane thing of trying to survive and therefore driving me to eat. **My brain was doing the totally illogical, insane thing of trying to make my body eat itself instead**, and therefore driving me to compensate and restrict.

The obvious thing to do when you realise the above, and begin to suspect that CALORIE COUNTING may not be helping you is to DO SOMETHING ELSE. **Now, the thing I should have done -** *that we all should have done* **- is to STOP. No more dieting. No more restrictions. <u>But when you have an eating disorder, that doesn't actually seem like one of the options.</u>**

"Lifestyle choice" diets

If you are on any other form of diet that claims to create weight loss without being calorie controlled, such as keto, intermittent fasting, BRANDED DIET PLANS, HCLF, Whole30, Paleo, you are also restricting your intake. There are rules about what you can and cannot eat and these diet plans are, usually, followed with the intention of losing weight. Technically, you would lose weight because it was still calorie controlled, right, but people love to ignore that. Ignorance is apparently bliss. I never found bliss in any of this, though, so I'm not so sure. But I did, in fact, try many of these things over the years. Cutting out carbs was something I did often (because I knew they were higher in calories). Cutting out fat was also something I did habitually (same reason). I would NEVER in a MILLION YEARS have actually tried out keto as I was SO afraid of fat.

The issue with these diets is that you often convince yourself that it's NOT a diet. It's a LIFESTYLE. It's HEALTHY. **You tell yourself that you aren't on a diet because you aren't counting calories, you're just following some rules to make yourself feel healthier and be healthier and get control over your appetite which is just, for some BIZARRE reason, out of your control.** Anyway. It's still restriction. Why?

Well, if you're on keto, you aren't allowed carbs. You might be telling yourself you DON'T WANT bread and pasta and potatoes and crisps, but is that true? If you're on a branded diet plan with a point system, you can EAT WHATEVER YOU WANT but only a CERTAIN AMOUNT. If you're used up all your points, you CANNOT EAT ANY MORE OF THOSE CRISPS. If you're doing intermittent fasting, the common result of this is that you eat less during the day. If you're doing 5:2, you're insane. If you're on Whole30, you can only eat 30 things. So you're obviously restricting the other 7893 things you may want to eat, which will *absolutely* include things like crisps and chocolate and crusty white bakery bread and lemon drizzle cake. Right? **All of these diets are restrictive because they all RESTRICT you from eating certain foods, eating certain amounts or eating above a certain quota.** So if you are doing any of these under the guise of "not restricting" ask yourself the question again.

<u>**ARE YOU RESTRICTING?**</u> Yes.

Do you *really* not like processed foods?

"Oh you eat SO HEALTHILY," the middle aged women in the staff room used to sigh at me as I ate my vegetables and salads for lunch followed by my protein oat balls or my coconut oil, dark chocolate and oat flour "bakes". They would be eating nothing, or they would be eating tinned soup. Then, they would eat a bunch of biscuits from the tin.

"I just enjoy it," I would say with a shrug. "Growing up, we always ate like this. I don't like processed foods because I never ate them."

And. The worst part? I *judged* them. I thought. *Look at them eating all those biscuits. Where is their self-control? If they just ate normally, they wouldn't get so hungry they need to eat all of those biscuits!* **It was the ultimate hypocrisy considering what was going on behind my scenes but, hey, the ED do be like that.**

Holier than thou. I was the type of person that I now, personally, find ANNOYING. Drifting around, acting like I was on some moral high ground because I rarely ate cookies. Except, of course, I DID. Sometimes three of four. Packets. At once. But you know. THEY didn't know that. THEY thought I LOVED clean eating and DISLIKED processed foods.

Did I? Do I?

That's still something I'm working through. I do, genuinely, adore fruits and vegetables. I do, genuinely, prefer sweet potatoes to hash browns. I LOVE brown bread. I LOVE bran cereal. But. I do like chocolate bars. I do like crisps. I do like white toast with butter. I do like cake. I do like fish fingers. And, when I would binge, can you guess what I would binge on? It wouldn't USUALLY be vegetables and tofu (although if that was all that was around, it was fair game). It would be processed foods. Pizza. Crisps. Chips. Biscuits. Cakes. Pork pies. Sausage rolls. Coleslaw. I could list every processed food in the supermarket, probably. I did it for five years. **There's a high possibility that I worked my way through the entire inventory of products during my time in active duty.**

I always used to say, also, that processed food gave me bad skin. The irony of this situation is that I NEVER had good skin. My skin was constantly breaking out, constantly dry or oily or spotty, swinging between extremes. And I had persuaded myself that it was BECAUSE my willpower would crumble and I would eat processed foods (either as part of "trying" to find balance, or as part of my binge episodes) that my skin was bad. But. Listen. ***Five months into recovery and there's not a single spot on my silly little face.*** I eat vegetables. I eat carbs and fats and proteins. I eat

whole foods. I eat processed foods. I drink water and hot chocolate and tea and fizzy drinks. All of this is balanced, now. And shocker. My skin has cleared up. So let's ask the question…**DID processed food give me bad skin? Or did my eating disorder give me bad skin?** The malnourishment? The stress I was placing on my body? One day, pumping myself full of nothing but veg and the next, eating endless amounts of processed foods in a binge cycle? One day, eating no gluten and no dairy. The next, eating it all. One week of intermittent fasting, followed by another week of eating all day, every day. Intense exercise. Hours a day. Sweating all over my skin; stressing my exhausted body even more.

So. Do processed foods give YOU bad skin? Have you actually tried to eat them whilst NOT engaging in an eating disorder? Because if you haven't, if you have only been "allowing" yourself them whilst also engaging in any disordered behaviours at all, how on earth do you know that the bad skin is a result of the processed food? It seems a little more likely it's a result of the eating disorder and the lack of consistent nourishment, if I'm being honest. It certainly was for me.

And, let's be real here. *Say it IS the processed food giving you spots. Is that really the worst thing? Or would it be worse, perhaps, to spend the rest of your life miserable, starving, restricted, out of control, scared, lonely and disordered AND have beautiful skin?* Because I certainly wasn't spending very much time engaging in the world, spots or no spots, when I was deeply disordered. Now, I go out without caring if my hair is a mess or I have a spot or whatever, because I'm going out to LIVE and DO STUFF and HAVE FUN and BE A REAL PERSON rather than a shadowy wraith with perfect skin. So maybe processed food DOES make you spotty. But an eating disorder ruins your life. And takes everything from you. Seems like a no brainer choice to me. *I would rather become a giant walking spot than return to the small hell world I inhabited for so long.*

But anyway. Think about your diet. Do you like healthy foods? Do you like eating clean? Do you enjoy the way it makes your body feel? Maybe, yes! The feeling part, most probably! But. Do you also want to eat OTHER things too but you don't? Do you want to have porridge, fruit and yoghurt for breakfast and then eat some biscuits at 11? Stir fried vegetables and tofu for lunch, and then a chocolate bar? Some days, for dinner, salmon and couscous and roasted broccoli, but other days, pizza? If you want to do those things but don't…

ARE YOU RESTRICTING? Yes.

Are you really not hungry first thing in the morning?

Intermittent Fasting. The answer to all of our problems, right? We can skip a whole meal, wait until later in the day, eat HUGE meals and still lose weight. Magic.

I managed at one point to persuade myself that I genuinely WASN'T HUNGRY in the morning. Of course I *wasn't*. Eventually. **I stopped being hungry because I systematically taught my body that I WAS NOT GOING TO FEED IT at a certain time.** Your body is smart, right? So if it figures out that you are going to IGNORE it crying out for food in the morning, it stops asking. It's a waste of its energy - precious and in need of conserving seeing as you're starving it - to keep up the processes that send those hunger signals. So it slows it all down. And your brain gets better at ignoring it. Practice makes perfect.

Some people may genuinely not be hungry in the morning. Is that you? Are you sure? Like FOR REAL? Or is it just easier to believe that because then you don't have to eat breakfast? And if you don't have to eat breakfast, you can push back all of your meals and save up food for later in the day. **When you're eating less than your body needs, it makes sense to try and eat it as late as possible so that you can feel hungry for the least possible time, right?**

Maybe you DO genuinely NOT FEEL HUNGRY IN THE MORNING. But let's be real here, okay? Let's be real. **People with eating disorders probably should not be trusting their hunger signals because years of following disordered patterns (bingeing, restricting, purging, over exercising) completely and utterly messes these up.**

Some people may have genuine medical reasons to need to intermittent fast. If you think you are one of these people, have you had this confirmed by a medical professional? Really? Or did you just Google your symptoms?

I did this for years, okay? I skipped breakfast. Saved my calories up for later in the day. Ate HUGE volume meals for lunch and dinner which then my body struggled to digest anyway. Why did it struggle? When you don't eat for hours and hours and hours, your digestion slows down. Logical and sensible, right? **A fire doesn't keep burning if you aren't putting fuel on it. And then if you try and get it to burn by suddenly dumping a WHOLE LOAD of rubbish cheap coal on it, rather than the right amount of quality fuel, that fire is going to take a little while to get going.**

I felt physically stuffed, with the food sitting there in my stomach. Churning. Uncomfortable. **And yet, although I was FULL, I was still HUNGRY because the food was taking years to digest AND I hadn't eaten anything satisfying (fats, carbs!) AND I hadn't listened to my mental hunger or tastebuds either.** And do you know how that used to end? I would end up bingeing because I was still <u>SO HUNGRY</u> and then I would lose control over myself and my impulses.

Sometimes I would try and eat breakfast. *I would think it MUST be skipping breakfast that is the issue. If I eat breakfast, maybe this problem will go away.* It didn't go away. So I would always cycle back to intermittent fasting, having decided (with incorrigible evidence) that eating breakfast did not, in fact, help.

But it wasn't eating breakfast that was the problem. Three guesses what the problem *actually* was?

You don't need three guesses, do you?

It's because **I was still restricting**. I was still eating fewer calories than I needed, just spread out more throughout the day now. Or I was eating enough, maybe, but not things I ACTUALLY wanted. Or I was eating some things I wanted but exercising to excess to BURN IT ALL OFF. Or I was still fasting: either by skipping lunch or dinner, or not eating after 5pm.

So the cycle would continue. I would eat breakfast. Restrict. Binge. Compensate. Restrict. Give up on eating breakfast. Restrict. Binge. Compensate. Restrict. Try eating breakfast again. Restrict. Binge. Compensate. Over and over and over.

If this sounds like you...

<u>ARE YOU RESTRICTING?</u> Yes.

<u>Why have you gone vegan?</u>

On and off throughout my life, I had been vegetarian. I was never particularly a big fan of meat anyway, and the idea of eating animals was, to me, not really a vibe. So by the time I was in my 20s, I didn't eat much meat at all - I only really ate chicken. Chicken breast, *obviously*, not chicken thighs. And that was only really because I had seen online that it was a good source of lean protein which would, of course, help me with the ultimate life quest to lose fat and build muscle.

When I was 26, I began to follow a bunch of vegan influencers online and couldn't HELP but notice that they all shared some very key similarities: they were all skinny, they all had abs, and they all seemed to be able to eat large quantities of food. That was my dream. So I decided to go vegan. It's important to note, though, that I DID agree with what they were saying. I still do.
I believe that the dairy industry and the meat industry are, due to capitalism and over-demand, horrendous. Ethically, I 100% support veganism. I stand by ALL of the righteous anger I exhibited towards meat and dairy when I was ONE OF THOSE PREACHING VEGANS. I still believe it all. I wish I had the mental stability to be vegan.

But.

I didn't go vegan because of those ethics and those morals. I knew, at the time, that I hadn't because when I would binge, I would binge on meat and dairy. Had my decision *truly* and *fundamentally* been guided FIRST AND FOREMOST by morals and ethics, I would have been bingeing on vegan food, right? I would have been unable to allow myself, even in the zombie binge mode, to eat the things I ate: pork pies, sausage rolls, fresh cream chocolate cakes.

I knew, deep down, why I had chosen to go vegan. **It gave me a socially acceptable reason to be volume eating meals that were mostly made of vegetables.** It gave me a reason to not eat cheese and chocolate - because EVERYONE knows that the vegan versions of those taste like trash. **It gave me a reason to turn down baked goods that people had made or bought to share. It gave me a reason to check the back of every packet at every party without looking like I was checking for calories.** And then TRAGICALLY be unable to eat most of the snacks because of milk powder. It gave me a reason to bring my own food so others didn't have to cook for me. It gave me a reason to select the lowest calorie option at a restaurant and to skip the fries at fast food places because they were *cooked in animal fat*. I got a thrill every single time a restaurant didn't have substantial vegan options and I was "forced" to have a salad.

It also gave me really, really bad gas but we don't need to dwell on THAT.

Are you vegan? Why? It may well, heavily, be to do with values and morals and ethics. But is there any chance, any chance AT ALL, that you chose to go vegan for any of the reasons I did?

Because if you did...
ARE YOU RESTRICTING? Yes.

Intolerant to dairy. I can't eat gluten.

Then there inevitably comes the INTOLERANCE phase. You read about dairy and gluten on the Internet and how they are, allegedly, awful for digestion and inflammation and your skin. Coincidentally, dairy and gluten are often contained in higher calorie foods like cakes and bread. Also coincidentally, you have awful digestion (bloated all the time, food sits in your stomach for what feels like days, you've very constipated) and terrible skin (spotty, dry, inflamed).

So, gleefully, you decide you MUST be gluten intolerant and dairy intolerant. You MUST cut these things out, at all costs. And then, *maybe*, you will look like the celebrities: skinny, perfect skin, drifting around ethereally without any hint of digestive distress. *I realise now, they probably didn't experience digestive distress because you actually need to have food in your stomach for digestion to occur* but, hey, I had to get there on my own. It was a process.

Anyway. No more bread. **No more dairy. No more gluten. Just like being vegan: an excuse to check the packets at parties; an excuse to not eat the food and bring my own; an excuse not to choose higher calorie options at restaurants; an excuse not to eat cheese or bread or chocolate. A socially acceptable reason to restrict.** And, at times, a way that I would deliberately isolate myself and avoid social situations: *that place isn't GF, I'll give it a miss this time* or *sorry I accidentally ate some milk earlier and can't get out of the bathroom now!*

Was I intolerant to dairy? And gluten? At the time, my digestive system *really did* seem to struggle. I really did believe, on some level, even if not the deepest one, that I was intolerant. But. But. But. *I was also starving myself, vomiting frequently and eating mostly vegetables. For years.*

If you think you have a gluten or dairy intolerance, go to a doctor. They can confirm it.

It's far more likely, if you have an eating disorder, that your digestive issues are a result of the eating disorder rather than a specific intolerance. You've kind of trained your body to be intolerant to food. All food. Gluten. Dairy. The whole broccoli and head of cauliflower you ate last night. Reintroducing foods slowly, and building up variety, will really help with this. Now, I eat yoghurt more than once a day. I eat bread every day. **And guess what? Either I'm Jesus and naturally healed myself or I was never intolerant in the first place.**

So. If you think you have a real bona fide intolerance, go to the doctor. If the doctor says no, ask yourself the question that we probably know the answer to.

ARE YOU RESTRICTING? Yes.

I LOVE EXERCISE IT'S SO GOOD FOR MY MENTAL AND PHYSICAL HEALTH

Exercise is a tough one. A really tough one. I play netball, I rock climb and I love a bit of yoga. And, genuinely, those things have always been entirely separate from weight loss or weight control. Netball is fun and I love the team element and made lots of friends doing it. Rock climbing was entirely focussed on being strong and flexible and developing technique, so weight was, largely, irrelevant. And yoga...I just really enjoy the feeling of a good stretch!

However. Over the years, I watched lots of YouTube and I followed lots of fitness influencers on various social media platforms. They boasted of how they could EAT SO MUCH FOOD because they had BUILT LOTS OF MUSCLE and MUSCLE NEEDS MORE ENERGY THAN FAT TO MAINTAIN. So, naturally, as someone with an eating disorder, the idea of being able to EAT LOTS and have a toned, socially desirable body was FABULOUS. So. I went in cycles. Buy a programme. Go to the gym. Lift weights, with no real idea what I was doing. Give up on the programme after a few weeks. Buy resistance bands in a bundle, along with a plan. Do the plan. Give up on the plan. Follow a YouTube challenge. Hate every minute of it. Wonder why my body wasn't changing. Cycle on cycle on cycle.

Some people enjoy weight lifting. Some people enjoy cardio workouts. I was NOT one of those people. But I kept pretending to be. I kept dragging myself to the gym, or to the YouTube playlist every day, forcing myself to do the workouts and hating them. I wasn't giving them my all because I couldn't. Why not? A) Because I didn't enjoy them and B) Because I still wasn't eating enough fuel for my body, let alone enough fuel for an over exercised body. **I really thought, somehow, that I was going to GET STRONG and BUILD MUSCLE whilst eating LESS than my body needed to have a healthy period.**

I hate the term 'calories in, calories out' like your body is some kind of maths equation. But. It makes sense to think about it here, just to conceptualise what I was doing to my body. I was not putting enough IN. And I was taking more OUT than I was putting IN. So even in the times where I was "eating enough" and "eating what I wanted" I was EXERCISING TOO MUCH and taking energy AWAY.

So, we know what THAT means, right? Restricting. Restricting my body of the correct amount of energy for the activities that I was forcing it to do.

Does that sound like you? Are you exercising a lot and still eating very little? Are you exercising to *earn* food?

ARE YOU RESTRICTING? Yes.

Are you really a thirsty person? No, really. Are you really THAT thirsty of a person?

I don't GET hungry first thing in the morning. All I want is a cup of tea. Or two. Or three. Now, after a while, this was true. I didn't get hungry in the morning. Why? Obviously, I systematically taught my body not to expect food. I drank lots of tea. No sugar, of course. A tiny splash of NO ADDED SUGAR OAT MILK. The warm liquid and the minimal calories from the splash of milk kept me "full" because I was filling my belly with lots of sloshing warm liquid. The mugs I drink from are BIG - about 500ml - and I would have 2-3 mugs of tea before 10am. That's 1.5L of liquid in my stomach, the volume of which is only about 2-4 litres. So I was basically just putting lots of liquid in and it was temporarily making my stomach feel like it was full. **Oh the betrayal she must have felt when she realised it wasn't food or nourishment I was filling her with.**

It's common diet advice, of course. We love a bit of toxic diet advice. IF YOU'RE HUNGRY, HAVE A DRINK. AN EXCELLENT APPETITE SUPPRESSANT. *Do you know what a better appetite suppressant is? Food.* But you know. We're all a little disordered here so who I am to say that? Personally, I was fully convinced that I wasn't hungry and that I was just an incredibly thirsty person.

You also hear that thing touted around that people often eat too much because they THINK THEY ARE HUNGRY when they are actually thirsty. And yes, some preliminary looks at the scientific research (because, when considering your body, health and nutrition you SHOULD seek out the research, not just what an influencer says online or a crazy leggings lady writes in her haphazard book of advice) does suggest that people confuse dehydration with hunger. But. **That's not you, my dear. You aren't dehydrated if you're slamming back litres of tea and diet cola and energy drink, okay?** You've had plenty of liquid. The "hunger/thirst" confusion occurs in those who HAVE NOT been drinking and who ARE dehydrated. You are, on balance, probably too hydrated.

I certainly was. Because my drinking (tea, fizzy drinks, water, hot chocolate - low calories duh - and squash…not an alcoholic…yet) continued all day. I would have about eight cups of tea, 2 litres of Pepsi Max, three or four hot chocolates…and all because everytime I would feel ANYTHING in my stomach (HUNGER, BABE, IT WAS HUNGER) I would decide I was thirsty and head off to OVER HYDRATE my poor body.

Drinking too much, I have learnt, is actually dangerous. Healthy adult kidneys can eliminate about 1L of water an hour. Cool. Have you considered, though, that given your eating disorder, your kidneys *may not be healthy kidneys?* Mine weren't. Mine were diseased. Anyway. Drinking too much water messes with the balance of electrolytes in the blood. Electrolytes (sodium, potassium, magnesium, chloride and calcium) need to be balanced to maintain healthy blood, heart rhythm and muscle function. Too much water dilutes these and puts you at risk of swelling of your cells, including in the brain, which can cause confusion and seizures.

It also stops you being hungry. Which means you become malnourished. So, check in with yourself. Are you REALLY a thirsty person? Or are you drinking all that fluid to suppress your appetite? *If, like me, you've been doing it for many years, you may find that you genuinely FEEL like you NEED all of that liquid. It's a habit, right? And your body has come to expect 10L of fluid a day so will be confused when you stop doing that.* So you may feel like you need to keep drinking that much fluid. But let me tell you. You need to eat far more than you need to drink 10L of liquid. You need to eat far more than you need to keep using drinks as an appetite suppressant. So, start slowly reducing your fluid intake. One week have 9L not 10. Then the next 8 not 9. You get the vibe.

Do you drink an excess of fluid? Do you find yourself feeling hungry before you want to eat, and thinking *I'll just have a drink to tide me over?* Do you have a liquid breakfast?

If so…

ARE YOU RESTRICTING? Yes. Not liquid though. Just food. Just the one thing your body needs to grow and survive and be nourished. At least you aren't dehydrated though. Just malnourished.

Was I restricting?

The hardest question that you actually need to ask yourself, though, is this one: what are you waiting for? No, but ACTUALLY, what are you waiting for? Most

people have this vague idea in their head that they will recover when they are "sick enough". But when will that be?

I hear so many people say that they do not feel that they are sick enough to recover because they have not been to hospital. So…what? Are you *genuinely* waiting to go to hospital? Are you *genuinely* trying to get sick enough that you need to be hospitalised? **Do you *actually* want to be stuck in a hospital for weeks on end, unable to see friends and family other than in tiny visiting slots; eating hospital food; being poked and prodded 24/7; being controlled by others; not being able to work or engage with hobbies outside of reading, crosswords and watching TV; and being surrounded by other ill and suffering people?**

It's probably not that you actually WANT to go to hospital. But our eating disorders are always looking for a way to convince us that we are not ready to commit to recovery. Always. A really common one is the hospital one. *How* can you be *sick enough* to be *ready to recover* if you have never been hospitalised? *How* can your eating disorder be *bad enough to recover from* if it's not even *bad enough to be hospitalised for*? *How* can you feel valid and tell people that you are recovering from an eating disorder if you never became *so frail and ill* that you needed *medical treatment*?

But. Let me tell you this as someone who used to think like that; and someone who was ill for a decade without hospitalisation; and someone who did, eventually go to hospital: I *wish* I could take it all back. I wish I could go back to me ten years ago and tell her: stop. You will never be sick enough. **Hospitals will not help you recover, either. Hospitals actually rather hate patients with eating disorders.**

So. I'm not actually going to talk anymore about my hospital experience. Why? It could fill a whole book. There is so much I could write about those days, the darkest days of my life. BUT. **This book isn't about that. The hospital was not part of my mending other than the fact that it locked me in place, froze me in time, and forced me to think.** But you are giving yourself a chance to think right now by sitting down and reading this book, hopefully with a cup of tea and a lemon flavoured snack. And then, you can go out into the fresh air, and go to the supermarket, and see your friends, and go to work, and *live your life* instead of being locked up in a beeping prison full of constantly changing staff, screaming patients and disgusting food. You can do your thinking in an environment where you have your freedom, still, and where you have the time to process your emotions *and* see the people you love.

You *don't* need to go to the hospital to do this work. And I didn't either: I just couldn't see it at the time.

I won't discuss my experience here because it is not necessary for bending or mending or never-ending recovery. I won't discuss it here because I do not want anyone to feel invalid or competitive about the fact that they never went to hospital OR that they went to hospital more than me. **I also do not want to add to the stereotype: I was wildly unwell for many, many years before I was hospitalised and going to hospital is not something that MOST people with eating disorders ever do. It was, in the grand scheme of my sickness, the smallest percentage of time and entirely irrelevant.** It didn't make me better. It did not help me recover.

If you have never been to hospital for your ED, take heed: you don't want to. Your ED may think you do. It may be telling you that you *aren't sick enough* and that you *aren't valid* and that *other people are better at their eating disorder because you've seen them dancing with an IV drip on social media*. If you are struggling with an eating disorder, you are sick enough. Going to hospital is not something to be ticked off a checklist of *I must reach these illness milestones before I can recover*. Because guess what? **I went to the hospital. And I still didn't feel sick enough**. I was sectioned under the Mental Health Act because I tried to self-discharge myself because I felt that "someone else needed the bed more than me" even though I was, quite literally, dying. YOU WILL NEVER FEEL SICK ENOUGH.

And when I got out of the hospital? I didn't feel sick enough either. And every day since? Not sick enough. Every time I see someone else, a little sicker than me? Not sick enough. Every time I see someone else, healthier than me? Not sick enough. If I eat? Not sick enough. If I don't? Not sick enough. If I gain weight? Not sick enough. If I maintain? Not sick enough. If I lose? Not sick enough. Every single day, I have eaten my meal plan and wished that I hadn't because I didn't feel sick enough. Every single day, I have looked at my body, and *existed in* my body, and I have not felt sick enough.

Hospital changes nothing about the fact that YOU NEED TO RECOVER. If you cut your hand whilst cooking dinner, you are injured. You don't need to go to the hospital. Most of the time anyway. Imagine bleeding all over your kitchen and refusing to clean the wound or put a plaster on it? Why would you do that? *Oh because John cut his hand open last week and it was worse than my cut. John needed to go to the hospital. I don't so my wound doesn't need treatment.* Very sensible. What will happen to you? For one, you'll have a LOT of mess to clean up later. And for the other? You may end up in hospital anyway, one day, from gangrene. Or dead. Or just living with an annoying wound that refuses to heal properly, and weeps and bleeds and oozes for weeks and weeks and weeks and then, eventually, scars over far worse than the wound.

The feeling will never come. You will never be sick enough. So that only leaves one logical option, right? If you are never going to be sick enough, you may as well start to recover RIGHT NOW rather than get any worse.

Don't ignore the wound. Clean it up now, not later.

Doing the work as soon as you are able means that there will be less work to do in the long run. Don't get me wrong: this is going to be a marathon, it's going to be gruelling, it's going to be the hardest thing you have ever done. But. **The sooner you start, the less time you are giving the thoughts and behaviours and habits to become part of the furniture in your brain. The sooner you start, the less time you are giving the ED to grow stronger, the parasite that it is, living in you and growing stronger as it sucks your life out every day.**

> There is no point in you waiting until you are "sick enough" because that is going to involve you waiting forever. **"Sick enough" is a train that never comes because there will *always* be someone sicker than you.** But...there are a lot of people who are *healthier* than you. And do you know what they are doing? Building careers, and families, and friendships. Eating cake. Sunbathing in parks. Reading books. Exercising in ways that they enjoy. Living.
>
> I don't want to be "sick enough" anymore. I want to be healthy enough to LIVE.

So. **After all that intense thinking about the last decade of my life, I did come to the conclusion that I was, in fact, going to have to recover.** I was going to have to recover because *otherwise I was going to have to live the rest of my life being sick, and trying to get sicker, and never getting sick enough.*

I also had to accept that I was in fact, restricting. On SO MANY LEVELS and in SO MANY DIFFERENT WAYS. <u>I had believed, for a decade, that my eating disorder was an issue with overconsumption.</u> That's the kicker when you don't trust yourself around food. **You ASSUME that it's to do with a lack of control around food that means that you EAT TOO MUCH.** You can't see that the trigger for that is, usually, related to restriction.

For me, it was a combination of restriction types in cycles over the years. Sometimes I was directly restricting intake: calorie counting. Others I was restricting food groups: veganism, whole foods only, no processed foods. Sometimes I was restricting energy: over exercising whilst under-fueling for the amount I was doing. **The WHOLE TIME I was restricting mentally because, deep down, I always wanted to be smaller.**

Every action I took around food was driven by the need to shrink my body. The things I ate, or didn't. The exercise I did. The vomiting. The bingeing. The starving. It was all with an underlying drive to Just. Get. Smaller. Ironically, for the most part, after the initial weight loss when I was 22, the endless cycles of bingeing and restricting meant that I basically stayed the same weight for years. Just going up and down slowly within the same range.

I didn't want to see the truth for what it was. I didn't want to admit that I was restricting. Because if restriction was the PROBLEM, that meant that the solution was to GIVE UP RESTRICTION.

We hear this advice all the time. I know I heard it a thousand times over the years. But I always dismissed it because I was so blindly convinced that I wasn't *really* restricting. It's time to be honest now, though. Healing only happens when you face what needs to be healed. So the first, most pivotal stage in the MENDING process was to accept it. So, yes. I was restricting.

I had to accept that I needed to stop. **Altogether. No more calorie counting, no more over exercising, no more veganism, no more fake intolerances, no more cutting out processed foods, no more restricting food groups. And, most importantly: no more trying to lose weight.**

This was terrifying to me. In my head, it would mean that I would GAIN LOTS OF WEIGHT and SPIRAL OUT OF CONTROL. After all, I KNEW I couldn't trust myself around food. I'd tried that and it didn't work.

But.

The rational voice whispered. It was quiet at first, the rational voice. So quiet I almost missed it.

You've never actually tried. You've never actually tried *to trust yourself around food - not properly. You've always been, on some level, restricting. You've allowed yourself to eat, sometimes, sure, but always returned to the self-disgust and restriction soon after. You were never actually committed to it. You always wanted, underneath it all, to lose weight.*

And it was true. Whilst I did, on and off, decide I was going to stop restricting, I never let go of the desire to lose weight and therefore I always returned to restriction in some form or another. I realised that my binge eating as a child and as a teenager had coloured my perspective: I thought that it was ME that was the issue. I thought that there was something written into my genetic code that meant that if I ate, I wouldn't be able to stop. Because, to be fair, that was my experience. But. What I hadn't realised was that I WAS restricted even then. Not in the same conscious way that I restricted as an adult, maybe, but food was not freely available in the way that it needed to be for me not to fall into a binge/restrict cycle. **As a child, restricted by adults and diet culture and all the messy rules around food. As a teenager, and an adult, by myself and the diets and the constant yoyo-ing back and forth.**

So. I had to let go.

Horrendous.

But.

I had reached the point where I could see that restriction wasn't doing anything for me. ***It wasn't getting me to lose weight. I was just cycling up and down in the same weight bracket, becoming more and more unhappy, more and more physically unwell, and more and more isolated.*** Restriction was meant to make my life better by making me thinner. Sure, at first, it *did* make me thinner. But it didn't make my life any better. **And then, eventually, my body adapted to the low intake and stopped losing weight and I got stuck in a cycle where I was restricting for NO REAL REASON other than that I was too scared to stop in case the weight piled back on.**

So I decided. I would try. I would commit to no more restriction.

<u>**I decided that I would do it for a month.**</u> That way, if I lost control and ballooned up, I would be able to go back to the eating disorder. It would be an experiment. I would commit to it for one month. After all, I knew that I could go from bigger to smaller. I knew how. I'd done it before. I was an expert at going from bigger to smaller. It was the small to smaller that I had struggled with. **I'm not necessarily recommending that you do what I did and set yourself a time frame because that might not work for you.** But for me, I had spent YEARS unable to REALLY commit to giving up restriction *just in case* I lost control. So by promising myself that if I DID lose control, I could go back at X point in time, I was able to make the tenuous first steps forwards.

7. THE PLAN OF ACTION: FOOD

So you have DECIDED to commit to recovery. You have done the foundational thinking: you have sat down, picked through your past and looked at the reasons why your eating disorder may have started and been sustained. You have looked at your hellscape in stark reality. You have accepted that you will never be sick enough. You can see that your choices are: recover, spend the rest of your life in hell, or die young. You have decided you are going to choose the first option. **Maybe you have committed to doing recovery forever or, if you're a baby like me, maybe just for a month as an experiment.**

But…now what?

What actually happens next?

I had gone home. I was sitting in my empty flat, alone. I had done the pre-work: I had thought about my past with eating and my body; I had identified that my eating disorder was, in part, a coping mechanism and also, in part, down to restriction; and I had committed, fully, for a month at least, to recovery. But what did that *mean*?

I needed a PLAN.

And everyone knows that the BEST LAID PLANS always fail, right? Because people make them too complicated. If you think about all of my "plans" to recover before, they were all *very* complicated. They involved me doing one hundred things at once. One of which was still restriction, of course, but you get the picture. As soon as I messed up one part of the plan, there seemed little point continuing with the rest. I was doomed from the start with those plans. Complicated plans allow a million different ways for you to fail. And when you *fail,* your eating disorder takes that as OBVIOUS PROOF that recovery is IMPOSSIBLE.

So I made a simple little plan based on all of the research I had done over the years, and things that people who had *actually recovered* spoke of doing. **I came up with a 5 POINT PLAN OF ACTION.** 5 is a good number, right? That's why 5 year plans are so popular, right? They hold strategic value - **a balanced timeline that is long enough for change, but not too long that it seems impossible**. And that's what *my 5 POINTS OF RECOVERY offered: a strategic approach that would allow me to balance the key areas of my recovery with a higher chance of success.*

Also, the fewer rules I had, the less likely it was that any of them were being driven by - or could be hijacked by - my eating disorder.

Finally, to be completely lame, I decided that I was going to write them around the points of a star. Why? To remind me of one of my main WHYs of recovery. This is a little self-indulgent, okay, so feel free to look away, or puke in your mouth or whatever, but: when I was a child, I had a primary school teacher who was SUCH A CHEERLEADER of mine. She was honestly a gem. She could probably tell that my home life wasn't very ideal - having been a teacher myself, you can always tell the kids that aren't being loved in the right way. They're always a little bit too much. Too happy. Too smiley. Too positive. A facade to hide the depth of the pain they can't yet name or understand. Anyway, at the end of the year, she wrote in my report: *Carla lights up every room that she walks into. She's got stars in her eyes when she smiles.* My mum said she was proud of me.

I had stars in my eyes when I smiled. And it was true - I was energetic and fun and bouncy and happy and people did gravitate towards me. I brought laughter with me. I was funny. I *HATE* writing all of that because it makes me sound arrogant, but I was a good person to be around.

Until I got sick. And then I wasn't. **Slowly but surely, as I starved my body and my brain, I starved away that happy-go-lucky girl with the sparkle and the pizzazz and the endless energy and the stars in her eyes.** I became someone else. I wasn't even a shell of myself - none of that old version of me existed at all in my malnourished body. **There wasn't room for her.** There wasn't any energy for her. **She was too much to be sustained. She was gone.**

But when I committed to recovery, I realised that I could have some of her back. Not her, of course, because she was ten years old and on a track to develop decades of issues. But a new version. I could create myself on the prototype, but this time I would be able to use all of my knowledge and my adult brain to fight the things I couldn't as a child. **And as I did that, and pruned away the parts of me that were no good and built new, healthy parts of me...the stars would come back. I had to believe that.**

The eating disorder period of my life had been dark. Where I was, there had been too much light pollution. London air. Clogging up the sky, hiding the light. Now I was going somewhere else, where I could breathe easier, where the sludgy, nasty pollution wasn't going to follow me. Of course, it would be a long journey so the stars wouldn't be visible straight away...but as I walked further...I would spot glimmers...and push onwards…towards a clear sky and the sparkles of the stars free from the darkness of pollution.

So. Five points for a five point star. Five points to get my sparkle back.

My 5 Points of Recovery:

1. **Eat three meals and three snacks a day MINIMUM. Eat these every 2-3 hours. If you are hungry outside of these times, eat EXTRA.**

It was important that this happened EVEN IF I wasn't hungry. Early on in my recovery, this was vital as I didn't have hunger cues. I had ignored them for so long that they had just kind of…gone away. *Eating regularly, every 2-3 hours, would begin to teach my body that I was going to feed it properly again.* It could learn to redevelop its hunger cues, and, at the same time, learn to trust me. **If it learnt to trust me, it would, in theory, be less likely to drive me to binge.**

I made a timetable. I'd always loved a timetable at school: I was a stationery girly. I drew it out on pretty paper, with my fine tip felt tips. I input the eating times into my calendar too and set alarms on my phone. I made a star chart, and stuck a sticker on it for every point of eating.

The six points of eating were a minimum but in order to ensure I was NEVER restricting, if I was hungry outside of those, I also had to eat. Waiting until the next designated slot would just be another form of restriction - more delayed eating, more showing my body that it couldn't trust me to eat when it was hungry. For a month at least.

2. **Every *meal* is to contain a protein, carb and fat source. *Snacks* can be whatever the hell you want, though.**

<u>**This one might not be right for you as it's a specific rule around food.**</u> However, with my history, I knew it was necessary. It was necessary because if I didn't make that rule, my meals could easily slip into being the mounds of vegetables and salad and low carb shirataki noodles that I used to eat. I was notorious for never eating any fats and eating as few carbs as I possibly could. Often protein would also fall away because it was just more appealing to my eating disorder to volume eat high fibre low energy foods like broccoli and cabbage. It was also necessary because it wasn't that I didn't WANT proteins, carbs and fats. Whenever I used to make a sad little meal, I would think about what I COULD have with it if I wasn't on a diet.

Stir fried veggies. I would wistfully think of how delicious they would be with quinoa or roasted sweet potatoes; with pan fried honey glazed salmon and a side salad dressed with olive oil and salt. My bowl of fruit for breakfast. How much yummier it would have been with a creamy vanilla yoghurt, drizzled hazelnut butter and granola. My egg white sandwich between two slices of low-carb bread, crumbling before I had even picked it up. Obviously I would have preferred thick brown crusty bread; whole eggs and mayonnaise and a bag of salt and pepper crisps on the side.

I knew that I could not trust myself. If I did not have meals with each component planned in, the eating disorder would find a way back in. It would start with the fats, I knew. It would convince me I didn't like fat sources. It would "forget" to add them in. And then slowly, slowly, the foods I was eating would begin to narrow all over again.

I drew up a meal planning sheet. I wrote out my favourite sources of each nutrient.Every week, I sat down and planned it out. But, here's the key: I did it in pencil. If, one day, I woke up and really didn't want what was planned for breakfast, I would have something else - because if I forced myself to have something I didn't want for the sake of *following the plan* that was also…you guessed it…restriction!

So I was going to do it. I was going to eat balanced meals. For a month at least.

3. **No restriction. Processed foods are on the table. Chocolate bars are on the table. Vegetables are on the table. Meat and dairy are on the table. Whatever you want,** *apart from nothing,* **is on the table.**

This obviously made me uncomfortable because I was worried that I would lose all control and eat everything and anything in sight. I, of course, had grounds to believe this as this is what I had done previously when bingeing. However, I had to continually remind myself that this time was different. I was no longer restricting and had no intentions to restrict even if I did go wild and eat everything. I had never tried to STOP RESTRICTION at the same time as accepting that I needed to stop losing weight. I figured that I owed it to myself to try. At least for a month anyway.

Veganism was out. I knew I couldn't do that. I told myself I would eat meat if I wanted it. I didn't end up wanting it very much at all, and never bought it to make myself, but the option was there. I knew, also, then I needed to let myself eat crisps and chocolate and biscuits as part of my daily food options. Because I knew that I had always wanted to eat those things. I had envied people when I saw them eating those things so casually, like it was nothing. So I needed to do it. I needed to eat them. However scared I was that if I had them in the house I would eat them ALL, I needed to try. For a month at least.

4. **Stop all compensatory behaviours. No purging; no laxatives; no exercise. If you binge, you binge. Your body needs the energy anyway to heal and restore.**

This one was the hardest one because, for years and years, I had always known that when I ate "too much" or when I ate "the wrong things" I could get rid of it. My body had also come to expect this. Food sat in my stomach for hours and hours, not digesting because my body was expecting me to get rid of it. That feeling made me *want* to get rid of it. But I knew that I needed to take it off the table. I needed to see what happened - to my body and my brain - if I REFUSED to give in to those urges and if I just stopped purging.

I rationalised that if I *did* go wild and eat a million UNITS OF ENERGY in one day, that was just me giving my body the energy it needed to heal faster. In recovery, you have to eat a surplus in order to heal the internal damage from restriction. So, I figured, I could look at any binges that happened as part of me eating this surplus rather than as EXCESS FOOD THAT I NEEDED TO COMPENSATE FOR RIGHT NOW. For a month, anyway.

5. <u>**Every time you have an EATING DISORDER THOUGHT, don't ignore it. Look it STRAIGHT in the eyes. Think about it. Understand it. Where does it lead? Why is it there? Reframe it. Think it away. Make it bog off. Don't ignore it: acknowledge it so that you can NOT ACT ON IT.**</u>

Whilst all the other points on the star were important ones for my physical recovery, I still believe that this point is the most important one for full recovery: and that's why it was always be at the top of my star. Because I could do all of the other things: I could eat regularly, I could have balanced meals, I could stop restricting, I could stop compensating. **But if the thoughts were all still there in my head, and I did nothing to combat them, it was only a matter of time before I slipped back off the cliff edge**. It was only a matter of time before the siren call of the ED lured me back into the unforgiving waves of its hellish ocean. **People say "why don't you just eat" to people with eating disorders. And that's why. We *can* just eat. Easy. Kind of. We can just do the things we know we need to do. We can gain weight. We can be physically healthy.** I was at a physically healthy weight for years. Sometimes I did all the eating things I was meant to do. But I never got well.

Because it's not *about* the eating. It's about the *way we think and feel about the eating.*

And if we just eat without addressing how we think and feel about it...we are always at risk. And I didn't want to live the rest of my life teetering on a tightrope, wondering if the extra weight of a single sandwich might tip me over and send me tumbling back down into the ED.

I needed the thoughts to be gone. Or, at least, bound up. Tied so tightly that they couldn't get out. Locked in a corner with swords pointing at them.

8. THE PLAN OF ACTION: COPING

Outside of the eating, there was also, of course, the glaring issue that my eating disorder was a coping mechanism. I therefore had to consider that I needed to find other healthy coping strategies: I needed other ways of managing my emotions and my trauma and all the icky yucky sludgy stuff in my soul. I put COPING STRATEGIES in the middle of my five point star and, actually, that seemed perfect.

How could I do all the rest, if I wasn't also doing the coping part?

How could I eat three meals and three snacks a day, and balance all of the macronutrients, if my coping strategy was an eating disorder? How could I stop restricting if my coping strategy was controlling my body? How could I reframe my thoughts if I didn't *want* to because they were helping keep me afloat? How could I stop compensating when I had no other methods of making myself feel okay? And so my star was born.

My Five Point Recovery Plan: Mission Stars in her Eyes

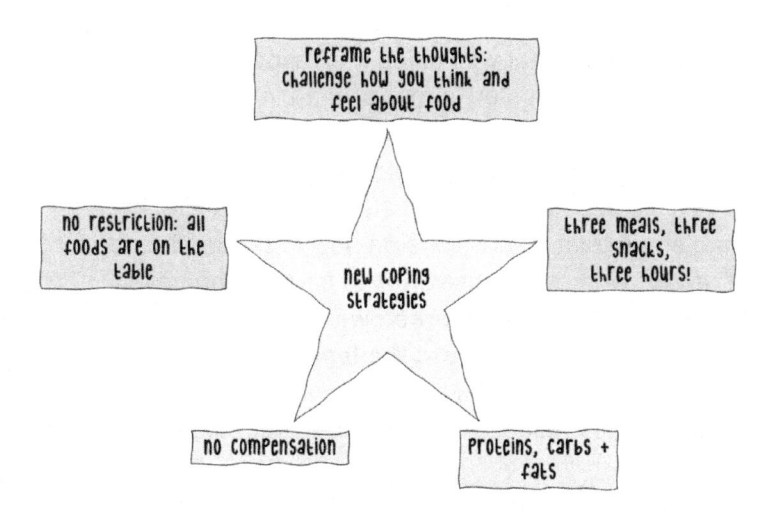

```
                    ┌─────────────────────────┐
                    │  reframe the thoughts:  │
                    │  challenge how you think and │
                    │      feel about food    │
                    └─────────────────────────┘
┌──────────────────┐         ★          ┌──────────────────┐
│ no restriction: all │      ╱ ╲         │  three meals, three │
│  foods are on the │     ╱   ╲        │       snacks,    │
│       table      │    new coping     │   three hours!   │
└──────────────────┘   strategies      └──────────────────┘
                        ╱       ╲
              ┌──────────────────┐  ┌──────────────────┐
              │  no compensation │  │ proteins, carbs + │
              └──────────────────┘  │       fats       │
                                    └──────────────────┘
```

Now, this bit will be different for everyone, naturally, based on what it is they may have been using their eating disorder to cope with. For this reason, I'm not going to delve too deep into the side of my recovery that doesn't relate to the food and the eating. However, as it is VITAL that you think about your own coping strategies to replace your disorder, I thought I would list some things that I found useful, just in case you decide you could take a flying punt at any of them:

1. <u>THERAPY.</u> You might be lucky enough to be offered therapy on the NHS. However, you might find this does not work for you. You may not be offered it at all. Both things happened to me: I dramatically failed at CBT-E and then the NHS were unable to offer another option as that was the only therapy available in my area. So I sought a private therapist. I was lucky enough to be able to afford this but I did sacrifice other things to be able to pay for this. I, however, chose to see it as an investment in my future self. What was the point in saving my money, if I possibly wouldn't be around to spend it? If my goal was to live a happy life, going without things for a period of time so that I could work on fixing my brain seemed like a sensible use of funds.

   People sometimes ask me how to go about finding a therapist and I would say: take your time and do not just choose the cheapest person you can find. I asked people I knew if they had any experience with therapy, or knew anyone who did. I asked them for their recommendations of therapists. I looked therapists up online. I joined local social media groups and asked there. Then, I researched the therapists. I looked up how long they had been practising, their training background, their qualifications, the reviews that people had left about them and any other random information I could find about them on the Internet -

and I'm from the generation that stalked people's crushes online so trust me when I say, I found out *everything* I needed to know. Anyone who was primarily on Instagram was a hard NO. Anyone that was using their experience for social media clout was, in my mind, more interested in money than in healing people.

Ideally, you need to be looking for someone that is not only trained in the area that you want to work on (if it's a specific issue) but also EXPERIENCED in working with it. Having had some training sessions on how to deliver therapy for SA is very different from having worked extensively with people who have experienced this. **The longer someone has worked within a particular area, the more they have learnt and understood and the less likely they are to say something potentially triggering.** That's the thing you do need to remember about therapists: they are just people too. And people are not perfect.

With the money thing, the cheapest therapists are often cheap for a reason. Sometimes, you may stumble across a gem of one that is really good and just starting out - but make sure you research them first and read all the reviews and understand their background. Equally, just because someone is *really expensive* doesn't mean they are really good either. So, again, make sure you research them first and read all the reviews and understand their background.

And remember: most importantly, YOU DO NOT HAVE TO STICK WITH THE FIRST THERAPIST YOU FIND. I get it. It's an awkward social situation to tell someone: *hey, I don't want to see you anymore. It's not me…It's you.* But come on. It's your healing, right? And you're paying them. And any good therapist will know that they will not be the right therapist for every person. They will let you go with grace. And if they don't, they aren't a good therapist and you had a lucky escape. If you can tell that they're not right for you, and it isn't feeling safe and productive and like it's a good space for you, stop. Find another one. It's too important to do this bit wrong, okay?

It's not a race to find a therapist, get through therapy and be healed. You've probably been struggling for a long time, right? And you want the healing to be real, deep and enduring? You don't want it to just be a plaster over the wound. You want to go into the wound, perform slow, careful surgery, sit with it whilst it heals from the surgery, do the pre-op care…Take all the time you need to find a therapist. Take all the time you need to do the therapy. **Because this time now, that you so desperately want to rush but need to take slow, is the *foundation* of your future.** You would be a bit concerned if a builder put the foundations for a house down in half an hour, right? You'd be a bit concerned about whether those rushed foundations had the integrity to hold that house up for years and years, right? So don't rush therapy - it's the same thing. You need a solid foundation to build on and this is going to take time.

If you cannot afford therapy or are not ready to access this yet, there are lots of charities and local support groups that offer support for specific needs. Again, research this on the internet - you would be surprised at what you might find available in your local area. The *mind* website is also something worth exploring as it has links to similar things as well as lots of information and guidance on how you can access support in your area and online.

2. <u>BOOKS.</u> Be careful with this one as I know a lot of self-help books that are INCREDIBLY damaging and FAR MORE HARM THAN GOOD. I know a lot of books on trauma that don't teach you coping strategies, or help you deal, but rather provide more fuel for the fire of the idea that you *are* broken and *should be acting like this.* I know others that try to minimise your trauma and reduce and invalidate your experience. Before I ordered and read any books, I researched them EXTENSIVELY online. I read review after review after review. I read the synopsis. I tried to read excerpts if I could - social media can be a good place to find quotes. I also asked people around me who I knew had experience with healing from trauma if they had any recommendations. I found three books particularly of use: Rupi Kaur's *Healing Through Words* + *The Sun and Her Flowers* + Oprah Winfrey's *What Happened To You.*

The first is a guided creative writing experience that encourages you to write things to address your feelings. It took me deeper into places I had never gone before, and allowed me to really sit with the feelings because, when you're trying to write poetry, you kind of have to spend a little while sitting with the pain to find the words to put on paper.

The second is actually just a poetry book. It is a poetry book about growth and healing. It puts some of the most painful emotions you could imagine into words and somehow makes them beautiful; it speaks of struggle and pain, but also of survival; and shows that even when you feel some truly horrific, dark and seemingly impossible emotions, there is a way out. You can be the sunflower, growing and growing despite it all. Healing can happen.

The third I love because it doesn't approach trauma from a place of pure emotional damage: it acknowledges the role of the brain and brain development on our behaviour and actions. **It helped me feel less crazy because it made**

me begin to see WHY I had done some of the seemingly unfathomable things that I had done. This book does what I could never quite do myself as I was operating for so long under the false belief that the problem was just intrinsic to me and always going to be there: it mixes the science of trauma with the emotion of it. By doing this, it creates the soil for healing because it PROVES that you aren't fundamentally broken, there wasn't just *something wrong inside you all along*. No. **In fact, things *happened* to you that impacted on your brain and the way you process things: but if it could be done, it can be undone.** There's no fixed state of "broken". You need to look at who you are. You need to look at *why* you are and *what happened to you* and then you can begin the tricky part. But being able to begin the tricky part, after years in stasis, is still progress. It's immense.

3. <u>JOURNALLING.</u> Doesn't sound like me, does it? That's because it's not. I don't mean journaling in the sense of what you see online: a nice dotted notebook, fountain pens, sitting at your breakfast bar with a matcha, dressed in gym wear, writing in your neat little writing. Or following little prompts like: *my summer bucket list, my favourite foods, books I want to read in 2023*. Or filling pages with beautiful drawings and cutouts and quotes written in fancy script. This practice always seemed, to me, like a massive waste of time. When I say journaling I mean this: I had a plain notebook and a biro. And whenever I had a thought or a feeling or something that was troubling me, I would get my notebook and I would SCRAWL IT ALL OUT ONTO THE PAPER. And when I say scrawl, I mean *scrawl*. Half the time, it wasn't even full sentences. Half the time, I didn't even manage to get the writing on the line. Wild, looping text; angry, sad, deranged - pain spat out onto paper in an entirely non-poetic and non-beautiful way. No breakfast bar, no matcha, no gym wear. No. J**ust a sad girl with tangled hair, dressed in jogging bottoms and a hoodie, hunched over a notebook and surrounded by dirty mugs and empty cola bottles**. I would write when I was reading the books above. I would write before therapy, and after therapy. I would write in five minute breaks from work. I would write before I got out of bed and before I went to sleep. Sometimes, I would wake from a traumatic dream in the middle of the night and write. **Call it trauma dumping**. I wasn't *journaling,* I was just *trauma dumping* in an ochre yellow notebook. As you do.

A particular favourite excerpt: *NO MY TRAUMA DID NOT MAKE ME STRONGER YOU BUFFOON, IT MADE ME DEVELOP OVER A DECADE OF EATING DISORDERS AND THOSE DON'T MAKE YOU STRONGER, THEY MAKE YOU QUITE WEAK ACTUALLY.*

4. MY SILLY LITTLE CALMING STRATEGIES.

I call them this because I have always been an incredibly sceptical, practical person. In the past, when people would mention any of these techniques, I would scoff: *how could THAT possibly help someone when they are feeling anxious or traumatised?* but…I had committed to recovery. And that meant that **I also had to commit to finding something - ANYTHING - that could help provide some kind of emotional soothing once I had pulled off my eating disorder blanket of doom-filled protection.** So I was willing to try anything.

And.

It's hard to ignore the fact that many of us here, many of us struggling with food and body and trauma and pain and suffering, have lived in a vortex for our entire lives. When you grow up in a chaotic environment, you feel like chaos inside. You are a storm. Always. You are constantly in fight or flight mode. You are a swirling hurricane. You have never stood on solid ground. **When you grow up like this, you don't learn to self-soothe because there is no time for that. There is no space for that. There is no room to be calm in a world where you need to be on high alert.** You were focussed on your survival.

But. When you're not there anymore, when you don't need to be in fight or flight mode, your body is still in the hangover. It doesn't know it's safe. How would it? It spent so long wired and ready. So anything, *anything* at all, that can help you feel calmer and more grounded instantly adds value to your life. It's a coping strategy because, as silly as it might sound, if it gives you a minute to pause and come back to yourself. It gives you time and space to *think* rather than to continue to act in a way that is *entirely driven by the emotions and the pain.*

The eating disorder was a coping strategy as it made everything numb. When the numbness begins to fade, you need *anything at all* that might help you stay calm as you begin to ride the waves of your emotions waking up again.

Fiddle toys
I have a whole collection. Fidget spinners, fidget cubes, tangles, pressure rings, Pop Its. **Now I'm not saying these particularly help me in the midst of an actual full emotional breakdown, or after a traumatic dream, or when I'm sobbing for god knows what reason. But they do help me when I feel anxieties and thoughts *begin* to bubble.** They do help me when I'm sitting

doing things like watching TV, or on meetings at work, or chatting to friends. They remind me constantly: I am here. In this body. I am here. They're really useful for getting rid of some of the anxious energy *before* it escalates. Sometimes I feel like a balloon that is being pumped full of too much air, and you just know that the next bit of air *could* be the air that bursts the balloon. The fiddle toys sometimes reduced that pressure in the balloon a little bit. I take them to therapy too, *obviously*. When you don't want to make eye contact with someone, they're an excellent excuse not to…

Soft Toys

I have developed an obsession with collecting unusual soft toys. My collection is growing: a frog, a bunny, a crab, an octopus, a lemon, a pretzel, a broccoli, two dinosaurs, a shrimp, a sunshine handbag, a frog handbag and a sloth.

Most children have a cuddly toy, right? When they are feeling sad or worried or scared, or at basically all times in the day, they cuddle their teddy and it makes them feel better. It brings them comfort. It soothes them. So why, then, is it that at some age it is decided that you are "too old" for teddies? How can you be "too old" to need comfort, and to need soothing? And this is the issue, isn't it? Adults are supposed to be tough. Adults are supposed to have it all together and *not need* a comfort teddy, and *not need* to be soothed.

Well - *I* need comfort. *I* need to be soothed. So I cuddle my teddies. I have them in a range of sizes - you can get some really tiny ones that fit in your hand. These are great to hold and squeeze and to take with you in your pocket. The bigger ones are great for hugging to your chest whilst you take some big ol' deep breaths. And all of them are just SO SOFT that when you sit there stroking them, that's soothing all by itself.

I don't even care that I sound a bit crazy - a grown adult talking about hugging her teddies - that stuff helps and I'm never going to stop talking about the things that we *shouldn't* talk about if I think they will help even one other person. So hug your teddy.

Tapping

Now this one is deranged. Or at least, I thought it was when I first heard about it. I was working in a specialist school for young people with learning disabilities and we had some training on EFT (Emotional Freedom Technique) or…*tapping*. TAPPING. LITERAL TAPPING. Now I'm not a scientist or medical professional (have I said that yet?) and I do think that all research needs to be taken with a huge bucket load of salt - as people always find what they want to find, and data is so very easy to manipulate.

However, I do know that there are scientific trials that support tapping as a way of easing emotional distress and managing stress. And I *did* see it work, time and time again, with the children in the school. You tap specific points on your face and upper body using two fingers - it's something to do with acupressure, and the tapping helps mute the fight/flight stress response somehow. I have no idea how. Like I said, not a scientist.

And one day, when I was mid freak out, locked in the bathroom at work, mind spinning, palms sweating, fight or flight rising…nothing else available to me…I snapped. And I tapped. And it helped. For me, the feeling of thudding helps me come back into my body. It draws me back to myself. The steady rhythm is something to focus on whilst everything else swirls.

Look it up. You may think, like I did at first, that it sounds completely deranged. I still kind of think that. But I also know that, when the world gets really swirly and dark and I feel like I'm not standing on solid ground anymore, a good old tap can help short-circuit some of the spirals.

And hey, tapping your face and upper body like some crazed body percussionist is a much better and safer coping mechanism than trying to starve yourself to death, right?

Breathing
Goes without saying. Breathe. Breathe. BLOODY BREATHE OKAY. I mean it. Like you feel that feeling building. You feel like a balloon. Pressure. About to burst. Stop. Stop. A BIG SLOW BREATH IN. A BIG SLOW BREATH OUT. This isn't working. AGAIN. BIG SLOW BREATH IN. BIG SLOW BREATH OUT. THis is silly. SHUT YOUR EYES. IN THROUGH THE NOSE. OUT THROUGH MOUTH. How could this help? AGAIN. BIG SLOW BREATH IN. BIG SLOW BREATH OUT. SLOWER. BIGGER.

Pretend you're in yoga class or something.

Pretend you're a horse.

I don't care what you pretend. Just take deep, big, slow breaths and shut your eyes. Keep going. What's your favourite number? Breathe for it. If your favourite number is like 1 or something smaller than 5, maybe aim for 13. It's my favourite. It's meant to be unlucky, right? But why do we have the right to demonise a number? It was just minding its own business over there between 12 + 14 and everyone started shunning it. I also like it because I have decided I will make my own luck. Relying on the universe didn't work for me. **So I chose 13. I choose it. 13 big, slow breaths.**

Now, whenever I get impulsive thoughts, I force myself to stop. I force myself to shut my eyes and I force myself to breathe. And, if I want to act on the thought after I've got some hella oxygen into my brain, cool. But I never really do.

Sometimes all it takes is a moment to restabilise. **When you were in fight or flight mode your whole life, even having a moment to do this can be revolutionary for your body and brain to begin to realise: it's okay.** I tell myself that too. When I'm breathing. I used to do it with the kids at school when they were dysregulated. Sit with them. Breathe slowly with them. Tell them over and over again: you're alright, you're okay, you're safe.

You're alright. You're okay. You're safe. Breathe in. Breathe out. You're alright. You're okay. You're safe. Breathe in. Breathe out. You're alright. You're okay. You're safe. Breathe in. Breathe out.

Focus on your locus
Often, what we are becoming stressed and anxious about is out of our control. Much of the world is out of our control. For those of us with mental health struggles, this is wildly unfathomable and unfair. If only we could control everything, life would be perfect.

I find myself, often, spiralling because I am thinking about things that I have no control over. Mainly, the past. Over and over again. *If only I had done this instead of that. If I had said something differently, maybe it wouldn't have happened. If I hadn't done that, maybe things would be different now. Why did I do that? Why didn't I do this? Why did I let this happen?* And then, the future. *What if it happens again? What if…What if…What if…*

When I did my Psychology degree, I came across the Locus of Control. This theory relates to whether a person has an internal locus of control or an external one. People with an internal locus of control think that they have a lot of control over their own behaviour and will be more likely to take responsibility for their actions. People with an external locus tend to think that things happen regardless of their actions - due to luck (good or bad!) and other external influences.

I realised that my locus of control was *too* internal. **I was blaming myself for things that were *not my fault* because they had happened due to actions NOT taken by me.** The trauma, the C-PTSD was all caused by actions and events that I had not had any control over. Believing that I had, and that I was somehow to blame, had been keeping me stuck. I needed to see that some of it was external. Some of it was outside of my hands.

And recognising that also helped me begin to see a way out of stressful situations. I would stop myself. I would ask myself: *what parts of this situation are YOU PERSONALLY able to influence?* **What could I, reasonably, do? I started writing lists of 'things I can change' compared to 'things I can't change'.** Again, in my deranged messy little journal of course. When the pressure and stress started to rise I would remind myself: I cannot change the past. I cannot change the way other people choose to act. I cannot change the words that people say. I cannot stop other people from being triggering. **But. I *can* change the way I live now: I *can* change the future. I *can* change the way that I respond to people actions. I *can* choose to ignore their harmful words: I don't *have* to listen and believe them. I *can* choose to actively fight the triggers and use my coping strategies. I *can* breathe and tap and journal and fiddle and be kind to myself long enough to process the waves of pain. I can. I can. I can.**

I would chant to myself: focus on your locus. Focus. Locus. Hone in on what *you* can *do* to make yourself feel better. The other stuff, the stuff you can't touch or change, ignore it. There's no point looking at it for long. Look for the flowers in the undergrowth.

Shower
This one is deceptively simple sounding because, as many of us with *mental health issues* know, getting in the shower can be the hardest thing in the world. However, if you reframe it, it can be easier. **I get in the shower sometimes as a therapeutic tool, not to get clean.** By telling my brain that I'm not *having a shower* but rather *using a coping strategy,* for some reason, that can make it easier to persuade myself to get in. And genuinely, when I'm having a mental health shower, I don't wash my hair or anything unless the mood suddenly strikes whilst I'm there.

I stand there, under the warm water, and I focus on the feeling of the water hitting my skin and I breathe. Deep and slow, obviously. Telling myself I'm okay. Telling myself I'm safe. Focus on trying to release the tension in my body. Relax your shoulders. Unclench your teeth. Wiggle your fingers.

Car sitting
If you can't drive or don't own a car, don't do this. You don't want to get arrested - that will only make things worse. But you could apply the same principle to sitting in a park or on a bench in the town centre.

When things are getting TOO MUCH, sometimes I get in my car and I drive. I don't go far. **I go to supermarket car parks. I park. And I watch people**. That sounds really creepy, but I promise I don't do it in an obvious way. I just sit there. People drift in and out of the supermarket and I just sit there, my music on. It's the same idea as just lying in bed in a dark room BUT I'm not in my bed. I'm OUT in the world. I get to sit and wallow and think and feel things and be still BUT I'm still in the world. **It reminds me that I'm still part of something bigger.** That even though the pain is loud, I'm not locked away in my pain. **There's a world of life out there.** A silly man in a fancy sports car who can't park between the lines. A mother carrying twins in adorable matching dungarees. A middle aged man in pink sandals - legend.

Unapologetic
I understand that I've probably made myself sound incredibly weird, right? **A fully grown woman, fiddling with her fiddle toys, cuddling her teddies, tapping away at herself and breathing like she's giving birth before running off to scrawl maniacally in a journal, take a long shower without washing herself and then go and sit in a carpark.** But. I don't care anymore what other people think, right? Because these things are strategies. I am in the middle of recovery.

We don't judge people doing strange looking physio exercises when they're recovering from a car accident. We don't judge people learning to walk again after a stroke. We don't judge people for using a wheelchair whilst their broken foot heals. **So I won't judge me for using what I need to use as I continue my own healing journey.** *And I remind myself: all of these techniques look considerably less weird than the things I was doing when I was using my eating disorder as my sole coping mechanism.*

If you are worried that people will judge you, don't. Because the alternative is that you DON'T do things that could help you cope. And then what? **If you can't replace the eating disorder as a coping mechanism, it's always going to be there tempting you back.** Surely it's better to look a little weird to the world than it is to spend another year locked in your eating disorder? Your healing is your healing. If people don't like the way you are doing it, WE DON'T LIKE THEM. Anyway. We don't want to fit in. The "normal" world is pretty toxic. We know this! Let's build our own world.

I regret all the years I wasted not taking steps to make myself better. I regret it all. **If I could go back in time and speak to old me, she would totally ignore me but I would tell her this: if you don't do it now, you won't do it for ten years.** And nothing will have changed. So you may as well do it now.

So. Here we are now. I had done the big things:
1. I had identified that my eating disorder was, in part, a coping mechanism. To address this, I had developed a range of strategies and ideas to help me cope with the issues I had been masking once the eating disorder was removed from the equation.
2. I had identified that my eating disorder was, in part, related to restriction. To address this, I had developed my Five Points of Recovery.
3. I had accepted that I needed to get better because my only options were to get better; to accept that the rest of my life would look like this; or die.

Now for the scary part. I actually had to...do it?

9. DOING IT: KNOWLEDGE IS POWER

I'm going to talk you through how I personally implemented my own recovery plan, in case ANY OF IT AT ALL can help you. I'm going to tell you what went well, what I found helpful and what I struggled with. But what I want you to bear in mind, as with the rest of this book, is that this is *not* a textbook or a self-help guide or a medical document. This is purely anecdotal. This is purely *my* experience. It may not work for you. It may not be right for you. But when I was deep in my disorder, reading self-help guides and medical sounding texts did not help me. It didn't sound real. I *needed* to see real life examples. I *needed* to believe that REAL people could, and did, manage to recover. So this next stage is me showing you that. It is me unpacking my recovery so you can see that it can be done. Hope is the most powerful thing. Hopelessness can keep us stuck.

My first step at every stage of my starry plan was to be the little nerd that I am and RESEARCH. No, really. I've always loved learning and studying and knowledge. And now I could use my love of learning to LEARN ABOUT THE WAYS THAT I COULD HEAL.

It's really simple but because I had never fully committed to recovery before, **I had actively avoided researching recovery** and the things that might actually help me. As I had no deep rooted intentions of recovering in any way other than continuing to live THE WORLD'S HEALTHIEST LIFESTYLE AND GET THE PERFECT BODY, I had never sat down and researched *true recovery information and advice.*

I treated it like some kind of deranged school project. I had a folder and everything. I made notes. I printed things out. I *mind-mapped.* It was glorious. I would have got an A*.

I encourage you to do this, too: sit down and dedicate time to RESEARCH. Research **recovery**. Research the reasons <u>why</u> you need to eat three meals and three snacks. Research the reasons <u>why</u> you should be eating proteins, carbohydrates and fats. Research <u>why</u> you should be eating whatever you damn want for your snacks. Research the binge restrict cycle and the science behind restriction and what it does to your body and your brain. Research why you must stop all forms of compensatory behaviours. Research digestion. Research the long term health implications of eating disorders. Research weight restoration. Research hormone health and why not having a period isn't a good thing, despite the convenience it may bring.

Make sure that your research is ALWAYS related to eating disorder recovery. Do not go looking for general health advice, okay? **Because here's the thing: what is "healthy" for other people is not healthy for you.**

Other people may be able to cut chocolate out of their lives forever because of the research on *ultra processed foods* and *too much sugar* and *blah blah blah.* But you can't. It may be healthy for other people to do that. But if you do that, what happens? The lens narrows. You start to hyper focus again. If you've cut out one food, you can cut out more. And you end up back there, back with the eating disorder. And listen. *Engaging in your eating disorder is always going to be the most unhealthy thing you could do.* **It is healthier for you personally to eat the chocolate if you want the chocolate. If someone tells you that it is *unhealthy* to eat chocolate, you tell them that it is *unhealthier* for you to restrict and risk relapsing in your eating disorder.** Remind them that lemon drizzle cake kills far fewer people every year than eating disorders do. Remind yourself of that too.

So you must NOT research anything about nutrition and exercise and wellness WITHOUT the words 'eating disorder recovery' added in. And even then, you need to be really aware. If anything you are reading is suggesting anything that sounds like restriction or labelling foods or compensating: cut and run. Get out of there.

Make sure that the research you write down and use to motivate you has come from multiple sources. **I would usually check that the same idea came up 3 or 4 times before I would believe it**, and I would look to make sure that it was coming from someone reputable - this was usually either a medical or nutrition professional with REAL certifications, or someone that I could ascertain had *genuinely* recovered from their eating disorder and wasn't in quasi-recovery or orthorexia land. Scientific research too - you can't really ignore the facts of biology, and lots of what the body does both during and after eating disorders is intimately connected to biology. Trust me.

When you've done your research, you can use the knowledge you have accumulated to inform YOUR OWN PERSONAL RECOVERY in line with the things that you personally struggle with and need to work on. I'm sure many of them will be similar to mine, which is why I will be sharing some of them, but you may also struggle with things that I don't, and vice versa.

The NHS focuses a lot on doing things *to* people in recovery from eating disorders, rather than *with* them. **There tends to be this general feeling that you are a *little* unhinged,** not quite *cognitively able enough* **to manage your own recovery. So they tell you WHAT to do but they never tell you WHY.** As intelligent people, this isn't very helpful. We don't like to be told WHAT to do if we don't know WHY we should do it. It almost elicits that rebellious child in us, when our parents say *You don't need to know why - JUST BECAUSE I SAID SO.* Which isn't a reason, of course, so the lack of a reason makes us assume that THERE ISN'T ONE.

But the WHY to all of my questions about eating disorder recovery became a fundamental part of my recovery. Why? Haha. Because, when my eating disorder got really loud, and started demanding that I should skip breakfast, **I was able to argue back because I knew all the reasons why I shouldn't**. When it tried to convince me that my digestive issues would go away if I purged, or restricted, **I was able to argue back because I knew all the reasons why that wasn't true**. When it tried to convince me that I didn't want the chocolate bar when I knew that I did, **I ate the chocolate bar because I knew all the reasons why that was so important.** When it tried to convince me to delay my meals because I wasn't STARVING yet, **I ate because I knew all the reasons why delaying meals was a bad decision.**

Eating disorders are desperately illogical. Fight them with logic. It stalls them. Confuses them. For long enough for you to get back in that driving seat and stuff that food in. **Food in = nourishment = brain gets stronger = easier to fight.** The eating disorder, that is. Not cage fighting. Unless you fancy it. But not until you're weight restored and nourished again because cage fighting when you're not would be dangerous.

10. DOING IT: THREE MEALS AND THREE SNACKS A DAY.

Regular eating. Normal eating. An eating pattern. The concept seems so normal - eat every 2-3 hours - and yet, at the time, so impossible. I hadn't eaten three meals and three snacks ever in my whole entire life. At best, I had maybe eaten three meals at some points in my *eating disorder career.* But at worst, I was eating one meal a day, or eating SO MUCH FOOD and not digesting it. **It seemed an impossible feat to go from avoiding food for as long as possible OR eating whole BANQUETS, to waking up, eating breakfast, only waiting 2-3 hours and then eating *again* but not even lunch, just a *snack,* and then in only 2-3 more hours eating *again?*** SIX points of eating? SIX?

You can imagine what I believed would happen. To go from barely eating to eating all of that food? OBVIOUSLY I was going to BALLOON UP. I was going to SWELL IMMEDIATELY and GAIN 200 POUNDS OVERNIGHT and keep gaining weight forever and ever and swing back into the days of the BINGE EATING. Six meals seemed like too much. An impossible amount of food to eat and then digest. Surely, *surely,* it was impossible that anyone NEEDED that amount of food to maintain their weight?

I was overwhelmed. I didn't want to do it. But. I had committed. I was doing it. So I did my research, made my notes, and printed my information. Highlighted and mind-mapped. Learned about why regular eating was important.

I drew up the following list. There are more reasons than this but these are the ones that were most relevant to me, and that I wanted to hone back in on when the going got tough:

1. It gives **structure** to eating so that **eating becomes a regular and normal part of life**: it can become something that you just do. Like going to the toilet. Or getting dressed.

2. It keeps your **blood sugar levels stable** which reduces tiredness, grumpiness and all the chaos that comes with low sugars. *It stops you from being a GRUMPY COW.*

3. By teaching your body that you are always going to feed it again soon, you are also teaching your body and mind that **there is NO NEED to binge because MORE FOOD IS ALWAYS COMING**. When you don't eat regularly, that's when your body drives you to the binge as it doesn't know when it's next getting the food that it so desperately needs to heal all the damage you did. *And also, just, to live, you know? Like we actually need food every day? Did you know that?*

4. **It will help your digestive system begin to wake up again.** Your digestive system may have got used to not having very much work to do: either because you were putting too little food in for it to bother, or because you were taking the food out before it could do anything with it. It's gone to sleep. Or on holiday. It's not doing much. It's on a go slow. **By putting food in regularly, over and over again, you are telling your digestive system: it's time.** It's time to come back to work. You've got lots to do now. All day every day.

5. **It helps your body begin to redevelop its actual hunger cues**. When you are engaging in eating disordered behaviours, these hunger cues go out of whack. Restriction puts your body under stress because it thinks there's a famine. So to overcome this, it alters your hunger and fullness cues to aid in survival: sometimes you may be ravenous because your body is trying to get you to eat and eat and eat whilst it senses that food is available. **Other times, you may feel no hunger at all because the body knows that, if there's a famine and no food there, producing hunger cues that cannot be responded to is a waste of the body's resources.** The body doesn't know that the famine was caused by you. A lot of us therefore do not have hunger cues at first. **And the only way to really help them come back and normalise is to help the body realise that there IS no famine.** So you may need to eat when you're not hungry. And that's incredibly difficult. But the more you do it, the more the body starts to figure out when it actually is and isn't hungry.

The end goal is that, one day, you will feel hunger and fullness properly again and be able to eat when you're hungry and not eat when you're not. But you're not there yet. You know you're not there yet because even the idea of being able to "not eat" a snack has just sparked that little eating disorder PING in your head. You were already thinking about how many meals you could skip, weren't you?

6. **Eating at six different points in the day means that you are getting nutrients and energy at six different points in the day.** This means your body is getting consistent and regular fuel that it can use to do your daily activities and to repair the damage of malnutrition. If you aren't eating enough - say only eating three times - your body has to choose. ***Will it use the energy to get you through the day, or to repair old damage? Obviously it will choose to get you through the day. That's the survival instinct. So the damage doesn't heal and you keep dragging yourself through life, malnourished and weak and struggling still.***

So, armed with the knowledge of WHY I needed to do it, I started to do it. I won't lie to you: it is hard. It is incredibly hard.

Personally, I found breakfast the hardest and also my snack after dinner.

Breakfast was hard because I feel like there's just SO MUCH RHETORIC ONLINE about how you don't *need* breakfast. You see a lot less stuff encouraging people to skip lunch and dinner and I think that my brain latched onto this. I was also concerned that if I ate breakfast, it would wake up my hunger cues TOO SOON and lead to me eating MORE THROUGHOUT THE DAY as I would become a CRAZED HUNGRY MONSTER.

There's also all this stuff about how intermittent fasting is healthy and good for you. The science actually suggests that skipping breakfast is actually inconsequential for the health of GENERAL PEOPLE and that, instead, the total picture of the food they eat is more important (shocker, right?). However, you'll notice I said general people.

What we are going to need to remember, and keep remembering over and over again is this:

Things that may be healthy for other people are not things that are healthy for someone with an eating disorder.

It may be healthy for someone else to intermittent fast (I'm not personally convinced but that's beside the point...). It may be healthy for someone else not to eat that soon after waking up. But you? You have an eating disorder. If you intermittent fast, if you delay breakfast, that's not going to be healthy because it's going to open the door for the eating disorder. Even opening that door a crack is dangerous. It's a slimy, slippery goblin and will seep through the cracks. Even the "unhealthiest" of regular eating habits is healthier than engaging in your eating disorder: and eating breakfast is NOT unhealthy in any way. So remind yourself: **_it may be healthy for THEM to skip breakfast but it isn't healthy for ME as it could trigger my eating disorder, and that's the unhealthiest option in the world._**

And the crazed hunger? Funnily enough, that didn't particularly present much of a problem. Because I ate breakfast and then...a couple of hours later, I had a snack. And then I had lunch. **So my body didn't get CRAZED HUNGER in the same way that it used to because I was giving it regular energy, which, it turns out, is a much more effective way of NOT GETTING HUNGRY than starving all day.** Who would have thought. And yes, I was eating more throughout the day than I HAD been but that was the point. I had never been eating enough - that's what you do when you're trying to make yourself smaller.

My snack after dinner was hard because many people normalise dinner being the final point of eating, and again you have all the ONLINE RHETORIC about how if you eat after a certain time if WILL ALL SUDDENLY CONVERT TO FAT. However, I know this is not true: so again, I fought the thoughts with logic.

Your body does not cease to exist when you are asleep. When you are sleeping, your metabolism is still working: your body is still doing stuff. Especially when you are recovering, but normally too: **sleep allows the brain and body to slow down and engage in processes of recovery.** *But how would it engage in that recovery without ENERGY?* Loads of biological processes are going on whilst you snore: your brain is storing new information from the day and getting rid of stuff it doesn't need, nerve cells are reorganising, cells are repairing and hormones and proteins are being released. Digestion is happening too. And if you're recovering, your body is working on fixing all that organ and hormonal damage that you might have going on. Mentally too - you've got a lot swirling around in that gorgeous brain of yours and the brain needs that time of sleep to process it.

Equally, if you go to bed hungry with a rumbly rumbly tummy, how on EARTH are you going to get a good night's sleep? **If your sleep is trash, your overnight recovery will be trash, and the next day will be trash and when we feel like trash, we tend to lean towards engaging in our behaviours**...SO NOT EATING AFTER DINNER MAY WELL BE A LOSE-LOSE SITUATION FOR YOU!

Anyway, we return to the point above:

Things that may be healthy for other people are not things that are healthy for someone with an eating disorder.

It might be healthy for THEM to not have an evening snack. But you? You have an eating disorder. Not having an evening snack is unhealthy for you. Because it opens the door. If you know that you need more energy at the end of the day (either because you haven't eaten enough yet today, or because you have but you are *still feeling hungry*), you need more food. Not having an evening snack is unhealthy for you because it looks like RESTRICTION. And we know what restriction leads to. A cycle that you're stuck in. But also…if you're hungry, you're hungry because your body needs more energy? So ANYONE that is ignoring that is IGNORING their body asking for more energy which is NEVER going to end well. **And so many people wander around talking about how they have bad sleep and never feel refreshed and always feel drained…but never consider that maybe it's because they ignore their body when it asks them for more energy?**

Everytime I considered not having my evening snack because it was "unhealthy" to eat late at night I reminded myself: IT IS UNHEALTHY TO ENGAGE IN ANY HABIT THAT MAY CAUSE ME TO RELAPSE INTO MY EATING DISORDER. EVEN THE "UNHEALTHIEST" TIME TO EAT FOOD IS HEALTHIER THAN ENGAGING IN AN EATING DISORDER.

Now for the things I *did*.

I *did* work flexibly around my own life and needs to figure out the best plan for ME.

Initially, I was aiming to have my first meal of the day as a traditional "breakfast" - so a MEAL. You know, your **wake up, go downstairs, make some pancakes or porridge type vibes**. However, I found that after a couple of weeks of recovery, I was waking up RAVENOUS. This was, to me, a good sign. After years of not knowing if I was hungry, and finding lack of hunger cues quite triggering, it was good to know that my body was finally able to start showing me when it needed food. Anyway, this RAVENOUS HUNGER meant that I did not have the blood sugar capacity to make a proper meal. This, combined with the fact that I am NOT A MORNING GAL, meant that I wasn't the *nicest* to my family when we shared the kitchen in the morning and I also wasn't making the *best* choices to fuel myself because I was ANGRY AT THE MORNING and TOO HUNGRY TO THINK LOGICALLY. And as we know…***if* YOU can't think logically, something else in your brain that thinks very illogically does so much like to slither into the driving seat…**

So, I decided to start with a SNACK to stabilise my blood sugars, get my body going and give me enough energy to get up, get ready for the day and then go and *calmly* make a meal rather than being a frenzied rhino crashing around the kitchen trying to figure out a balanced meal whilst TIRED and HUNGRY. This would be something like a flapjack and a piece of fruit, or a couple of yoghurts grabbed straight from the fridge, or a protein bar, or a couple of pieces of toast. Food I could lay my hands on and have in my stomach within five minutes, basically. With a cup of tea, obviously, because we need to be HYDRATED AND CAFFEINATED around here.

I *did* draw up a timetable of eating times.

This was for several reasons:
1. I wanted to teach my body to develop hunger cues and **regularly expect food**, which it wouldn't be able to do if I was eating in some crazed, chaotic pattern
2. I wanted to **reintroduce routine into my life as my mental health is better (not good, it's never good) when I have a routine.** I opted therefore to wake up at the same time every day - including weekends - to begin establishing regular healthy patterns in my life.
3. **I knew that I was, without negotiation, eating between X and Y time.** So even if my eating disorder tried to persuade me that I wasn't, I absolutely WAS. I would write what I planned to eat down the day before and go through ticking it off. That way, I felt like a small child with a sticker chart and it was honestly a vibe.

It is important to note, however, that I drew it up with TIME SLOTS. So my pre-breakfast snack was to happen *between 7 and 8 for* example. And my breakfast *between 9.30 and 11.00.* The exception to that, of course, was if I was hungry SOONER, in which case GO FOR IT BABE. Why a time slot? Two reasons. **Firstly, so that I couldn't become disordered and obsessed with an eating time and refuse to eat outside of the specific time.** I was, by this point, obviously aware of the ED ability to latch onto ANYTHING AND EVERYTHING and make it disordered. **Secondly, so that, if things happened which delayed the time past 7, for example, I wouldn't then be able to decide that I had "missed" the time and therefore should "wait until the next meal".** Again. ED weaselling in. No thank you.

11. DOING IT: PROTEIN, CARBS AND FATS.

Balanced meals? With protein, carbs AND fats? Surely not. Surely people don't actually *eat like that?* Surely people subsist on vegetables and protein alone? That's healthy right? Vegetables have vitamins in them and everyone knows you need to eat *ten a day* and not just *five a day any more*. Throughout my illness, I had, at pretty much every point, avoided both fats and carbohydrates. For obvious reasons - they are both demonised by the media. Fat makes you fat. Carbohydrates got a bad rap and became part of diet culture obsessions with the low carb diet: and again, they make you fat. Apparently.

But that was all I knew. I had no concept of *why* I was not eating carbohydrates or fats other than that THEY MIGHT MAKE ME FAT. **But I had decided that I would rather be healthy and non-eating-disordered than *anything else* and that, therefore, had to include being skinny**. So if I had to eat carbohydrates and fats and that made me fat, well, so BE IT. SO BE IT. **I would rather be fat than dead. I would rather be fat than starving, sitting in my room alone, not going anywhere, not building a career, not having friends or relationships or hope or *anything* other than constant thoughts about my body and food.** I would rather be fat than disordered.

Anyway, the next step was obviously to EQUIP MYSELF WITH THE KNOWLEDGE THAT I NEEDED to FIGHT. We ride at dawn. <u>**Again: not a dietician. Not a medical professional. No qualifications. Just a random mentally ill internet girly who used Google a lot to educate herself into recovery.**</u> Some of these reasons may lack scientific rigour. They may be based on pseudoscience. However, they are all backed up by numerous sources *and* having this rationale is what helped me to start eating and living again so, for me, that's enough. For you, of course, do your own research and draw your own conclusions: as you should!

And remember - these will ALWAYS BE MORE REASONS THAN THESE. **There are one hundred reasons to eat. And one hundred more.** These are just a few that particularly resonated with me as motivators for my continued push into recovery land.

Why do I need protein?

- Let's start with the best one. Foods containing protein are YUMMY. I sat down and made a big old list of all of my favourite protein sources, as well as a list of ones I needed to challenge and try. Currently, my favourites include: salmon, prawns, tofu, tempeh, protein yoghurts and mousses (in lemon or raspberry mostly), edamame beans, protein flapjacks, eggs and Greek yoghurt. I'm not a fan of protein bars: I would much rather have a big bowl of greek yoghurt with fresh fruit and crunchy cereal and honey than shove a powdery tasteless log into my mouth. I used to swear by them though. I wonder why.

- Proteins are known as **the building blocks of life**! They break down into amino acids, and amino acids help the body to repair and to grow. Therefore, to have healthy bones and muscles, we need to be eating protein. *Weak muscles and bones are no fun: do you want to be prematurely aged, unable to walk around for very long, at risk of breaking a hip in your 30s?* Not if you can help it, I imagine.

Including a protein in every meal would mean that **my body would be able to repair itself better: I would stop feeling constantly tired and achy**, I would stop breaking my fingers left, right and centre, and I would stop feeling my legs nearly give out after walking up a flight of stairs. I would, one day, be strong enough to body slam a full grown man.

- Your hair, skin and nails are made from protein. *If you want healthy hair, lovely non-brittle nails to scratch people with, and gorgeous glowy skin, ram those eggs down*.

So including a protein in every meal would mean that **my dry, broken, balding hair might start to grow back thick and healthy.** Including a protein in every meal would mean that **my dry, spotty patchy skin might start to clear up** a bit. Including a protein in every meal would mean that **my endlessly broken nails that never grew an inch would stop snapping** at every twist and turn and start growing long enough for me to paint them pastel colours.

- Digestion! Protein goes into making enzymes which aid in the digestion of your food. This in turn helps with making new cells and body chemicals. But if you've got any digestive issues at all - like, for example, your 1kg bowl of vegetables sitting in your stomach for hours and hours and being so bloated you could join a prenatal class - maybe eating a bit of protein could help.

So including a protein in every meal would mean that **my very broken, very sad digestive system might start to be able to function in a slightly more normal fashion.**

- Stops you being hungry. Now I'm not saying you should be eating NOTHING BUT PROTEIN and TREATING IT LIKE AN APPETITE SUPPRESSANT. But. Lots of us with eating disorders are often incredibly hungry at times. And rather than eat, we often just…drink water…or look to other appetite suppressants like pills and low-energy volume eating. And then wonder why we are still hungry. <u>*The best appetite suppressant is food. But not low energy food. The best*</u>

appetite suppressant is the food that your body needs, with the nutrients that you body needs: and protein is one of those things. Protein is the most filling of the three food groups.

So including a protein in every meal would mean that **I was no longer going to have to live with gnawing endless hunger** that made my eating disorder feel so happy and victorious AND prompted me, often, to fall into those ***binge restrict compensate cycles*** that had kept me trapped for all those years.

<u>**NOW. LISTEN. BECAUSE YOUR EATING DISORDER HAS BEEN READING ALL OF THE ABOVE ALONG WITH YOU AND IT IS STARTING TO FEEL THRILLED. IT IS THRILLED BECAUSE IT IS THINKING: I don't need to eat carbohydrates and fats. I can just eat LOTS OF PROTEIN and it will help me BUILD LOADS OF MUSCLE and FIX MY GROSS SKIN, HAIR AND NAILS so that I STILL LOOK AESTHETICALLY PLEASING and NEVER GET HUNGRY.**</u> But. If you only eat protein, *you're still restricting and you know exactly where that road leads you.* And…despite what the fitness influencers want you to think, a diet that is TOO high in protein is bad for the kidneys and liver. They can't be processing all that, alright? Give them a break. And, overloading protein can cause excessive loss of calcium which can in turn increase your risk of osteoporosis - this would be counterproductive as you were, after all, trying *not* to be a thirty year old with a hip replacement.

Plus, have you tried to eat out at a restaurant and eat only protein? There's something overwhelmingly lame about eating the meat off the top of your pizza whilst your friends eat like normal people. And it's incredibly sad to go out for burger and chips and just ram a meat patty down your neck whilst everyone else has their burger in a bun and their fries on the side. Don't be lame and sad.

Besides which, there are reasons why we need more than just protein…

Why do I need carbohydrates?

- Let's start with the best one. Foods containing carbohydrates are yummy. Again, I made a list of my favourites and ones to challenge. My current favourites include: sweet potatoes, mashed potatoes, crisps, chocolate bars, biscuits, oats, bran cereal, wheat cereal, bread of all varieties (bagels, croissants, seeded bread, wholemeal bread, TIGER bread), noodles, quinoa and millet.

- And a real close second for me…**ENERGY! Carbohydrates are the main source of energy for our bodies - they're its favourites!** They provide the body with glucose which is converted to **ENERGY *for all of those bodily functions and all of that moving and thinking and living and breathing that we are doing.*** This energy is important: fuel for our nervous system, our muscles, our organs and our brain to work properly. We *can* use protein and fats to get energy too BUT the brain's primary energy source IS glucose. **So…if you want to be at your optimum…give that brain those carbs!**

- Energy that isn't used can be stored in our muscles to be used later on - glycogen deposits - SO WHEN YOU EAT YOUR CARBS, YOU DON'T NEED TO PANIC AND THINK YOU NEED TO GO FOR A RUN IMMEDIATELY. ***Your body will use that energy throughout the day so you can be a fabulous sparkly human.***

- Because of the fact that they are the body and the brain's favourite source of energy, carbohydrates have a protein-sparing effect. That means that if you have ENOUGH CARBOHYDRATES in your body, **your body won't decide to start munching on your muscles to use that for energy**. So that, in turn, means you won't end up weak and shrivelled and will instead, again, be able to ***wrestle a grown man to the ground should you ever see fit to do so.***

- Fibre. Fibre. Fibre. I don't think I need to go into depth about why you probably want more fibre in your life - but dietary fibre from carbohydrates is essential for maintaining digestive health. Fibre promotes gut microbiome diversity, gut health and digestion - **resistant starches are good food for our gut bacteria. And they need it - they've been through a lot.** Have some porridge, it might reduce the time you're there on the toilet with your feet on the squatty potty.

- They are satiating. Eating a salad isn't going to satiate you. You're going to be hungry all day, obsessing about food, wondering what your next meal will be and getting closer and closer to another binge-compensate-restrict cycle. Carbohydrates, due to their energy, bulk and fibre content and their ability to regulate your blood sugar levels, STOP THIS happening. They are far more likely to keep you full for a few hours until your next meal. ***Again, I come back to my point above: if you are looking for an appetite suppressant, a balanced meal might just be able to do that.*** Appetite is your body asking for what it needs. Surely the most sensible way to stop it is to give it that?

- Blood sugar stabilisation! You may be used to being an INCREDIBLY ANGRY PERSON when you have an eating disorder. It's probably because you've got low blood sugar. The anger, the inability to focus, feeling weak…all common side effects of being hungry. Regular carbohydrates throughout the day (note - throughout the day, not just at one meal!) helps your blood sugar levels stabilise. That comes hand in hand with *you not becoming so ravenously hungry so as to potentially trigger a binge. And…it makes you happier*.

- Carbohydrates **RAISE YOUR SEROTONIN LEVELS NATURALLY**. Say what? Carbohydrate consumption - acting via insulin secretion - increases serotonin release. Serotonin is important for a whole bunch of things including mood, digestion, nausea, healing and bone health. All of those things are pretty damn important, right? And EVEN MORE SO IN RECOVERY. *So eat that bread so you can be happier, poop better, feel less sick, heal quicker and reduce the risk of being that 30 year old with a broken hip.* **CARBOHYDRATES MAKE YOU HAPPIER.**

- Carbohydrates enable your body to produce melatonin - they increase levels of a protein called tryptophan in your brain. Tryptophan is a building block for melatonin which helps support a regular sleep cycle. Not eating enough carbs means you're not getting enough tryptophan which in turn means your body is not producing enough melatonin. **Did you ever wonder why you used to lie awake at night? You would be SHATTERED during the day - you had NO ENERGY to do ANYTHING EVER and so you were always convinced that you would SLEEP WELL TONIGHT. How could you not? You were exhausted**. But sleep isn't moderated by those exhaustion levels in the way we think it is - those chemicals in the brain are vital. And to have enough melatonin, you need enough carbs.

Now I don't want to go too far into this murky swamp of diet culture weight gain chat BUT. Lots of people are scared of carbs because of the myths that you hear constantly: eating carbs will cause you to gain weight. Not true. Eating MORE FOOD than your body needs *might* cause you to gain weight. It doesn't matter if that food is a potato or seven broccolis, if your body is often getting more energy than it's using, you *might* gain weight. **It's not the case that you eat nothing all day and then eat a single potato, you instantly gain 1 kg due to the carb effect.** Equally, carbohydrates have the SAME AMOUNT OF ENERGY PER GRAM as protein. Both of them provide 4 calories per gram. 4 units of energy per gram. So **realistically, carbohydrates are no more likely to make you gain weight than protein**: it's just that people are more *likely* to eat more crisps and biscuits than they are to get snacky at night and reach for a boiled egg. I would like to state that the above should not matter. We should not be paralysingly afraid of weight gain. If we gain weight, we gain weight. However, being someone with an eating disorder, *I know that the fear may always be there and I also know that I* *need to remove the aversion to carbs that has rooted itself deep in my strange little brain.* And one key way to do that? Remind myself of the truth: **carbohydrates are an important source of nutrients and energy and do not spontaneously cause weight gain.**

And again - hello you. I see you there. **I see your eating disorder thinking AHA SO IF I EAT PROTEINS AND CARBOHYDRATES, I can have a body that is COVERED IN MUSCLE and FULL OF ENERGY and ABLE TO SLEEP AND BE HAPPY and my appetite will be REGULATED and ALL URGES TO BINGE WILL BE GONE and MY DIGESTION WILL BE FAB.** To you, that sounds *recovered. Does it?* Because to me, it sounds like my eating disorder is saying: well if carbohydrates and proteins do all of that...*why do you need fats?*

Why do I need fats?

- Let's start with the best one. **Foods containing fats are yummy.** Again, I made a list of my favourites and ones to challenge. I'm going to be honest here - the list of my favourites wasn't a list at all. I had systematically avoided all sources of fats for years with the exception of the occasional avocado toast moment when I was in a "clean girl aesthetic" phase of life. However, NOW, my current favourites include: salmon, olive oil (cooking all sauces, curries and stews; frying eggs and tofu; roasting vegetables - oh my!), hazelnut butter, avocado, YOGHURT YOGHURT YOGHURT, fried chips and CHOCOLATE obviously.

- Fat is an essential source of fatty acids - the body, wise as it is, cannot make these itself. They help the body stay healthy in a bundle of ways including heart health, cancer prevention, cognitive function and skin health. *So if you want a healthy heart, reduced risk of illness, a smart brain and glowy skin...eat those fats!*

- **Some vitamins - A, D and E - are fat-soluble which means that they can ONLY BE ABSORBED with the help of fats.** So if you, like many of us I suspect, have at any point become overly concerned with your "health" and consequently started taking vitamins (usually gummy ones that you can pretend are dessert, I see you)...you may just have been pooping those vitamins right back out again. Sorry!

    We need Vitamin A as it *helps our organs work properly*, is important for **healthy vision, reproduction, growth and the immune system**. We need Vitamin D because it **helps your body absorb calcium, for strong, healthy**

bones - protecting you against the broken hip! We need vitamin E because it helps **strengthen your body's response to illness and infection** and it helps **maintain healthy skin and eyes**. So eat those fats to get those vitamins absorbed *to be able to see, have pretty skin, keep your hips intact and STOP GETTING A COLD EVERY FIVE MINUTES.* Again, I see you.

- Fats are a high energy food. They contain more energy per gram than protein and carbohydrates. Now you're probably thinking *why would I want that*? I know. I thought that too. But let's go with the logic: <u>higher energy foods give our bodies higher energy. Do you want to be a low energy, lethargic, boring person? Or do you want to be high energy, bouncy, and full of pizzazz?</u> Besides which - because of their higher energy content, fats are a really good thing to add to your meals because they will be providing your body with the energy it needs more easily. No need to chew through eighteen bananas to get your X amount of energy for the day. Just have one banana with some peanut butter; and a handful of broccoli with a nice fillet of salmon with the skin still on!

- Your digestive system might thank you too: whilst typically fats aren't known for aiding digestion, if you are eating LOADS OF FRUIT AND VEGETABLES and fibre rich foods to fill up because you're not getting the satiety that fat can offer, your digestive system is not going to be loving life. **By eating fats, increasing satiety levels and reducing those fibre-heavy volume foods…you might be surprised!**

- Hormones! Not eating enough fat decreases the production of oestrogen and progesterone because these hormones are made from cholesterol. This can lead to deficiencies which can impact fertility, but also cause symptoms such as insomnia, night sweats and palpitations.

I'll be the first to hold my hands up and say that, whilst I considered myself an "expert" on nutrition, I was wrong. I was an "expert" at calories. I knew how many calories every food under the sun had. But an expert in nutrition? How could I have seriously thought that when I was eating tinned hot dogs and egg whites? When lunch was a tin of diet plan soup? When I genuinely ate a bowl of broccoli, cauliflower, spinach and cucumber and called it a meal? **I was an expert in eating as much as I could for as little as I could.** And that, it turns out, is not the same as being an expert on nutrition. In fact, it's kind of the opposite: how on earth could I have ever been meeting my body's nutritional needs when I was not eating anywhere near enough food?

I didn't know any of the above. I had no idea what carbohydrates did: in my view, they just made you fat. I didn't have a clue what protein did: I thought it was something you needed only if you wanted to build bodybuilder muscles. And fat? Well I just thought that was a pointless addition to your diet as a means to eat tasty foods but with absolutely no nutritional value whatsoever. All I knew was that certain foods were much lower in calories than others, and those were the foods I wanted. Well. Not *wanted.* But the foods I *needed* to get the body I *wanted.* Unsurprisingly, most of those foods are low in protein, carbohydrates and fats WHICH IS WHY THEY ARE SO LOW IN CALORIES. Because they do not provide the body with very much energy content at ALL.So I ate a diet that barely contained ANY of those main three macronutrients.

And I wondered WHY I felt like trash: I wondered why I was tired and drained and weak. I wondered why my skin was dry and spotty, or greasy and rashy. I wondered why my hair was falling out, and my nails brittle and snapping. I wondered why my bones ached. I wondered why I lost my periods, and why I was always grumpy and angry and unhappy. I wondered why, as I started to lose weight, I didn't end up looking slim and toned: but rather loose and flabby because my body had eaten my muscle in response to not getting enough protein. I wondered why I got colds all the time. I wondered why I walked around in a constant state of brain fog. I wondered why my digestion was, for want of a better term, absolutely screwed.

Once I was armed with the knowledge of WHY I needed each of the three groups, it was much easier for me to argue with my eating disorder when it started trying to persuade me to remove one from a meal.

- *You don't really need sweet potatoes in this salad.*
- Yes I do. Carbohydrates provide energy. They are the body's favourite energy source. And I like sweet potato.

- *You don't really need almond butter on top of your porridge.*
- Yes I do. Fats are necessary to produce fatty acids for heart health, cognitive function, hormone health and skin health. And I like almond butter.

- *You don't really need salmon with your vegetables and quinoa.*
- Yes I do. Protein is satiating and helps the body to grow and to repair, and is vital for muscle maintenance. And I like salmon.

When I sat down to plan my meals, therefore, I made sure that I planned the protein, carbohydrate and fat source into each one. As time went on, this became easier as I knew what things I liked and went well together - but initially I did lots of research and looked at lots of infographics of the sources and amounts of each macronutrient in foods to make sure that I was getting enough of each. And every time my eating disorder tried to convince me that I didn't *need* that macronutrient *this time,* I returned to all the reasons why I did. Over and over again.

And I will be honest, it was hard at first. It was strange, after decades of eating wildly unbalanced meals, to suddenly be eating proteins, carbohydrates and fats all in one go. It seemed like too much. Too much food. Too much energy.

My eating disorder did a very good job initially of getting me to skip out on the fats. And sometimes the carbohydrates. On some days, I wouldn't use oils or peanut butter or avocado in any of my meals. On some days, I would use zero carb noodles in my stir fries, or cauliflower rice. But do you know what I began to notice? On those days, my digestion was no way near as regular. In fact, I was bloated and retaining a lot more water than on the days where I ate balanced meals. On those days, too, I was a lot hungrier: within an hour of eating, usually, my stomach was rumbling again. I was ravenous. By the end of the day, my appetite was wildly out of control. **But on the days where I ate balanced meals? I was able to go about my business for 2-3 hours without even thinking about food: because my body was satisfied that it had got what it needed.** When you restrict your food groups and don't eat a nutritionally balanced diet, ***your body will keep asking for more food, trying to get the things that it needs that you won't give it***. When you start giving it enough of what it needs, that gnawing endless hunger fades: it doesn't need to ask for things it already has!

Not that responding to the gnawing hunger is a bad thing: if you get to the end of the day and are ravenous, EAT. I did and I will. But: you don't *want* that to be the way your body operates, do you? Eating small unbalanced meals throughout the day, getting hungrier and hungrier, and grouchy, and unfocused, to then eat LOADS at night? ***What's the point in that? Why not just try and eat LOADS throughout the day? Why not try giving your body energy when it needs it?*** I'm being silly. Of course I know it's never that easy. But. It works. Sit with it. Small steps. I started with breakfast because, in my view, breakfast is the best food (in terms of yumminess, of course, not moral value!). I made sure that my breakfast was substantial and that it always included each of the three groups. Start as you mean to go on. Then, when I had established that and got (*kind of, sort of, a tiny bit*) comfortable with it, I shifted to lunch. Again. It needed to be substantial and it always needed to include each of the three groups. And then we went to dinner.

And actually? ***I began to realise that it was an enjoyable way to eat. There was so much more variety and enjoyment to a meal when it had different components***, rather than just chewing through a big bowl of the same mushy food. Each meal had different textures now, and different flavours, and all of my meals were different from each other because of the huge variety of new things that I could eat now that proteins, carbohydrates and fats were all back on the table.

I would also say that you don't need to stress too much about making sure that you have to have the full three within the *meal as a single thing*. What do I mean by that? Well, one day you may really just be craving a big salad made with roasted veggies (roasted in oil) and salmon. You don't *want* to shoehorn a carb into it because it's not what you fancy. So each your salmon and veggie salad, and then have a piece of toast afterwards. Or make yourself some chips and ketchup before. Or…my personal favourite…just eat your salad with a side of crisps. You aren't in a Michelin star restaurant. **Nobody is going to judge you: other than your eating disorder, and JUDGE AWAY BABE because YOU HAVEN'T MADE IT THROUGH TO JUDGES' HOUSES.** Breakfast was often one where I struggled to get the protein and fat element in if I wasn't fancying yoghurt and peanut butter on my porridge. So I would have my porridge, and I would have berries and yoghurt and peanut butter on the side, or a bowl of branflakes and some scrambled eggs and avocado on toast. Simples. And it looks extra cute on a tray, if you have some nice little bowls. Almost like being on holiday.

When it came to snacks, I just ate whatever I wanted because I knew that I was getting what I needed from the three main meals. This meant that when I wanted a snack, I COULD reach for a chocolate bar or biscuits or crisps without worrying about MAKING IT BALANCED. It didn't need to be because I would be eating a balanced meal in a couple of hours anyway so all my snack needed to be was some quick energy that would satisfy any cravings I had. Sometimes it *was* balanced: I'm a lover of fruit and yoghurt and old lady cereal. But often it really was just a big mug of tea and a bunch of biscuits - especially on work days!

There's one final important thing that I need to stress about each of the macronutrients above. One final reason WHY you should always eat protein; WHY you should always eat carbohydrates; and WHY you should always eat fats. It's probably the most important reason, too: more important than digestion and skin health and bone health and sleep and hormones and satiety. Do you know what it is? **THE MOST IMPORTANT REASON YOU NEED TO EAT PROTEINS, CARBOHYDRATES AND FATS? If you are avoiding any of them…you are restricting.**

Some of my FAVOURITE combinations? Oh go on then, if you insist.

- Salmon, noodles and veggies cooked in ginger and garlic paste, soya sauce, peanut butter, honey, lime juice and SESAME OIL topped with kimchi

- Smoked salmon and cream cheese on bagels
- Tofu or tempeh sandwiches, with roasted peppers, spinach, cucumber, pickled onions and garlic and herb cream cheese, with chopped fruit and crisps
- Porridge or pancakes topped with Greek yoghurt, hazelnut butter, defrosted frozen berries and fresh fruit
- Toast with almond butter and bananas, sprinkled with cacao nibs and salted, roasted peanuts

12. DOING IT: NO RESTRICTION

I've talked about restriction a lot in chapter 6 so I will just briefly reiterate the key points here about why you HAVE to take ALL RESTRICTION off the table.

- If you are restricting certain food groups, **you are not providing your body with the full range of nutrients that it needs**. Refer to the above section to see why we don't want that!

- Restricting certain foods and having rules about what you can and cannot eat makes the brain obsess about these foods even more. If you struggle with bingeing, this is likely to trigger a binge. And a binge is likely to trigger compensatory behaviour of some kind, and thus you find yourself trapped in over a decade of the same cycle over and over again. **Restriction isn't going to take you anywhere other than the binge-compensate-restrict hamster wheel that you have been running on for too long.**

- Even if you don't struggle with bingeing, the more you restrict, the more your hunger cues start to dull down. Whilst sometimes we do feel hunger, many of us with eating disorders will have reached a point where we say *I'm not hungry* and probably mean it. **We are, of course, hungry. We are starving. But our body has given up on telling us that, so it feels like, even if we *want* to, we don't need to eat.** Restriction then becomes a trap: we don't eat more because we aren't hungry and because we aren't eating more, our hunger cues slow down even more and we become extra convinced that we can somehow survive on thin air. Restriction in any form can become addictive. The feeling of being empty can become addictive. So if you open the door just a little bit to it, it won't be long before it seizes full control again. I always told myself this time would be different: it would just be a small, *normal person diet.* How hard could it be? Other people did it ALL THE TIME. Dropped a couple of pounds here and there and then went back to eating again.

But remember: **Things that may be healthy for other people are not things that are healthy for someone with an eating disorder.** And every single time I tried to restrict "normally", it always spiralled. It started off fine, and then as my eating disorder saw it working, it wanted MORE and it wanted it FASTER. Every. Time.

- If you are restricting the amount of food you eat, you are restricting your body of the energy that it needs to function. In recovery, you also need energy to repair all of the damage to your organs and to restore the weight that you should never have lost. **Therefore, if you restrict in recovery it's double bad: you won't have the energy to function OR to heal. So what will you do? Continue to suffer. Continue to exist, but barely.** Continue to be stuck in your hellscape.

- You have an eating disorder. So restriction is a disordered behaviour. And if you keep doing it…how will you ever stop?

Why do we do it, then? Initially, for the obvious reasons. Being smaller. Controlling our body. But we have made the decision to recover, right? So why are we still tempted to restrict? Why are we still accidentally (kind of) restricting?

For me, I was nervous about gaining weight too fast. The NHS don't help with that: they like to say **they want you to gain weight, but not too much weight, and not too fast either.** They basically validate all of the fears that your eating disorder has: that you will gain weight rapidly, lose all control of it and become "too big" in your estimation. Having been someone who had been obese in the past and who had, in my view, lacked control over food, this fear was incredibly prominent for me. The fears were multifaceted: I hadn't liked my body when I was bigger; I felt like people would judge me when I went RAPIDLY from underweight to obese overnight; society does not value people who "lack control" and "let themselves go"; and I didn't like the *feeling of my body changing size.*

I was also nervous about giving up the control that I had had for many years. It's like an abusive relationship, right? It was bad for me. So bad for me. But I needed it. I needed it because it was the only thing that I knew. **It was stable: it was the constant in the**

constant chaos of my life. Solid ground. Sure, the ground was at rock bottom, but it was still. I knew where I stood. It was predictable. Calm, even. My strength and stay, if you will. If I let it go, I would be letting go of that dull, predictable, endless struggle of life and throwing myself into the unknown: of what? **Chaos, probably. Feelings. Change.** There would be a big empty hole in my life: what would I *do* with all the time? I spent endless time researching food and watching other people eat online and following threads about people with eating disorders and exercise and researching the newest ways to build the body I wanted. With all of that gone, what would I *do*? The control would be gone and the emptiness would be there. Time, pointless, stretching out forever.

I didn't know how to be okay. I didn't know how to be okay. I had never *been* okay. I had always been messed up: my childhood, my brain, my specific set of circumstances had meant that every day of my remembered life, I had been walking around with a great deal of pain. Every day was a **low** day. I was used to suffering. I was used to the feeling of existing only so that other people were not hurt by my leaving. I wanted to die. Every day. And if I let go of the eating disorder, and maybe tried to work on the things that had triggered it…and the pain reduced? Or I found ways to hold it better? What then? I would be *okay*. And I didn't know how to do that. I didn't know how to be a person in the world who ISN'T haunted by the constant desire not to exist. **I didn't know how to be someone who was happy and balanced and healthy. It felt like, if I gave up my eating disorder, I would be giving up a job that I could do really well for one that I had no qualifications for.**

I was worried about losing my identity too quickly. My friends and family didn't know about my eating disorder for many years. When they finally did, it had been for such a short period of time that it almost felt silly for me to commit to recovery so fast. **From the outside, it might look like I had barely been ill at all.** And…dark as it sounds…I kind of *liked* it when they knew. Because suddenly everyone was checking in on me. Suddenly everyone was being incredibly lovely and caring, and trying their very best not to say triggering things about food and diet culture around me. I felt, for a few brief moments, like my illness made me more lovable. But, aside from that, it was also the identity that I had held for myself for all of those years. It wasn't necessarily an identity I wanted: I hadn't *wanted* to be a bulimic. But that didn't change the fact that every day for years I had known the undeniable truth about myself: **I had an eating disorder. I was someone with an eating disorder. And it took up so much of my life that it became who I was. I was someone with an eating disorder.** Part of me, however grim this is, didn't want to let that go. Again, I think it comes back to the fear of change. **But also the fear that, without the disorder, there was nothing remarkable about me at all.** Without the disorder, I was boring. I didn't know who I was, what I enjoyed or what hobbies I had: because for years it had all just been my body and food. So if I let go of that identity, it would mean trying to figure out who I actually was underneath it all. **And what if I didn't like her?**

I didn't know how. It had been part of my life for so long that I wasn't even fully aware of how deep it ran. When you have always been restricted or restricting to some degree, it can be quite hard to actually see where it begins and ends. I didn't *know* life without restriction. So I didn't always *know* in an obvious and tangible way that I *was* restricting. And to go against all of the rules and ideas that I had lived by *for as long as I could remember* felt like an impossible task. How was I meant to *know*? How was I meant to separate what I actually wanted and needed from what I *thought* I wanted? And how was I meant to know if *I* was thinking, or if it was my eating disorder or diet culture?

But. I knew that I had no options left. I had reached my breaking point and I was ALL IN FULLY COMMITTED TO RECOVERY. For a month, remember? So. I had to stop restricting.

So, first of all, I tackled all of the reasons why I was afraid to let it go. In my crazy journal, of course.

Reason: nervous about gaining weight too fast.
Counterpoint:

- *If you do gain weight quickly, it's because your body needs to.* You are following the guidelines recommended for weight restoration so whatever happens to your body is what is *meant* to happen to you body. It's not too fast if it is what your body decides to do.

- Initially, weight gain **will** appear to be incredibly rapid because you go from being very underfed and probably dehydrated, to eating lots of food that your body is being *incredibly slow at digesting.* Your body holds on to a bunch of water weight, both because it was so dehydrated and so that it can start the processes of repair, and also holds on to a bunch of poop - the constipation weight gain is real!

- *Stop focusing on the weight. Focus on how you feel.* Sure you may have jumped XXXkg overnight, but you can also now get out of bed without nearly dropping to the ground. Sure, the scale may say you are XXkg more than you were three days ago, but you can also go downstairs and eat something to satiate the intense hunger you've woken up with, rather than spend the morning tired and weak and shaky from low blood sugar. Sure you may be XXkg heavier, but your life is 100 times better.

- **The quicker you gain the weight back, the quicker you gain your life back**. Your cognitive function and your physical health restore as you weight restore, so the sooner you gain weight, the sooner you gain your brain and strength and pizzazz back.

- Gaining weight doesn't change anything. You didn't like your body when you were big, or when you were small so the size of your body is irrelevant. **Gaining weight won't make your family or friends feel any differently about you: they loved you before and they'll love you after.** And if they don't? They're the kind of shallow people you need to pop in the bin.

Reason: nervous about giving up the control that I had had for many years.
Counterpoint:
- *My eating disorder was controlling me*. I may have started out in control, but I definitely didn't end up that way. Being unable to eat birthday cake on my own birthday. Being unable to eat my best friend's wedding cake. Being unable to go out with my friends on a night out in case they try to make me eat. Eating bowl after bowl after bowl of cereal in the kitchen in the middle of the night. Throwing up hundreds of pounds of food. That's not control.

- Anyway, **what good is being in control when all the control has the potential to bring you is a smaller, weaker body?** That doesn't seem like a fair deal, actually.

- Plus, I reasoned, I didn't know what life was like if I let go of trying to control my body and food. I had never tried it. It might be less scary than I thought. And it would certainly be less boring than the endless daily drudgery of my disorder.

Reason: I didn't know how to be okay.
Counterpoint:
- This is a silly reason. You probably won't be okay anyway. You've still got all those crazy mad sad thoughts in your head. Don't worry babe. You don't have to go around skipping and singing just because you start eating again. Your life can stay sad and gloomy.

- Joking. But that's why you're going to *work on it*. You're not just going to spontaneously recover and SUDDENLY HAVE TO BE OKAY. You've got a plan, remember? Coping mechanisms. You're going to have therapy and you're going to sit and think about EVERYTHING and LEARN how to be okay. You're going to LEARN.

- Anyway. If you decide that you can't recover because you *don't know how to be okay,* that means you're accepting *not being okay* for the rest of your life. That doesn't sound very okay.

Reason: I was worried about losing my identity too quickly.
Counterpoint:
- **Do you REALLY want your identity to be someone with an eating disorder?** Like, REALLY? Would you want someone to say to your best friend, "Oh do you know X?" and them turn around and say, "Oh yeah I know them. They're really good at being sick. They're unwell. They do a really good job of being ill." No! I don't want that. **I want to be described as someone who is FULL OF ENERGY, and who is kind and funny and full of LIFE. The girl who wears the crazy leggings and the crocs and the quirky earrings. The girl who will go out of her way to help anyone who needs her. The girl who inspires people by her drive to do good.**

- I thought about if my friends were sick in the same way that I am. Would I be *impressed*? Would I think *anything positive about it at all*? Of course not. I would be incredibly worried about them, sure. I would want them to get better. I would want them to shed the sick identity as soon as they possibly could. I wouldn't think "oh wow how amazing, they are a person with a disorder".

- I want a new identity. *I want my identity to be: someone who got better. Someone who fought, really hard, for a really long time, and WON.* Someone who was strong enough to overcome one of the hardest battles. Someone who did not give up. Someone who knew that sickness was not an aspiration. Someone who has the ENERGY and the FOCUS and the PASSION to do good things for people and make other people's lives better. Not someone who is dull and drained and unable to do anything for anyone, least of all myself.

Reason: I didn't know how. It had been part of my life for so long that I wasn't even fully aware of how deep it ran.
Counterpoint:

- Not knowing how much control something has over you is terrifying. You always said knowledge is power, right? So, let's take that power back. Figure it out. Look at your life and your habits and every thought and feeling you have towards food and your body and ask yourself: is this important? Is this driven by me, or by my eating disorder? **I decided that I didn't want to be living in ignorance any more**. I wanted to figure out how deep it ran. I wanted to find out *how* to stop.

- Anyway, it's not that hard, actually. It's not rocket science. Everything I thought about food and my body was clearly spelled out for me on the Internet, and in the things my mother would say about food, and in the things that random strangers would say about larger bodies, and the DIET CULTURE SWAMP that we subsist in. To figure out what many of my rules were, all I needed to do was start actively thinking about the media I was consuming and listening properly and sceptically to the things people around me were saying.

So what happened?

I'm not going to pretend that it was easy and one day I woke up and gave myself full and unconditional permission to eat. I tried it. I engaged in behaviours. I took a few faltering steps forwards and a few huge slides backwards. But. I did something differently this time. Even when I did binge and then compensate, the next day **I followed the plan anyway. I ate three meals and three snacks every single day, regardless of whether or not I had binged the previous day.** I removed one of the compensation elements because by doing that, I removed the restriction element.

And so my body started to feel safer. It was finally, after years of the opposite, getting consistent nourishment. Slowly, slowly, those urges to binge started to reduce. They would come as abstract thoughts sometimes, but they were no longer compulsions that I couldn't ignore. **It was then that I realised: the stupid advice you read online had been right all along. My bingeing was, in part, largely impacted by the fact that I just wasn't eating enough.** My body was just trying to get more food in and bingeing was a quick and efficient way for that to happen. And my body didn't trust me to do that myself, for obvious reasons, hence why the urge became compulsive. This wasn't a quick process, by the way. It took MONTHS. It took fighting my brain EVERY DAY to force myself to make and eat those meals. It took WHITE KNUCKLING my way through urges to compensate. *It was the hardest thing I have ever done and, bloody hell, the hardest thing I hope I ever have to do.*

But. It was worth it. Because I went from where I was - bingeing and compensating every day - to barely doing it at all. And the crazy thing? **I had gone past my month**

deadline. And nothing that dramatic had happened. So I decided to just keep going for a bit longer and see what happened. After all, I reminded myself, I could turn back whenever I wanted.

Once the binges had reduced to barely there, I decided I needed to eliminate them completely. So I looked at them and thought about why they happened. And do you know what it was? It was on a day where I had "allowed" myself a chocolate bar for a snack but then wanted more chocolate later on. It was on a day where I had put crisps with my lunch and then wanted a bag of crisps in the evening. It was on a day where I had already had a sweet meal for breakfast so forced myself to have savoury lunch even though I was craving another sweet meal. I think this kind of recovery is all too easy to fall into. **You think you are eating unrestricted because you are eating the chocolates and the crisps and the pastries and the chips. But you aren't *allowed* to eat them whenever you want. So that's *not* unrestricted.** *There are still rules:* one a day, or at a certain time, or an over-focus on "good" foods needing to make up the bulk of the day.

The solution? No more rules. One morning, I genuinely started the day with two white chocolate wafer bars. It was, initially, very tricky. On that day, I think I ate five chocolate bars. But the next day? I didn't have any. And I didn't have any the day after, either. Or the next. I had, on average, one chocolate bar a day. And it wasn't because I wasn't *allowed* one the next day. It was because I didn't *want* one. I had got my chocolate fix and instead quite fancied some tea and toast instead. It was, honestly, shocking. I had spent YEARS convinced that if I allowed myself to eat what I wanted, I wouldn't stop.

But this time was different. *It was different because I wasn't approaching unrestricted eating from a place where my body no longer felt safe.* I was eating three meals and three snacks every day, consistently, without fail, even when it was hard. And it was. Most of the time. But I did it. Every day. **Over and over. And so my body…it began to trust me.** The urges to binge went down. Slowly, of course, because it takes time to rebuild trust when you've broken it quite as deeply and systematically as I had. But when my body began to feel safe, it didn't feel the same desperate urge to EAT AND NEVER STOP because it knew that it didn't need to do that anymore. It knew that food was always going to be coming soon. And my brain knew that if I really wanted 100 chocolate bars in one day, I would have them. But it becomes a different ball game when you know you're going to be digesting them all. You get to about three in a row and you feel nauseous and have to stop. And then later, you start craving something *really* savoury like salmon and potatoes. Because: your body knows what it needs. **When it asks for chocolate, it needs A SUGAR HIT for some QUICK**

ENERGY and for a PICK ME UP. When it asks for salmon, it needs some fats and some proteins.

Try listening to it because, hard as it is, you tried listening to your brain all this time and it didn't really work out that well did it?

Once I had reached the point where I was eating regularly, and was allowing myself to eat whatever I wanted, I knew I had reached the next hurdle: working out what I - me - actually **did** want. Of course, as I mentioned above, I had no real idea how deep my restriction actually went. I needed to figure it out so that I could be really sure I was listening to myself and not my eating disorder.

That's when I decided to start doing food challenges. Each week, I set myself a new challenge and, for the entire day, I planned my food around that challenge. By making it a whole day rather than just one meal, it meant that I was forced to address more than one small thing at once and that I was giving myself a chance to do things over and over again. **In the same way that your body needs to learn to trust you again, your brain needs to learn to trust all the foods you told it were bad, and to trust that the stupid rules you made up were, in fact, stupid.** The only way to help it do that is to show it, over and over and over, that it's okay now. *You're safe, you're okay.*

The challenges also removed some of the intense anxiety around the things I found difficult. Like, how difficult could rice feel on ORANGE FOOD DAY when it was *tomato and basil rice* with orange salmon and orange roasted vegetables and an orange Sriracha mayo dressing? A plate of sunshine is FAR LESS SCARY than some rice, salmon and broccoli, right? How difficult could sandwiches feel when it was a beautifully aesthetic STRAWBERRY AND CREAM JAPANESE DESSERT SANDWICH on a day full of sandwiches? A cute little puffy white and red sandwich is FAR LESS SCARY than a dry and sadly empty meal deal sandwich, right? How difficult could PIZZA feel when it was on the day I shopped at THE MOST EXPENSIVE SUPERMARKET for a day so felt like a boujee queen? A sourdough antipasti pizza topped with rocket is FAR LESS SCARY than some £1 oven pizza, right? How difficult could NUT BUTTER BE when it was cooked into the *most delicious* South African Peanut stew on NUT BUTTER DAY? A hearty, creamy stew is FAR LESS SCARY than a single piece of bread spread with peanut butter.

And why are they LESS SCARY? Because they are FUN. Because they are CREATIVE. Because they are NOT IN ANY WAY SIMILAR TO RESTRICTION MEALS. There was no way you could look at my glowing plate of orange rice, fish and veg and see a gym bro meal. There was no way you could look at my cream and fruit sandwich and see a sandwich that you selected because it had the lowest number on the packet. There was no way you could look at my fancy pizza and see a children's dinner. There was no way you could look at my peanut stew and see a carefully measured tablespoon of peanut butter.

Thinking of new and fun ways to eat foods BAFFLED my eating disorder. It distracted it, actually. I was too busy trying to think of yellow snacks, or how I could use processed vegan foods for a day, or trying to make recipes with only three ingredients: I had less time to go over *why* the foods were challenging. I was too busy thinking about how the challenge was challenging me to think outside the box and be creative.

Some of my challenges included:
- Colour challenges: eating all red food for a day, for example. I did red, black, orange, yellow, green, purple…one of my FAVOURITE new recipes came on purple day - red cabbage miso soup! On black food day, I discovered that I did, in fact, like raisins. On green food day, I realised that greens powder tastes like grass and should be avoided. On yellow food day, I ate my first iced biscuit in years.
- Making all of my meals using oats for a day (we had baked oats, savoury oats, overnight oats…if you haven't tried savoury oats…I know it *sounds* dubious but TRY IT!)
- Shopping at specific supermarkets for a day, to get me to try new products that I hadn't come across before
- Eating sandwiches for a day (we had Japanese fruit sandwiches, BRANDED SANDWICH SHOP, hoisin tofu sandwiches, sandwich biscuits, a breakfast sandwich made out of a full English cooked breakfast, a PB+J!)
- Using nut butters in every meal (we had nut butter on toast with fruit, African Peanut Stew, rice paper rolls with almond butter dipping sauce, and porridge and yoghurt bowls drizzled in the stuff).
- Trying savoury breakfasts for a week (there were lots of poached eggs! Also, I discovered balsamic glaze, the wonderful combination of halloumi and chilli jam, and PESTO EGGS).
- Bagel day (smoked salmon + cream cheese, classic combination; sweet bagels; bagel French toast; and the heavenly combination of a simple toasted bagel with butter)
- Rice day (rice pudding, the viral salmon and rice bowl, rice porridge - surprisingly a yes from me, rice cakes - a no from me)

The challenges also meant that I had to stray away from the foods that I had become comfortable with and ate all the time. **There's only so much that you can do with**

porridge, yoghurt bowls, fruits and veggies. So, every challenge was opening me up to new foods and new ideas and also showing me what I did and didn't like. I found new meals and snacks that I loved - meal prep ramen jars, savoury oatmeal, peanut stew, almond butter satay sauce, hummus prawns on toast, chilli jam and halloumi on toast, anything and everything lemon. I also realised that some of the things I used to think I did like and just wasn't "allowed"...actually weren't that great to me. I didn't *love* most nut butters. I didn't like Nutella at all. Crumpets were not as delicious as I remembered. Cheese was, in my opinion, a bit overrated. Not bad, don't get me wrong, but not as good as I had once believed it to be in the days where I hadn't eaten it for 80 years. Pasta was…just a vessel for sauce. Not something to be idolised. And porridge? Still good, but no longer what I wanted for breakfast *every single day*.

In fact, I suddenly found myself eating so many different things day to day and week to week that it would have been incredibly hard to describe what my favourite meals and foods were anymore. **And that's when you know you're making progress: I think if you asked most people with an eating disorder what their death row meal would be, they would be able to tell you instantly.** When you only eat a select group of things, it's not hard to be certain what your favourite is. But does that make sense? There are literally thousands and thousands of different things we can eat - how does a single favourite make any sense?

Back in the day, I would have told you mine: starter of barbecue tofu bao buns and pumpkin croquettes; main of pizza and garlic bread and coleslaw; dessert of vanilla cheesecake with fresh berries and cream. And a pint of hot chocolate to drink.

But now that I was eating different foods every day and every week? I wasn't sure anymore. Because the starter could have been any number of things: bao buns and croquettes, or creamy soup with chunky fresh bread and butter, or garlic mushrooms, or poppadoms and a chutney tray, or cauliflower wings, or feta, watermelon and mint salad. The main could have been pizza, or stacked sandwiches on seeded bread, loaded with pickles and roasted veggies and tempeh, or Thai red curry with lime and coriander rice, or pasta bake, or egg and chips with lashings of ketchup, or a vegetarian Full English, or smoked salmon and avocado on toast. The dessert could have been vanilla cheesecake, or lemon cheesecake, or lemon posset, or a chocolate oat muffin with yoghurt and fruit, or a raisin and biscuit chocolate bar, or GOLD chocolate bars, or a white chocolate and raspberry glazed doughnut or birthday cake.

<u>Because when you no longer feel like you are on death row, you no longer need a death row meal. When you *can* eat anything, there's no longer *one last day to make it count*.</u>

13. DOING IT: EATING IT NOT YEETING IT.

We're building up a picture here, okay. So. I'm now eating three meals and three snacks a day, plus more if I'm hungry. I'm making sure that my meals contain proteins, carbs and fats but eating whatever I want for my snacks. I had started to address my restrictions and identify all of the rules that I hadn't even realised I had.

So. I was gaining weight. And I was feeling very full, physically. And some days, when I did have the three chocolate bars a day, or something that I hadn't planned, or something that I hadn't particularly enjoyed…the urges to compensate were THERE. I had urges to do it all: to vomit, to engage in compulsive movements, to go right back to restriction the next day. When I had bad body image days, my first thought was WELL LOSE WEIGHT THEN.

But. I reminded myself constantly: *if you lose weight, you lose yourself. If you lose weight, you lose yourself.* Remember what it was like? You were tired and weak and snappy and angry and cold and sad and alone and, essentially, practically dead. *If you lose weight, you lose yourself.* Now you are a little bigger, sure, but you are so alive: you can laugh and walk and be present, you can go to people's birthday parties and EAT with them, you can SLEEP again, you can sit and drive without the bones in your bum bruising. Is that worth body image? WHEN YOUR BODY IMAGE WASN'T EVEN GOOD ANYWAY? YOU ALREADY LOST THE WEIGHT. AND YOU STILL DIDN'T LIKE YOUR BODY. Instead, you lost yourself. Constant reminders of what I lost versus what I gained. *If you lose weight, you lose yourself. You have gained weight, but you have gained life too.*

I also reminded myself constantly of the logic and the reasons WHY I couldn't compensate:

1. **The obvious one: do you want to live the rest of your life engaging in compensatory behaviours in order to not feel too full and to live in a smaller body? <u>That's the cost. The rest of your life</u>**. And the prize? A smaller body. Because the feeling full thing will go away. When your body gets used to digesting again, and it all gets revved back up to where it SHOULD BE, the amount of food that you think is *so very much* right now…will just be normal. Or not enough. You won't feel full forever. **But if you compensate…you might just be ill forever.** THE REASON YOU NEED TO STOP COMPENSATORY BEHAVIOUR IS, BECAUSE IF YOU DON'T, YOU WILL NOT GET BETTER.

2. **Compensating will make your digestive issues worse.** If your body doesn't trust you because it thinks you will start restricting food again, or it thinks that the food will be removed from your body, or it's expecting laxatives, or overexercise, your digestion is going to do what it did before: slow itself down in response. If it doesn't trust you to be consistently eating and resting and healing, it's not going to see the point in expending its energy being ready to help you. It's not your therapist - they're *paid* to stick around when you start acting crazy. Your digestion isn't. It's just there to protect itself. Your body will conserve energy at all costs.

    And think about it like this…that's just going to make your body image worse, too, because you'll go back to being bloated and retaining fluid like crazy!

3. **Compensating means that you are never actually removing restriction.** It doesn't count as allowing yourself to eat whatever you want if you know, deep down, that after you've eaten it you are going to get rid of it or account for it or make up for it. Your brain and your body know that food is not free. Your brain knows restriction is there. Your body feels the consequences of that.

4. **Compensating will continue to mess with your hunger cues.** Your body is trying to learn how to feel hungry and full again. If you are compensating, you're just going to be confusing it. It thought it was full five minutes ago, right? But now it's like…empty? Is it hungry or not? Should it send a hunger cue or not? There's so much complexity going on with hunger cues, involving all manner of hormones and biological processes and if you go and stick a big oar in there, you're just going to disrupt the flow. **You will not get those hunger cues to normalise if you continue to do abnormal behaviours.**

5. **It's addictive.** This might be a controversial statement but I believe that, at least for me, purging was addictive. And I think that goes for any kind of compensation: whether you use pure restriction, vomiting, laxatives or exercise. **I think it's all too easy to become addicted to the feeling of compensation.** Because it feels good. It feels like you have done something wrong, and now you are doing something right to fix it. You think you'll only do it once and that it's just a slip, but then what happens next time you want to do it? One more time always turns into one more time, always turns into a full blown relapse. You cannot ever just have one more time. You just have to stop. The last time needs to be the last time.

The ONLY WAY for my body and mind to reap all of the benefits of eating three meals and three snacks, of eating proteins, carbs and fats, and of removing all of my restrictions and eating a huge variety of foods was to EAT IT ALL AND KEEP IT ALL. If I didn't do that, the other things would be meaningless.

At first, it was really, really difficult. And I mean REALLY DIFFICULT.

The dangers of purging are well documented but you never really imagine they will happen to you. But that's why it's so dangerous. I knew a girl in my outpatient service who, like me at the time, was not underweight. She was bulimic, however. Purging depletes the body of electrolytes - potassium is one of these, and potassium is responsible for heart rhythms. Low potassium caused by purging can quite literally cause your heart to stop due to irregular heart rhythms. And the scariest part? You wouldn't even know. You would be wandering around, running off the adrenaline, convinced you felt fine and then one irregular rhythm would be enough and you would be dead. <u>That's what happened to this girl. She swore blind she was fine. She swore blind she "wasn't that sick" because she wasn't underweight. But she's dead now.</u> It was this death that knocked me for six and made me realise how dangerous what I was doing was. My own abnormal ECGs hadn't been enough to freak me out, nor had my nights in hospital on IV drips, hooked up to heart monitors. It wasn't real enough. But seeing someone who looked like me, and acted like me, *die*? I realised that my eating disorder was HELLA WRONG when it was telling me that I personally wasn't at risk.

I was.

And so I reminded myself of that every time I got the urge to purge.

THOUGHT: *It's just once though* the voice would whisper. *It's not that dangerous if you just do it this one time because you ate too much at your mum's birthday dinner.*
ARGUMENT: You've said that to me before. Every single time. And as soon as I do it once, and remember how it feels, I want to do it again. The next time I am stressed, I need to do it again. And you'll say it's just this once, AGAIN. One more time is never one more time. So it IS that dangerous because I have walked down this path before and I KNOW where it goes. When you start walking that way, it's almost impossible to turn around. **And at the end of the road? A grave.** And so what if I ate more than usual? My body needs this extra energy to heal.

As well as the constant reminders, I did also do a number of things that did help:

- I moved back in with my mum. This wasn't an easy decision for numerous reasons but it did mean that it was easier for me to resist the urges. I didn't want to accidentally block up her toilet and had no idea if her drains would be able to handle it. I also didn't want to risk her or my brother hearing me. So in making it HARDER to purge in private, that removed one of the layers of temptation. Not completely, obviously, as it was always possible to do it - it just wasn't as wildly easy as it had been when I lived alone. If you have the option to live with other people rather than alone, it can be life changing as a circuit breaker.

- I stopped drinking a ridiculous amount of fluid when I was eating. This wasn't necessarily a disordered thing: I've always been someone who just LOVES a little drink. Tea, hot chocolate, squash, cola, lemonade…I would get a pint of fizzy drink and have it finished in about two minutes flat. I just LOVED drinking. However, having all the liquid in my stomach with all the food did make purging easier. So I stopped. I had a cup of tea and that was that. I wasn't dehydrating myself - I would still drink enough to sink a small ship *after* my food had been given 15 minutes or so to start digesting.

- I would schedule activities immediately after meals: when I sat down to eat lunch, I would text a friend and ask to call them in 15 minutes. When my mum was home, I'd ask her if she wanted to watch an episode of the show we were watching as soon as I had finished dinner. I would get in the shower and stand under the hot water. I would meal prep. I would put my headphones on, blast music and sit in the garden. I would go and do the food shopping. Or I would do the recycling. Or I would go and drive my car to a random park and sit on the bench. If it was raining, I would go to a car park and I would sit and watch people walking by. I would be doing *something* after eating. There was never any dead time. The further I got without purging, the more I was able to not do this. **But it was fundamental at the start to make sure that BEFORE I sat down to eat, I knew EXACTLY what I was doing AFTER.** I would also leave the kitchen in a state of disrepair - instead of cleaning up after myself, I would leave the knife where it was, the chopping board unwashed, and the food out of the fridge. That way, Step One was always to do the dishes and reset the kitchen. And then on to the PLANNED ACTIVITY. And hey presto, before you know it…you've done it. You've white knuckled it. You've won.

- The most important thing, though, was when it *did* happen and I *did* slip: I had to EAT again. That was hard. Not *again* at snack, *again for that meal*. And then the snacks and meals for the rest of the day. So if I purged lunch, I forced myself to have another lunch. Because I NEEDED my body to know that this WASN'T happening again. I WASN'T going to deprive it of food again. I wasn't going to restrict. No more compensation, no more restriction. As I taught myself that purging was USELESS because I was ALWAYS GOING TO EAT AFTERWARDS, my eating disorder became less obsessed with purging. Why would it want to do that, if it knew I would force myself to eat *more* in response?

You won't believe me.

I know you won't. Because I didn't believe the people who had recovered either. For years, I looked at people who said they were able to stop and thought it didn't apply to me. I thought *you're different from me*. I thought *you didn't have it as bad as I have it*. I thought *we aren't the same*.

But do you know what? I was right. They WERE different. They WEREN'T the same as me. But they probably had it just as bad. They were different because they had STOPPED RESTRICTING. They had stopped COMPENSATING. And I had never done that. So that's why, hard as I tried, I was never able to stop. **Until you do the one thing that you feel like you *can't*...until you try the *impossible* and let go of that chokehold you have on restriction...you will always be at risk of being drawn back.**

Once I, *finally,* FINALLY decided to try it - for that single month, of course - and GENUINELY gave up on ALL restriction and ALL ideas of losing weight...well. Knock me down with a feather. It worked.

Three months later - a whole two months past that arbitrary deadline I had set to relapse if I needed to - I was finally a month clean of purging. A MONTH. 30 DAYS. Does that sound impressive? Maybe not. But before that, I had done it every day for over six years so...30 days? A revolution.

14. DOING IT: FACING THE GOBLIN. REFRAMING THE THOUGHTS.

And then the final point of my star. And my favourite one, and the only reason I was able to do any of the above.

I didn't just miraculously find myself sitting at the table, happily eating my three meals and three snacks, humming a happy little tune. I didn't find myself springing out of bed every morning, running downstairs and drizzling nut butter freely on my pancakes. I didn't find myself eating as soon as I was hungry, every time I was hungry, and allowing myself to eat absolutely everything that popped into my head. I didn't wake up free of the eating disorder thoughts. It came slowly. It came DELIBERATELY. It had to.

I think a big issue with my initial attempts at recovery, and what a lot of us do, is that we EXPECT it to happen IMMEDIATELY. We know what we need to do: eat regularly, remove restriction, stop all compensatory behaviours. And then when we wake up and we have eating disorder thoughts, this can destabilise us. We think that maybe we aren't ready after all. **We tell ourselves we can't recover yet because the thoughts are still there.** So we wait for the thoughts to go away. But they don't. And we're still trapped. Restricting and compensating and listening to the thoughts. But it's fine, you tell yourself, because when the thoughts go away, then you'll be able to start your recovery.

I'm going to tell you what you don't want to hear.

They don't go away.

Or at least, if they *do* go away, it's going to take a very, very, very long time. As I write this, I have been in active, committed recovery for just over a month. And the thoughts are still very much with me. Not just every so often. Always. Every minute of every second of every day. Like bees. Swarming. Endlessly.

You know when you're trying to lie in on the weekend and it's 6am and the birds wake you up with their incessant chirping? That's what it's like in my head. Every decision about food. Every meal. Every time I'm hungry. Every time I'm not. Every time I go out to eat. Every time I go to the supermarket. Every time someone says anything about diets or health or body size. Every time I walk past a mirror. Every time an item of clothing clings to part of my body. Every time I see someone exercising. Every. Single. Moment.

I have taken to treating them like an annoying goblin, or small child, that is following me around (same difference, right?) and muttering irritating things at me non-stop. I COULD try and ignore it, right? Just tune it out, put my headphones on and blindly pretend it's not there. But goblins, and children, tend to be rather persistent. If you try to ignore them, they're just going to get louder and louder and louder until you *have* to listen to them. So what's the alternative? Listen to them.

You're probably thinking WHAT?!?! WHAT KIND OF RECOVERY BOOK IS THIS? THIS GIRL IS TELLING ME TO *__LISTEN__* TO MY EATING DISORDER THOUGHTS? Well, in my defence, I *did* tell you at the START that you *shouldn't* be taking advice from a random mentally ill girly off the Internet…

No but look.

If you listen to them - like PROPERLY listen to them - you will start to realise that they are, in fact, utterly deranged. You know how kids cry when you won't let them eat mud? Or how they cry if they ask you for something, and you give it to them? Or when they tell jokes that aren't funny and want you to laugh? It's all UTTERLY DERANGED. When you listen to kids, you start to realise how WEIRD and SENSELESS they are. And when you listen to your eating disorder thoughts…you might start to notice the same thing.

Once you have listened to them, you can then do the fun part. If a child was crying about wanting to eat mud, I would let them eat it. Joking. I'm a trained teacher, that would be *irresponsible.* I would explain to them, logically and calmly, why eating mud was a bad idea. They might still decide to eat the mud. But, it's a lot less likely that they will when they know there might be worm poop or dog wee in it. If a child cried because they wanted a toy and I gave it to them, I would explain that they had what they wanted and if they were upset, they could just give it back. If they told me an unfunny joke, and got angry when I didn't laugh at it, I would probably explain to them why it wasn't funny and suggest ways they could improve their stand-up skills. This is why I won't have children, you see, as they wouldn't appreciate my abject refusal to humour them and instead fight every one of their statements with PURE LOGIC.

And that's what you need to do with the eating disorder. Because, listen and trust me: there is not a SINGLE THOUGHT that your eating disorder has that cannot be refuted with actual logic.

How did I do it?

Thinking.

I caught every thought and I *thought* about it. Then I imagined that someone else had said it to me, like it was a fact. And that was enough to get me going.

I asked myself: WHAT DO YOU MEAN?

WHAT DO YOU MEAN NOBODY WILL LOVE YOU IF YOU'RE NOT UNDERWEIGHT?

WHAT DO YOU MEAN YOU WANT TO BE SICK ENOUGH? SICK ENOUGH FOR WHAT?

WHAT DO YOU MEAN YOU'RE THE ONLY PERSON WITH AN EATING DISORDER THAT IS NOT GOING TO SUFFER LONG TERM EFFECTS?

WHAT DO YOU MEAN YOU'RE HUNGRY BUT YOU'RE NOT GOING TO EAT BECAUSE YOU'RE GOING OUT TO DINNER IN SIX HOURS?

WHAT DO YOU MEAN YOU CAN'T EAT ANOTHER APPLE BECAUSE YOU'VE ALREADY HAD ONE TODAY?

I would write the thought down. And then I would find a REFRAME that helped me to rationalise why the thought made no sense. I would write all the reasons the thought wasn't a helpful thought. And all the reasons it was stupid. I would research anything and everything that might help me counter argue against the thought. **I became a lawyer, essentially, locked in battle against the trickiest client: my own illogical, hurt and wounded self.** I kept them in the notes section on my phone so that I could revisit them if I needed to.

Often, though, there wasn't time to do that. The thought would pop into my head immediately and I would have to stop myself from acting on it FIRST. So, for example, I might be walking down the street and the thought might say *hey you've only been walking for half an hour, if you keep going and do another loop, that'll be good for you because you've been lazy recently.* I wouldn't have time to whip out my phone and journal my arguments and my reframes. So, to stop myself in the moment, I developed an immediate strategy. As soon as a thought popped into my head that even HINTED at being disordered, I would say to myself: **DON'T BE TOXIC CARLA.**

Maybe you should buy those smaller leggings and try and fit into them.
DON'T BE TOXIC, CARLA.

Maybe you shouldn't eat breakfast because you're not that *hungry after you ate out last night.*
DON'T BE TOXIC, CARLA.

Choose option A because it's lower in calories than option B.
DON'T BE TOXIC, CARLA.

I want to look like her. I should get a gym membership and start eating more protein.
DON'T BE TOXIC, CARLA.

You're not that hungry this afternoon so just wait until later when you get back from your errands to have your lunch.
DON'T BE TOXIC, CARLA.

So: the strategy was set. An immediate *don't be toxic* **response to the mind goblin, followed, later on, by the rational and logical** *what do you mean* **of it all.**

Thinking. Yeah. I *thought* my way into recovery. **Or rather, I negotiated my way out of the prison my eating disorder had created for me.** I was caged in, surrounded by more bars than I had ever realised. But, day by day, I hacked at one of the bars. It loosened. Weakened. The next day, I hacked at another. And the next, another. And then one day, I returned to the first and hacked at it again. And little by little, the bars weakened and - slowly but surely - I began to *remove* them.

SECTION THREE: THE NEVER-ENDING ERA

Doing It is done. The Mending Era ends there.

You are probably confused. You are probably thinking *Carla, you aren't sounding very mended.* You are probably thinking, yeah, *sure you're eating three meals and three snacks, you're not compensating and you're eating in a balanced and non-restrictive manner, and you're reframing your thoughts* BUT *you are CLEARLY still struggling immensely to do those things. That's not mended. You need to stay in the MENDING ERA for longer until you are FULLY MENDED. Having thoughts and fighting them all day every day is not recovered.*

Correct. It's not recovered. But it *is* recovering. It is *doing*. But now here's the thing. It's not the bending part that's the hardest. It's not the mending part that's the hardest. Those things are really hard, and reaching the point where you UNDERSTAND your disorder and are DOING what you need to do to recover is A PHENOMENAL ACHIEVEMENT. But it's Everest, yeah? Your journey so far has taken you to base camp. Now it's time to climb.

It's the next bit. The never-ending era.

When you've got the understanding and you've got the knowledge and actions in place, you're ready. For the rest of your life. **And you are going to have to commit, fully, to the possibility that your battle will be never-ending.** It may not. You may, one day, be fully and entirely free from all thoughts and feelings and behaviours in any way, shape or form connected to your eating disorder. But if you, like me, have been unwell for a long time and as you will, unfortunately, be walking forth into a disordered world, **you may also find that some of the thoughts and feelings linger with you for a long time.** Not in the same aggressive, controlling way they do now: not like an open, pulsing wound, maybe, but like the softening of the scar, the cut sealing over and turning purple and then, with the years, fading to a gentle white.

I have tried to be complacent before. I have tried to *just let it go and be free and live.* And it didn't work. So as I go forth onto the next leg of my journey *this time* I am going to do so with vigilance. I am watching myself. **Every move I make, every breath I take. I am watching.** Why? So that I can catch all the thoughts. So that I can stop them and reframe them and challenge them and unlearn them and rewrite them and undo them and continue creating myself as someone *I* want to be rather than the shell of a person I was for ten years.

People may say this is a bleak outlook to take: the idea that I may never be "recovered" and may always be in a "never ending era" of my disorder. But I don't see it like that. What I see as *bleak* is the fact that I wasted 10 years of my life to eating disorders. What I see as *bleak* is any possibility of a future where there is room for the goblin to get back in. I don't see myself being aware and focussed and determined to catch any signs of faltering as *bleak*. In fact, I see it as quite the opposite: I see HOPE. And I see it as something I will get better at, and stronger at, as the time goes by. Practice makes perfect. Repetition builds muscle.

In the first months and years, I expect that this process will be very deliberate. As time passes, and I grow stronger - both mentally and physically - it will become more automatic. I will learn to guard myself in a way that becomes second nature, and slowly, slowly, slowly, the never-ending era may just blend into an *ended* one. But it may not.

And if it doesn't, if I never get to close the book fully and place a final full stop at the end of '*I recovered',* the sentence '*I am in remission'* will do just fine. Because the other alternative, of course, is: *I have an eating disorder.* And I know which of those options is the bleakest. There can be a lot of pressure to say *I fought this and I won*. It sounds more impressive to have *won* and for the battle to be over. But in a world that is constantly at war, if you don't keep your eyes open, you could be back on the battlefield without realising it. I think it's just as impressive to say *I am fighting, I am winning and I will not lose this battle.*

Laid out in the next pages, you will find:

- Examples of common reframes that I use that you may also be able to use. If you cannot use them because they are not relevant to you and your own thoughts, that's fine: it's the thinking process behind them that is the important part. If you can take what I do for my thoughts, and try the same process with yours, it may help. This will never be a complete list as there may always be new situations and contexts that throw thoughts up. You may think you've dealt with a particular thought and it may pop back up. But that's okay. You just keep going. Eating and reframing. Keeping on keeping on.

- Tips and advice for how I navigate the difficult parts of ongoing recovery

Again: I will reiterate that I am not a professional. I am not saying that any of this will apply to, or indeed help, anyone other than me. I am simply sharing them on the off-chance that anything at all that I learnt from my horrible experience may be able to help another person to suffer a tiny bit less than I did.

15. REFRAMING: CALORIES

ED thought: Choose the lowest calorie option. I should eat X instead of Y because it has fewer calories. I can't eat THAT because it's SO HIGH IN CALORIES.

Reframe:
- Calories are energy. **High calorie foods are high energy foods.** Low calories foods are low energy foods.

- <u>**I am going to choose high energy foods because I want to be a high energy person.**</u> Having enough energy throughout the day means that I can be energetic, happy, bubbly and involved in life.

- Low energy foods make me tired, lethargic and weak. I don't want to be a low energy person.

- I want my BODY to MOVE in a high energy way: I want to be able to walk and run and climb and play sports. I want to be able to paddleboard and do yoga and ride a bike and hike. I want to be able to climb up the stairs and carry my own shopping and hold my friend's baby. I want to be able to do *all of those things* without feeling like I might faint or like my body might crumble at any minute. **To MOVE in a HIGH ENERGY way, I need to FUEL in a high energy way.**

- I want my BRAIN to THINK in a high energy way: I want to be able to remember things from the previous day. I want to be able to do crosswords and read and write and create and work. I want to be able to laugh at jokes and join in with conversations and watch Quiz Shows. **To THINK in a HIGH ENERGY way, I need to FUEL in a high energy way.**

- You KNOW that choosing low energy options when you WANT the higher energy option is restriction. Restriction opens the door. Keep. The. Door. Shut.

- How do you want people to describe you?
    - "Oh yes I know her. She's lovely but always tired, you know? Doesn't really seem present, or involved in life? Distant. Reserved. Oh yes, I know her! She knows all the calories in every food!" OR
    - "Oh yes I know HER. She's so full of life, isn't she? Always on the go! I don't know how she has the energy to fit everything in!"

ED thought: I am hungry but I can't eat anymore today because I have eaten my calories for the day.

Reframe:
- If your body didn't need food for something, why on *earth* would it be telling you it's hungry? **Your body wouldn't be wasting precious energy sending hunger cues to you for a joke.**

- You *know* that the online calorie calculators are utter trash. You *know* this. <u>How could a random number, that millions of other people would also have been given, be the EXACT SPECIFIC NUMBER of calories that your UNIQUE and INDIVIDUAL body needs?</u> The amount of calories you need compared to someone else depends on your age, lifestyle, height, weight, body composition, health, genetics, metabolism, hormones, medication and so on.

- Do you move around the same amount every single day? Do you do the same amount of difficult thinking every day? Do you socialise the same amount every day? Do you sleep the exact same number of seconds every single night? Do you blink and breathe and cough and smile and sneeze the same number of times every day? *GENUINELY do you believe that you would need the SAME amount of energy on a day where you go for a two hour hike as you would need on a day where you read an entire novel without moving all day?*

Your energy expenditure is DIFFERENT every single day. So the energy your body needs on every single day will be DIFFERENT.

But then how do I know the number?

YOU DON'T. YOU DON'T **NEED** TO KNOW THE NUMBER BECAUSE IF YOU NEED TO EAT, YOUR BODY WILL TELL YOU BY BEING HUNGRY OR TIRED OR GRUMPY. **IF YOU TURN INTO A LOW ENERGY PERSON, YOUR BODY IS TELLING YOU THAT IS HASN'T HAD ENOUGH.**

- You KNOW that not eating when you are hungry is restriction. Restriction opens the door. Keep. The. Door. Shut.

ED thought: Okay, but I didn't do ANYTHING today. I have been laying around reading that book all day.

Reframe:
- AGAIN. If your body didn't need food for something, why on *earth* would it be telling you it's hungry? **Your body wouldn't be wasting precious energy sending hunger cues to you for a joke.**

- If you've done a lot in the previous days, you may well feel hungrier in the following days even when you are resting. **This is because your body didn't get enough energy on those previous days and, now that you're slowing down and resting, it can see that.** And it trusts you, because you're resting, that now you're able to give it the energy it needs to recover and repair from doing a lot. This doesn't have to be running marathons, by the way. **Lots of things take more mental and physical energy than you would imagine:** cleaning the house, driving long distances, a day full of meetings at work, a lot more social interaction than you are used to, a day wandering around parks on a Sunday.

- Even if you don't *think* you've done enough physical or mental activity to warrant your levels of hunger, you are wrong. **If you are hungry, your body needs**

energy. It does a lot, inside, that you don't know about. Repairing, healing, fighting illnesses, metabolising, digesting, breathing, *keeping your heart beating*...if you need more energy one day and you decide not to give it to your body, your body is going to be unable to fuel all of those activities properly on top of your life activities. And BOOM. Low energy person again.

My core affirmations:
- Calories are energy. Eat high energy foods to be a high energy person. Eat high energy foods to move and think and live with high energy.

- Your body wouldn't be wasting precious energy sending hunger cues to you for a joke. **If it's asking, it's needing.**

- Not eating when you are hungry is restriction. Restriction opens the door. Keep. The. Door. Shut.

16. REFRAMING: I NEED TO BE SKINNY FOR OTHER PEOPLE TO CARE ABOUT ME

ED Thought: People will only like me if I am skinny. If I am skinny, I will be pretty and popular.

Reframe:

- **Are you friends with anyone because they are skinny?** No, really. Think about all of your friends. <u>Why are they your friends?</u> Are they your friends because they are skinny? I don't bloody think so. That's insane. Why would ANYONE have "be skinny" on their list of what makes a good friend?

- Being skinny doesn't make you popular because, eventually, it makes you try your very best to STAY AWAY FROM PEOPLE. It has the OPPOSITE EFFECT. You isolate yourself and lock yourself away so that people cannot make you eat. You withdraw from the world. Go to a party? Where there might be FOOD? NO. Go out to a restaurant? Where there will be FOOD? No. Go to a bar and drink ALCOHOL and EAT FOOD? No. **WHAT IS THE POINT, THEN, IN BEING SKINNY IF YOU WILL JUST BE SKINNY AND SAT ALONE IN YOUR BEDROOM**, SHIVERING UNDER A DUVET COVER WHILST THE PEOPLE YOU WANTED TO LOVE YOU ARE OUT IN THEIR HEALTHY BODIES EATING CHIPS?

- ***When you are "skinny", you are not a good person to be around. You are not a person that will be popular.*** You go to social events and you drain the life out of them by wandering around being morose and irritable. You snap at people. You think all of your friends and family are annoying and you start to hate them for existing. Your fuse is as short as a fuse can get. Nobody understands why you keep rolling your eyes at them. You don't find anything funny. You are so focussed on the hunger and the weakness in your body that you cannot focus on anyone else. You don't notice things: your best friend looking sad; your friend who has a new necklace on that they keep fiddling with like they want you to comment; smart quips that you once would have loved. You are too tired to join in properly. You go home early.

- You are not pretty because you are pale and haggard, with balding hair and dry skin and acne. You are not popular because you have shut yourself away.

ED Thought: I need to lose weight for someone to love me

Reframe:

- **I do not want to be in a relationship with someone who loves me for the size of my body or my physical appearance.** This is not a stable relationship. This is not a safe relationship. I would always be worried that they would leave me if my appearance changes, which it will: as I get older, my body and my face and skin and wrinkles will CHANGE. **I want to be in a relationship where I KNOW that the other person values and loves me for things that aren't superficial and won't change with time.** Can you imagine waking up every morning and looking in the mirror, paranoid that if you see a change, the person you love might pack their suitcases and leave?

    Besides which…<u>why would *I* want to be with someone superficial enough to love someone based solely on their appearance? That's not my kind of person.</u>

- **I want to be loved for HOW and WHO I am.** I want to be loved for how kind I am. How caring I am. How much I give to other people, and how much I will always give. I want to be loved for how much of a family person I am, for how I will drop everything in the middle of the night to go to a friend in need. For my empathy. For my depth. I want to be loved for how funny I am (modest, I know). I want to be loved for my heart. I want to be loved for my mind.

- I'm NOT A LOVEABLE person when I am malnourished and underfuelled. I am grumpy, unreasonable, tired, lacking passion and interest in life, and sad. I am not a person who anyone would WANT to be in a relationship with anyway. I would not be able to sustain a positive relationship whilst in a relationship with my eating disorder.

- I have never once loved any of the people that I have loved BECAUSE they are thin. I have found them attractive, but *only* because they were beautiful people. Personally, I look at traditionally "gorgeous" people who act like they are God's gift to the world and they make me a little sick in my mouth. That's not attractive to me. What is attractive to me? Kindness, humour, softness, gentleness, ambition, drive, curiosity, the ability and desire to question and learn and grow. **If I have never loved someone because they are thin, why do I think I need to be thin to be loved?**

- **In relationships, I want my partner to be the happiest, healthiest version of themselves. I want to be in a relationship where my partner feels the same about me.** If my partner came to me and told me that they had been undereating for a while to get a body that I would love them for, I would tell them that I love them and then we would *sure as hell be on our way to get some pancakes.* **I want to be with someone who wants me to be fed and nourished and healthy, rather than weak and hungry.** I want to be with someone who wants the best for me, always.

- You stopped looking for love anyway. You stopped going on dates because there would be food and alcohol involved. So now, what? ***You wanted to be skinny so that someone would love you, but now you won't go out to try and find that love because you want to stay skinny?*** HOW DOES THAT MAKE ANY SENSE BABE? And what? Do you want a relationship where you both go out and you don't eat? They do, but you don't. Or do you want to be able to go out, eat, FILL YOURSELF WITH ENERGY to be able to go and do fun stuff like mini golf or bowling or exploring new cities or driving a boat down a river or pottery painting?

ED Thought: people only care about me when I am skinny because they know I am sick.

Reframe:

- **Do you only care about your friends and family when they are sick?** When they get better, do you stop caring about them? No. When they are sick, you don't love them *more* than before: you just *worry* more. Do I *want* to make my friends and family *worry more? Do I want my friends and family to be stressed and unhappy?* **That wouldn't be very caring of ME to want that for THEM.**

- It's not *me* that wants people to care because I'm skinny and sick. My *eating disorder* wants that because then it's winning. Then people can *see it*. But **I want people to care about me because I bring something meaningful to their lives: because I make them happy, and I am kind, caring and gentle.** I want people to CARE about me because losing me would be LOSING SOMETHING GOOD in their lives, not because I am sick and dying.

- <u>If people ONLY care about me when I'm sick, they are not people who I want in my life long term.</u> That's not real love. That's not real care. I care about my friends at every minute of every second of every day. I would do anything for them, at the drop of a hat. If you have people in your life that *wouldn't* do that and would just come for the obligatory hospital visits when you are sick (and, let's face it, probably splash it all over social media to show the world how good a person they are) THEY ARE NOT REAL ONES. You don't *need* those people in your life. If these people ONLY care and ONLY show you they care when you're desperately unwell…they don't CARE ENOUGH. You deserve better people than that in your life.

- My real friends and family cared about me before I was sick. They cared about me when I was sick, too, and they will care about me after. **But when I *was* sick**…my best friend sat in her car for an hour after seeing me and cried. Another friend had to STOP seeing me altogether because she found me too triggering. My mum came into the hospital and flinched. My ex boyfriend would hug me goodbye everytime he came to visit and I would feel his hands anxiously checking my bones as he touched my spine. My sister didn't come to see me at all: I imagine because it hurt too much. How do you force yourself to go into a hospital and see your sister shrunken and grey, dying in a hospital bed? That's not the image you want with you forever. ***When I was really sick, people cared about me just the same, but they HURT more.***

- It felt, for a while, like my treatment teams (both inpatient and outpatient) cared about me. It made me feel a little better on the days where I felt like people had let me down and didn't care about me enough. BUT. It's important to not get hooked on this feeling. **Because…whilst they *do* care…it's their job. They're**

paid to care. And they probably DO care about you BUT it's their job. They're not going to be there forever. They'll get another job, move away to a different city, get married, build a life, care deeply about their friends and families and children...it sounds harsh but you are just a part of their 9-5 or their 8-8 maybe. When they go home, they go home. S<u>eeking the care of professionals is a dangerous game to play because you're forming attachments to people who are not yours to be attached to.</u> At first, it feels okay. **But you will soon realise that you cannot spend the *rest of your life* seeking care and validation from people who are paid to be there.**

Because another hard truth is this: the OLDER you get, the less they *do* care. You become "severe and enduring". A revolving door patient. A grown woman is far less endearing than a teenager or a young, fresh-faced girl in her 20s. They don't see you the same. They don't believe you can get better. The care does feel a little bit less caring. It feels sharper. More like an obligation. They feel like you are wasting their time.

- This is the same, unfortunately, with friends and family. **There's only so many times that you can convince them that you are going to really try to get better this time.** There are only so many times that you can relapse before they get tired of it. They don't UNDERSTAND, of course, because it's a mental illness that they do not have so they will never - thank god - be able to put themselves in your shoes. It doesn't make it *right* but it does make it *true:* as time goes on, they still CARE, but you see it and feel it less because **the care becomes overshadowed by the frustration of spending so many years being patient with a disease that will never listen.**

- I want people to care about me because I care about them and because I add positive things to their lives. I want to have the energy and be well enough to ENGAGE in their lives, and JOIN IN with them, and care for them properly and have them care for me too. I want to be able to go out into the world and KEEP meeting people who will care for me, and who I will care for, and building real enduring relationships with them rather than with the superficial, anxious care that comes with an eating disorder. That alway has a tinge of pity to it anyway.

<u>**My core affirmations:**</u>
- If people only love and care about me because I am skinny and/or sick, **they do not care about me in the way I want to be cared about.**

- **_Relationships based on physical appearance are not safe, stable relationships and they are not relationships that I want to be in._**

- I have so much to offer friends, family and lovers beyond a weak, skinny body.

- I am NOT a good friend, sister, daughter, lover when I am engaging in my eating disorder. Nobody likes me very much. I am moody, irritable, snappy, unkind, rude and selfish.

- Your friends and family do not *care more* because you are sick. They just *worry more*.

- People *will not humour your eating disorder forever.* Sooner or later, they will start to get tired of it. Their *care* will become sharper. Less forgiving. Don't waste time chasing this: instead, spend time chasing your real connections and building new ones with new people who you can care for and who can care for you.

17. REFRAMING: FOOD

ED Thought: This food is a Fear Food. I don't eat that food. It is scary. If I do eat it, I need to plan it into my day and compensate for it.

Reframe:
- If you ask another person with an eating disorder what their fear foods are, they are likely to list something that ISN'T a fear food for them. If you tell them YOUR fear foods, you are likely to list something that they label a SAFE food for them. Different people have different fear foods. **_Surely if the food you fear is ACTUALLY SCARY, everyone would be afraid of it too?_** See: FEAR FOODS ARE ILLOGICAL. Your brain has chosen something to fixate on and is now convincing you that the food is bad. It makes NO SENSE to be afraid of specific foods. **All foods are safe unless they are laced with arsenic, they have been touched by a young child or you have an allergy.**

- Further evidence: years ago, you used to be afraid to eat oats. Now you want to eat them every day because they are a safe food. Years ago, you wouldn't eat apples but you would eat grapes; now you can eat apples but grapes are Not Okay. Rice cakes used to be a safe food, but now you have an aversion to them and instead choose bread which, before, you would rather have died than eat. **HOW CAN YOUR FEAR FOODS BE *GENUINELY* SCARY if they have**

CHANGED over the years? If something were actually scary, it would stay scary. Like spiders. They've *always* been scary.

- It is not the food that is the problem. It is the way that you THINK about the food. It is the beliefs you hold about the food. It is the fears you have about *how the food will impact* your body or your health. We cannot change the food. The food will stay the same. We cannot blame the food either: it is innocent. But we CAN blame the thoughts. They are NOT innocent. The thoughts are trying to KEEP US STUCK IN OUR EATING DISORDER. We can, and should, change those. How?

- Well, think about the food that you fear. Specifically. What IS the food? And why do you fear it? We fear most foods because they are HIGHER ENERGY foods, right? So anything that has lots of THE C WORD: typically things that are higher in sugar and fat and carbohydrates.

  Why do we fear these things? Because we fear we will lose control over our bodies. We fear we will lose control over our lives. We fear being larger. We fear people's opinions of us. We fear our opinions of ourselves. We fear letting go. But listen. If you don't start to eat those foods you are afraid of, you HAVE lost control over your body. You are NOT in control if there are foods you CANNOT eat. **You are NOT in control of your body if your disorder is driving you to CONSTANTLY underfuel yourself and make yourself malnourished.** You HAVE lost control of your life. You cannot do the things you want to do anymore: you cannot focus on work, you cannot focus on a social life, you cannot focus on love or hobbies or passion or the future. <u>Sure, you may not have become LARGER. You may have become smaller. But your LIFE has become smaller.</u>

- **All food is energy for your body, no matter what it is.** If it has calories in it, it has energy in it that your body can use to FUEL you and be a HIGH ENERGY PERSON. There is nothing to FEAR about ENERGY.

But there is something to fear about NOT GETTING ENOUGH ENERGY. Do you know why? Because you won't just lose weight. You'll drain your life away. Slowly but surely. The days turn into months which turn into years and you don't notice until it is too late. You don't notice because you don't have the ENERGY to notice. Your health goes slowly too, or quickly sometimes. Your bones weaken. Your skin sags. Your teeth start to rot. Your heart starts to waste. Your digestive system starts to atrophy.

Do you know what IS scary? Do you know what you SHOULD fear? Waking up in ten years time and still having an eating disorder. **Waking up and realising that because you spent all that time being SCARED of peanut butter or eggs or apples or blueberries or yoghurt or whatever loony thing your brain chose, you also spent all that time LOSING time.** You didn't eat your best friend's wedding cake. You lost friends steadily over the years because you cancelled every meal out. You never found a partner because you never went on dates because you were scared of restaurant food and alcohol. You haven't eaten an Easter egg in years. You've ruined every Christmas.

To be honest, losing a whole LIFE to a sad existence of fear is MUCH MORE SCARY than putting the goddamn almond butter on my goddamn porridge.

Being **prematurely young in my 40s**, with **crumbling bones** and grey, wrinkled skin, **unable to walk without hurting**, unable to sit down comfortably, unable to even make it around the supermarket without my heart *hurting* is MUCH MORE SCARY than bread. The idea of being **alone**, most of my friends and family having given up on me long ago, along with all of the eating disorder services and medical professionals who labelled me a revolving door...*THAT'S* FEAR. My friends, tucked up nice and cosy in their homes with their successful jobs and their families and their pets and their social lives...and me at home, alone, with my inspirational placemat that I ignore and my rice cakes and my miracle noodles. That's the stuff of nightmares. And whilst it seems like that's so far away from you now that it will never happen...I never expected to be 28 and still here.

You'll notice that, in the above, I never mentioned being underweight. That's because it doesn't matter. If you are underweight or not, the longer you are under-fuelling your body, the more malnourished you become. **People die from malnourishment at all weights. Organs give up at all weights. Bones crumble at all weights. Suicide happens at all weights.**

When I was 18 and they asked us *where do you see yourself in ten years time* **I wouldn't have liked to say** *sat in my mum's box room feeling anxious because I'm going to eat fish and chips.* You think you have all the time in the world but if you don't get out now, when will you?

Look. This was meant to be about FEAR FOODS. But it's turned into a rant about EATING and LIFE. Because...the foods aren't the problem. The foods are never the problem. The problem is the way you think about the food and what will happen if you eat it. **So instead, start thinking about what will happen if you don't. And then every Fear Food becomes less scary.**

- Sandwiches? Energy to stop you ending up prematurely old, alone, weak and sad. Pizza? Energy to stop you ending up prematurely old, alone, weak and sad. Chocolate? Energy to stop you ending up prematurely old, alone, weak and sad. Processed food? Energy to stop you ending up prematurely old, alone, weak and sad. Processed foods? Energy to stop you ending up prematurely old, alone, weak and sad.

We can also reframe each food specifically, through the lens of: as well as stopping me from ending up in the above hellscape, what can this food GIVE me now?

- **ED Thought:** I can't eat sandwiches.

Reframe:

My eating disorder informed me for many years that sandwiches weren't healthy. Instead, for lunch I needed to have meal prepped containers of SALAD or QUINOA that took AGES to make and AGES TO EAT and made me look like a REAL HEALTHY GAL. But. I wasn't a healthy gal. I was a hungry gal. I was a hungry malnourished gal that wasted hours preparing food. All because I couldn't eat a sandwich. To me, sandwiches were bad because they were BREAD. And bread was bad. No but listen. It's not the sandwich that is the problem. The sandwich is innocent. It's the way we think about the sandwich. **This is how we SHOULD think about the sandwich: a sandwich is a cheap, quick and easy way to provide your body with energy and nourishment. Bread** is a source of **carbohydrates**. Carbohydrates are our bodies' **number one source of energy**. Your body needs carbs if you're gonna be a high energy person! Carbs also give us **fibre** to help us do what we gotta do, and keep our **blood sugars more stable** through the day. You whack some eggs or meat in your sandwich, you've got some protein for healing and repair and muscle maintenance. Chuck some cheese on there too or avocado or mayo and you've got some fat for healthy hormones and to help vitamin absorption and for vital fatty acids as well as for pure yum. **All a sandwich is is another opportunity for energy. Another opportunity to give your body those things it needs to thrive.** And let me tell you, now that I've tasted a footlong melted toastie, there is no way I am going back to eating the exact same incredibly disordered and wildly sad six inch sub that I ate for years.

Sandwiches also give you time. Time in the evening to spend on your hobbies. Time on your lunch break to destress and take a few moments of relaxation in the middle of a busy day. Time to think about things other than meal prepping the lowest calorie portable option you can think of. Time when you're out and about with family and friends because you *can* just grab a quick bite to eat and then get back to what you were doing.

Also…they're bloody yummy. Have you TRIED a hoisin tofu sandwich, with plum sauce, coriander, cucumber and lettuce? A cheese and tomato baguette? A FISH FINGER sandwich with pickles, ketchup and tartar sauce?

- ED Thought: I can't eat pizza.

Reframe:

Pizza. What is pizza? Well, when I was DEEP in my eating disorder, pizza looked like: sweet potato or cauliflower crust that took at least an hour to make, bitter tomato passata, vegetables, and either nutritional yeast or some kind of nut creation "cashew cheese". Or it looked like a wrap with the above on top of it. It looked like me ordering the gluten free option when my friends and I got takeaway and getting it with no cheese because "I don't like cheese". It looked like me sitting there, pretending it was JUST SO YUMMY and TASTED JUST LIKE PIZZA when, in fact, it did not. It looked like me still being hungry afterwards. Or mentally hungry, if not physically hungry as my brain and body did not WANT a bunch of vegetables piled on top of MORE VEGETABLES or a CARDBOARD LIKE BASE. It meant me spending evenings with my friends stressed about the energy I had consumed, feeling like it was a waste of calories anyway because *it hadn't even tasted any good.*

But listen, again. The pizza is not bad. It's the way you *think* about the pizza. Let's break it down.

- **Pizza base.** Made from dough. What's that? Carbohydrate. Body's main source of energy. High energy food for a high energy person. Also, fibre. Helps your digestion. Carbohydrates help keep blood sugars stable.
- **Cheese.** Protein AND fat. And calcium! Protein for healing and repair and muscle maintenance. Fat for hormone health and absorption of key vitamins and for fatty acids. And for flavour and happiness, obviously. Calcium for bone health. Very relevant.
- **Meat or prawns or extra cheese or veggie protein:** again, protein. Healing and repair and muscle maintenance.
- **Sauce and veggie toppings:** if the sauce is made from tomatoes, extra micronutrients. If it's not, extra flavour and extra energy. Veggies on top - or fruit, I'm a pineapple gal - for those micronutrients and vitamins.

- **Yummy**

When you think about it, pizza is basically just a whole meal with all of your required nutrients just...already in a circle. All ready for you to eat.

It also gives you TIME. When you get in from a long day and you're tired and hungry and just need to recharge and have some down time...the last thing you want to be doing is smashing some cauliflower into a circle shape and baking it in the oven for 30 minutes just for a big mouthful of soggy disappointment. Chucking a pizza in the oven from the freezer, or ordering a takeaway, takes SECONDS and then you can give yourself that SELF-CARE time of lying on the sofa in a dark room. Or scrolling on your phone...watching my silly little videos...

I saw a man walking down the street with a pizza box the other day. It was a simple image. But it was profound. Because my heart said: *that* is the future I want. I want to be someone who is hungry, and goes to get a pizza, takes it home, eats it and moves on with life. That's my goal.

But it also gives you MEMORIES. **And FUN. I have too many memories of nights with friends that I didn't enjoy because I was stressed about pizza.** I have too many memories of eating something else, concocting some lie about why I couldn't have the pizza, SMELLING the pizza and wanting it desperately...or wolfing the pizza down so fast I didn't enjoy it so that I could go and compensate for it...**I have so many ill-formed memories of nights with friends because the anxiety around food had taken up too much space in my brain for me to focus on what was actually happening.** And because I was too tired and lacking energy to join in properly.

- ED Thought: I can't eat chocolate.

Reframe:

Chocolate gets a very bad rap. It's bad for us and it causes weight gain. It's not got protein: chocolate is basically a delectable mix of fat, carbohydrates and sugar. But then so are lots of things. And, may I remind you, we *do need all of those things* for our body. In fact, **the sugar content in chocolate makes it PERFECT for those moments where you are lower in energy and needing a sudden BOOST** (no, not the bar...well...that's probably where the name comes from, right?). HIGHER ENERGY food for a HIGHER ENERGY PERSON and a HIGHER ENERGY LIFE. And people say things like "chocolate doesn't fill you up". No, cool. But it DOES give me a boost of energy for an hour or so and then, guess what I'm allowed to do? When I get hungry again, I'm allowed to eat. And if I want to have some protein and slower releasing carbs then, because that's what my body is asking me for, then that's what I'll have.

Don't forget all of the benefits of fat, of course, and why we need some fat in our diet.

Now, let's go back to the "chocolate causes weight gain" bit. It doesn't. Weight gain happens when you eat MORE ENERGY than your body needs. In that line of thinking, I could say: broccoli causes weight gain. Cucumber causes weight gain. Quinoa causes weight gain. The reason *why* people blame chocolate is because they often end up eating RATHER A LOT OF IT. In fact, the number of people I know who say: "I don't want this anymore but I can't stop eating it", or "I feel sick but I can't stop". They aren't listening to their bodies in the moment. But why? Not because, as some dodgy research on rats might imply, that sugar is addictive. **But because they are going to go back to RESTRICTING chocolate aren't they? Most people have decided that they cannot have chocolate whenever they want it.** They will have set limits. Once a week, maybe. Once a day, for slightly less diet-cultured people. Only at lunchtime. Only on special occasions. You would struggle to find someone who will *genuinely* eat chocolate whenever the craving strikes. And that's why, when they *do* start eating it, the brain urges them to carry on. Because of the boost of sugar, the flavour the brain enjoys…it knows it might not get that again for a while, so it's capitalising on it whilst it can. When I made the shift and decided I would eat whatever I wanted whenever I wanted it…some days I ate three chocolate bars. And then I wouldn't eat another one for days. Because my body had got its fill of short, sharp sugary energy and wasn't currently interested in it anymore.

Chocolate does not make people gain weight. Eating too much of *any* food makes people gain weight. **I would rather live a life where I eat chocolate and potentially gain weight than a life that sets me on a trajectory that is always going to end with me being small, miserable, alone and unwell.**

And let's not forget: chocolate also gives us love. People LOVE to buy each other chocolate. As presents. On bad days. As quick ways to show they care. Too many times, people have done *the kindest thing of thinking of me and bringing me chocolate they know I loved* and INSTEAD OF ME FEELING LOVED, and INSTEAD OF ME FEELING HAPPY, I felt panic. And stressed. And, more often than not, threw someone else's love in the bin. The eating disorder takes away the chance to FEEL the way people want you to feel: like they love and appreciate you. You deserve to feel those things. You may not think you do, but other people do or they wouldn't have bothered!

- ED Thought: I can't eat processed foods.

Reframe:

Processed foods: anything other than whole foods. Anything other than lean meat, vegetables, whole grains and fruit. So that's like…pizza and chocolate and sandwiches and crisps and sausages and cereals and biscuits and ready meals. But also…milk and yoghurt and canned beans. Anything that has been frozen, canned, cooked or dried has been *processed*. Many people with eating disorders fear processed foods because the WORLD fears them. Diet culture hates them: *processed foods are high in sugar and salt and fat and chemicals. Processed foods are addictive. Processed foods cause weight gain. Processed foods are unhealthy.*

A big part of my recovery has been reframing what we see about processed foods in the media. Sure, they probably aren't the BEST, MOST HEALTHY thing for you. But when you have an eating disorder, there is something FAR WORSE for your health than a piece of bacon or a chocolate bar. Do you know what that is? **Malnutrition. Behaviours. Restriction**. Having rules like "no processed foods" and labelling foods "good and bad" opens the door to the eating disorder. It loves to slither in through the cracks, the goblin. Processed foods PROVIDE me with energy and nutrients and allowing myself to eat them REMOVES restriction. Therefore, for me, eating processed foods is far healthier than my alternative would be.

But…processed foods ALSO CONTAIN the things that we need. They still contain fats, proteins, and carbohydrates. Your body can still use them for energy and nourishment. We DO need some salt and sugar in our diets. **Processed foods give us a CONVENIENT way to get those nutrients in without us having to spend hours in the kitchen or transport a small larder around with us every time we leave the house.** On those nights where we are too tired, mentally or physically, to cook from scratch…jarred pasta sauce and meatballs from the freezer are a lifesaver. Quite literally, if they stop you going back down your path of restriction. Or, if we are out and about, we can grab something to eat rather than going hungry because there's nothing "whole" in that motorway service station.

ED Thought: I want a sandwich right now but I can't have a sandwich because that's not breakfast food. I want pancakes right now but I can't have pancakes because those aren't dinner food.

Reframe:

- You are going to put the food in your mouth and chew it up. By the time you've chewed it up and swallowed it, your stomach is not going to know what it was you were eating. **Your stomach does not know the difference between breakfast, lunch and dinner food.** It just sees it for what it is: food coming in that needs to be digested. Energy and nutrients! Your stomach isn't going to go: oh no thank you, you've put a pancake in me and it's not the right time of day for pancakes so now I REFUSE TO DIGEST THIS UNTIL THE NEXT MORNING.

- **Around the world, breakfast foods are all different.** Same for snacks, lunch and dinner too! In England, we might eat cereal and toast, or porridge. In Turkey, common breakfasts might look like bread, cured meats, cheese, olives and pickles and lots of oil. In France, it might look like pastries. In China, breakfast might include soybean milk and deep-fried dough sticks, steamed buns, tofu pudding, noodles or rice dishes. In America, you might see chicken and waffles or pancakes and bacon. In all of those places, you will also see people eating TOTALLY DIFFERENT THINGS. But look: if someone can eat cereal in one country, and someone else can eat a steamed bun in another, and someone else can eat salami and olives in another, and someone else can eat chicken in another...I think it's safe to say that the body does not care what food you put in it at certain times. *In fact, the only time it's going to care about what's for breakfast is when you HAVEN'T had breakfast and it's trying to tell you that it's HUNGRY PLEASE.*

- **If you are craving a particular food at a particular time, it is probably for a reason.** If your body wants a nice egg mayonnaise sandwich for breakfast, you may be missing some carbohydrates or some of the vitamins in eggs. If your body wants pancakes for dinner, you may not have had enough fat throughout the day to meet your body's needs. If you really, really want to eat something, also consider that **you may not have been allowing yourself to eat that thing often enough** to remove the mental hunger associated with it. **You may be craving a food because you need the nutrients it contains**, or **you may be craving a food because you enjoy it** and you want to eat it. Either way, the food will give you energy and freedom.

- If you want a sandwich for breakfast, and you don't have a sandwich, what will you do instead? Eat nothing? That's not good: you will have no energy and nourishment for the morning, your body will stop trusting you to feed it regularly again, and all those age old issues with digestion and hunger cues and low blood sugar will rear up. Force yourself to eat something you don't want? And then spend the rest of the morning wishing you had eaten a sandwich. Waiting for lunch so you can have a sandwich. Feeling like you wasted the meal because you ate something you didn't want. Unable to enjoy the morning because now you are thinking about food AGAIN.

    But if you do eat the sandwich for breakfast? Your stomach digests the sandwich, just as it would digest any other food. Your hunger goes away: mentally and physically. You have the energy and nourishment to go about your morning and you aren't thinking non-stop about food because you have eaten what your mental hunger asked you for. Instead, you have a good morning and in a couple of hours, once your body has successfully digested the sandwich, you will feel hungry again and go for a snack.

ED Thought: I can't try new foods because if I don't love them, it's a waste of calories

Reframe:

A big thing for me when I was deep in the disorder was the idea that food had to be perfect. I had to LOVE every meal or it wasn't worth it. If I didn't LOVE it, it was a waste of calories. This idea is also another diet culture idea, right? I'm sure at some point you have heard some sadly misguided human say, "oh it wasn't worth the calories" when they didn't enjoy something as much as they wanted to.

But listen. Listen. Listen.

It IS worth the calories. Because, as we know, my high energy pals: calories are energy. So HOW could consuming some energy when you needed some energy NOT BE WORTH IT? **What's it worth, to you?** To me, the energy is worth: me joining in with my friends. Me being able to do my hobbies and see my family and my friends, and do my work, and build my passions. Me being able to be out in the world, rather than at home, locked away, starving. Me having the mental focus to read and learn and grow. Me not returning to my eating disorder. Me not being a low energy person who is cold, grumpy, and focussed on nothing other than food. **So actually…ALL FOOD is WORTH the calories.**

Even if you eat a meal and you don't love it, it has given you nutrients, it has given you energy and it is, therefore, not a waste.

Do you know what *is* a waste? All of the time you spent thinking about how little food you can eat. All of the time you spent looking at yourself in mirrors and hating what you saw. A LIFE that goes down the drain because of an eating disorder. The nights you didn't have fun with friends. The birthday parties you hated because there was cake nearby. The events you never went to because there would have been food. **Instead, you sat at home and you ate a perfectly weighed and measured portion of voluminous food…now** *that* **is a waste of calories. Because** *those* **calories really won't have been giving you very much. Little energy, little nourishment, little enjoyment, little life.**

So…trying new foods is actually a win-win situation. I *could* find a new food that I love, right? So I win. Alternatively I *could* eat something that I don't *love* but that is still providing my body with energy and nourishment. So that's a win too, right? It's a continual reminder to myself that food is energy and nourishment for my body and therefore that it IS perfect even if it's not the best thing i've ever eaten. It's also given me new information: I am learning what I do and don't like OUTSIDE of the rules set by my eating disorder. I am free to *like* what I want to like and *not like* what I don't like! No more forcing myself to enjoy the flavour of egg whites and insisting that protein bars taste *just like chocolate if not better.*

And to be honest, the more you are allowing yourself to eat, the less important those perfect meals become because they're not the focal point of your day anymore. If you know that you are going to eat again in a couple of hours rather than in a couple of days, the PERFECT FOOD doesn't matter. Because: there's always going to be another chance to eat something you do love. **You aren't on death row anymore.**

My Core Affirmations:
1. No foods are fear foods. The problem is not the food. The problem is the way we think about the food. There is nothing to fear about food.

2. There is no such thing as wasted food because any food has GIVEN us things that we need, and PREVENTED US from losing things to restriction. There is always going to be another chance to eat.

3. All foods GIVE us things: proteins, carbohydrates, fats, nutrients and energy. Key things that our bodies NEED to survive and thrive. Food also GIVES us time and

memories and love and enjoyment. Key things that our minds NEED to survive and thrive.

4. Fearing food only TAKES things from us: energy, health, friends, family, time, opportunities, focus, happiness. Years. Life.
5. The only thing to fear about food is not getting enough energy and becoming a low energy person with a low energy life.

18. REFRAMING: SOCIAL EVENTS

ED Thought: My friend has invited me to meet them for coffee and cake at this coffee shop. I don't want to go because there won't be anything I can eat. You can't even get a single thing with your five a day at a coffee shop. And liquid calories in the drinks are such a waste!

Reframe:
- **The food you can get at coffee shops provides you with vital macronutrients even if it doesn't have any of those micronutrients typically found in fruits and vegetables.** If you get a toastie, you will probably be getting carbs, proteins and fats in one! If you get a cake, you will be getting carbs and fats (and maybe some protein too if it's cheesecake!). The food will provide you with the most important thing that your body needs: ENERGY.

- Not every meal needs to contain fruits and vegetables. **You have several other opportunities to eat throughout the day.** If you are craving your five a day, you can incorporate those things into your other snacks and meals.

- **Liquid calories are not a waste.** If you have a hot chocolate, or a coffee that isn't black, or a milkshake, or a frappe…*that's* going to be made with milk. Milk is a good balance of proteins, carbs and fats and also contains a whole bundle of important nutrients like calcium, phosphorus, vitamin D and potassium. Even if you don't have any milk in your drink, and you have one of those fabulous iced cooler drinks or whatever - they will contain sugar (carbohydrates) for a quick energy hit to keep you going for an hour or too before you eat again. Or, you know…you could pair it with a toastie or a cake to give your body more to digest!

- Soup is a liquid. Smoothies are liquids. Protein shakes are liquid. If you put a roast dinner in a blender and pulverise it, it's a liquid. Okay maybe don't do that. **But if soup, smoothies and protein shakes are liquid - which they are - and you see all of these *health nut gym types* yeeting these back like nobody's business: it's probably safe to assume that it's not the *liquid* that's problematic.** Once again, it comes down to the same old story: liquid calories do not make you gain weight. People gain weight when they have more energy than their body needs. *Often, they over consume liquid calories because they are in a cycle of restriction followed by bingeing: they don't allow themselves the drinks when they want them, leading to them craving them more than they would if they just incorporated them into their lives.*

- Being able to go to a coffee shop and sit down and have a drink and a snack with a friend is going to bring so much more to your life than staying at home so you don't gain weight. **How much weight could one coffee shop trip make you gain, anyway? But what if *not* going makes you lose a friend? That's the weight of a whole person. A whole friendship.** Gone. Sure, it won't happen *immediately* if they are a good friend. But if you keep letting them down…if you keep making them feel that seeing them is not a priority for you…if time after time they reach out and you refuse…**one day you will wake up to find that your ED won: no more coffee shop invitations for you.**

Is that a life you want to live? Where your friends eventually stop inviting you to places because they know you won't come?

- And what if you are in town running errands and you suddenly get hungry? There's a coffee shop right next to you. I mean, most towns have a coffee shop in every other space on the high street, right? Look around you. You can smell the toasties. You can smell the coffee. Your stomach is rumbling. What are you going to do? Wait? Get in the car and drive home HUNGRY? That's dangerous: not just for you, but for other people. **If you make a judgement error because of your low blood sugar, you endanger not only your life but the lives of those on the road too.** You wouldn't drive drunk (I hope) so you shouldn't

drive hungry either. You and I both know that's not a dramatic statement: when you have an eating disorder and your blood sugar crashes, your body and mind become undeniably erratic. Go into a coffee shop and eat a toastie: protein, carbs, fats. Sit in a big cosy armchair for a few minutes and sip a steaming cup of hot chocolate: sugar and tastiness and relaxation. Then you can get back on with your day in a much calmer way, drive safely and go about the rest of the afternoon without obsessing over food and *how you wished you had eaten a toastie because they smelled phenomenal.*

ED Thought: I'm going out for lunch so I won't need to eat snacks and dinner after that.

REFRAME:

- What are you going to have for lunch? Food. What does your stomach do with food? Digests it. If you were at home, and you made yourself a cheese salad baguette and crisps, or prawn stir fry, or pancakes, you would still eat your snacks and dinner. Because you would get hungry. Because that's what human bodies do. They digest food, they use up energy, they ask for more energy a couple of hours later. Food eaten at home is digested and used for energy. Food eaten in restaurants is digested and used for energy. The energy is not infinite. Your body will need more.

   Here's a secret: there is nothing wonderfully special and different about restaurant food that will mean you do not get hungry a few hours after eating it. ***It doesn't contain some special appetite suppressant that switches your body off for the rest of the day***. You *are* going to get hungry again after you eat lunch out. **Because you aren't going to *cease to exist* once you have eaten your lunch just because you ate it in a restaurant instead of at your own table.** You are going to move around, and do things, and USE ENERGY throughout the afternoon and your body is then, naturally, going to get HUNGRY again because it will need energy again.

   It is still just food. Food eaten in a different location does not act any differently in your stomach.

- The fear around eating out often comes from the fact that we don't KNOW what's in it EXACTLY. Why? Because it might be higher in energy? But...we want to be high energy people, right?

- If you don't eat for the rest of the day, you aren't going to enjoy the rest of your day very much. Don't bother making evening plans, or aiming to be productive and get chores done. Don't even bother planning to relax and chill and catch up on TV. Your brain isn't going to have space or energy for any of that stuff. Instead, you're going to be grumpy, lethargic and daydreaming about food for hours.

- **And what happens tomorrow?** You're either going to wake up RAVENOUSLY HUNGRY and start the day feeling stressed about food and the possibility of bingeing (as a direct response to the restriction of the previous day) OR you're going to wake up with no hunger cues whatsoever because your body doesn't really trust you again. So then what? Will you skip breakfast? And then go about your day with steadily less and less energy? And less energy and motivation to fight the disordered thoughts? The options look different but they're the same: the next day, you will wake up and you will be at high risk of falling back into a cycle of restriction and compensation. You're already halfway there. You already did the restriction part.

ED Thought: I'm going out for dinner so I shouldn't eat much throughout the day to save my calories and make sure I am hungry enough.

Reframe:

- **Your body is going to need energy to get through the day BEFORE you go out for dinner.** If you don't eat all day, you're going to have a rubbish time. Your day will seem INCREDIBLY LONG and you will be grumpy, tired, lethargic and unfocussed. You'll spend all of your time trying to ignore your hunger. You'll probably go on the restaurant website a good ten-twenty times to gaze at the menu and think about the food you will, eventually, be able to eat. **Why suffer all day long for a couple of hours in the evening?** All you're going to do is make the evening seem like it wasn't worth it. Maybe you'll even dread going; maybe you'll resent the people who invited you. Instead, if you *eat like normal,* your body will have energy *like normal*. You'll have a nice day and you'll be EXCITED to go out for dinner and see the people you are dining with.

- If you haven't eaten beforehand, what's going to happen when you get to the restaurant? People don't typically SIT DOWN IMMEDIATELY AND ORDER THEIR FOOD RIGHT AWAY. They want to CHAT. They want to ask how you've been, talk about what they've been up to, go at a relaxed, leisurely pace. If they wanted fast food, you'd be in a burger shop. If you go in and you're all like "right let's order immediately", they're going to think that you're in a rush to leave.

People don't typically know *exactly what they're ordering* and *they haven't spent hours and hours in the lead up to the event reading and rereading the menu.* They are going to need time to LOOK at the menu and THINK ABOUT WHAT THEY WANT and um and ahh about all the different options. If you are ravenous because you haven't eaten all day and your blood sugar has crashed, you're going to get SNAPPY AND IRRITATED with them for ACTING LIKE NORMAL PEOPLE. You might get snappy and rude. Or you might just not have the energy to participate in their pre-dinner chat at all, and just sit there, lamely, staring into space. **What's the point in being there if you can't enjoy it?**

And then…it's a restaurant, right? It's highly likely you're going to have to wait quite some time to get the server's attention. And then quite some time after that for your food to arrive. Whilst that's all happening, too, other people's food will be being brought out and you'll be able to SMELL it and all that irritation and snappiness and lack of focus is just going to get WORSE AND WORSE AND WORSE.

THEN your food will finally arrive. The thing you chose off the menu several days ago and you don't really fancy but it's low in energy. Your friend will have their burger or their pasta or their pizza and you'll resent them for that, too. Then you'll WOLF YOUR FOOD DOWN so fast you barely even taste it, let alone enjoy it, because you're SO DAMN HUNGRY. And you'll have to sit and watch your friends finish their much yummier looking food.

If you keep stuff like this up, one of the things you will lose, along with weight, will be your friendships. People aren't going to stick around forever if, every time you go out to eat with them, you act like you're on the clock and like you would rather be with anyone else in the world.

- And do you want to know what the WORST PART OF THIS WHOLE SCENARIO IS? When you go home, you're probably still going to be hungry because your body will not have got all of the energy it needed for the whole day and *it knows that.* So you'll have saved up ALL DAY for a meal you DID NOT GET TO ENJOY and YOU WILL BE HUNGRY ANYWAY. And you'll be massively bloated, properly, and wonder *why* and probably try and blame *the salt or the high energy content in the restaurant food* when in reality…you're bloated because your digestive system slowed down because you weren't putting anything in it all day and now you've OVERLOADED IT so it doesn't know what to do.

- And...what happens tomorrow? Compensation? Restriction? The more you listen to the ED, the louder its siren call can become.

ED Thought: I can't go to X's birthday meal because there will be cake there and people will think I'm eating too much.

Reframe:

- You are bored now, probably, but that's good. Because you KNOW the first thing I'm going to say. **Cake = food = energy.** Cake = carbohydrates and fats (and possibly some protein!) which your body NEEDS in order to function and thrive. Cake can be high energy. High energy food for a high energy person. High energy food for a high energy life.

- People are very unlikely to give much thought to what you are eating. People are, by nature, inherently quite focussed on themselves. Especially in the diet culture world we live in, it's highly likely they're too wrapped up in THEIR own silly thoughts about how much and what THEY are eating to be overly concerned with you.

  If they DO by random chance happen to think that you are eating too much, that's stupid. How could they possibly know? They don't know anything about your body, your hunger levels, your healing needs or what you have and haven't already eaten that day. You're at an establishment literally DESIGNED for eating: so if these people are *surprised* that you are *eating so much food* they clearly need their head checked.

  NOT EATING is going to draw MORE attention to you anyway. It's far more unusual to be the only person NOT EATING at a dinner than to be someone who is EATING AN ADEQUATE AMOUNT OF FOOD FOR THEM.

- **Think about the person whose birthday it is.** Think about the photo they are going to take of the group: you know the one, everyone along the long table leaning in with a big smile on their face. When the birthday bean looks back at the photo, they are going to remember the lovely dinner they had with their friends. They are going to remember the jokes that were told, laughing until their face hurt, the gossip about people you used to go to school with, the food they ate, the way they felt *loved* and surrounded by the best people in the world. **Do you know what they *aren't* going to remember? You and how much food you ate. You and whether or not you looked "fat".** They are just going to be glad that you were there.

Unless, of course, you show up and refuse to eat and decline their birthday cake and sit in the corner like some pale, morose and hungry little ghost. Unless, of course, you are too hungry to join in properly and too snappy to have a good time. **Unless, of course, once again you sit on the outskirts of life, watching it happen in front of you but unable to join in.**

ED Thought: It's X's engagement party. It's in the afternoon and they said there would be "nibbles". What about snack time? What if the nibbles are too much? Maybe I should skip lunch first? What if I don't like any of the nibbles? Maybe I should skip the nibbles altogether?

Reframe:

- Snack time isn't a problem because the nibbles *can* be your snack. It doesn't matter *what* they are. They don't need to be your normal "snack" food or a perfect balance of protein and carbs, okay? Because, whatever they are, they will be some form of *energy for your body*. **Nibbles are often high energy too, which is great because you are going to need more energy for all of the wandering around and socialising.** *Making small talk with strangers takes more mental work than you probably realise!* Those nibbles are going to give you the opportunity to have a much more fun and fuelled time, and to be an energetic and engaging person!

- Take a snack in your bag. Then, if you genuinely don't like the nibbles - or there aren't enough nibbles to keep you full - you can pop to the toilets and eat it.

- In ten years time, you don't want your core memory of that event to be you lingering by the nibbles table for hours, being tormented with the choice to *eat them or not to eat them.* You don't want your core memory to be you turning up hungry and dizzy because you skipped lunch and then wolfing down nibbles that you couldn't even taste or enjoy. You don't want your core memory to be you turning up and *wanting* to eat the nibbles and *lying* to everyone around you about why you can't eat them. You want your core memory to be you, celebrating your friend and her love, whilst you have a nice, relaxed and well-fuelled time.

- Remember: if you want the nibbles and you don't eat the nibbles, this is *restriction.* And any restriction, even something as small as not eating some nibbles, opens the door. **If you are in a room full of food, and it smells delicious, and you are hungry, and everyone else is eating…but you aren't…your body isn't going to feel safe. It isn't going to trust you.** Again. And it's going to get very confused: it's hungry, it's surrounded by food…why can't it have any?

ED Thought: I've been invited to a party. But there will be alcohol there and we are ordering pizza. Alcohol IS empty calories and with the PIZZA added to that, I will gain so much weight.

Reframe:
- People gain weight when they REGULARLY consume more energy than their body needs. You aren't going to be REGULARLY consuming alcohol energy. **Anyway, you are going to be USING more energy than usual because you will be up late, dancing and talking and laughing and socialising.** *That takes up more physical and mental energy than you are usually using at 2am so the extra energy will be useful!*

- Anyway, what's more important to you? Not gaining weight *or* getting to have fun with your friends? Right now, you probably think THE FIRST ONE OBVIOUSLY. I HAVE AN EATING DISORDER. OBVIOUSLY NOT GAINING WEIGHT IS THE MOST IMPORTANT. Okay. But what about in a year's time? Two years? Three? **You'll have watched time go by** - you'll have seen all the pictures of parties that you didn't go to on social media, or you'll have collected a series of sad, tepid memories of you, hungry and sober at a party where everyone else is merry and full of energy. **You *may* have stayed the same weight, or lost some weight. Your friends, mostly, will have stayed at very similar sizes too.** But they will also have pictures of the parties they went to, and memories of hazy nights laughing and dancing and laying drunk in the garden, gazing at the stars. You couldn't join them in that because your bones hurt too much to lie on the ground.

You might be choosing NOT GAINING WEIGHT as better than FRIENDS now but trust me. **In ten years' time, after ten years of missed chances, you will begin to question if it was worth it.**

What you lose in weight is never worth what you lose in life.

If you keep going, and rejecting all of your friends' invitations, or turning up and being a bit of a mood hoover party pooper, eventually you will be left with one option only. Not gaining weight. And who wants to sit at home on a Saturday night and their *only option* of activity is…**trying to *stay small*?**

- Sure, alcohol may be *empty energy* in the fact that your body can't really use it in the same way that it can use that yummy pizza that will be fuelling you through the night. BUT. It's not empty calories if it brings you joy. It's not a waste of energy if it helps you create funny memories to laugh about for years to come. <u>**It's not empty if it makes your life more full.**</u>

ED Thought: My friend has invited me to stay at their house after the party. But I need to be able to get back into routine with my eating straight away and I don't know when and what I would eat at their house.

Reframe:
- There are two options here: if your friend is close enough that you are staying at their house, they may be close enough that you can ask them what the plan is for food the next day. And, listen. **THAT'S NOT ACTUALLY A WEIRD OR DISORDERED THING TO DO. They won't think *why are they asking me that, that's so strange?*** It is, in fact, quite common for human beings (who need food in order to survive) to try and plan when and where they will be able to eat. It's actually less common, despite what you may think, for human beings to decide they *don't need to eat and that they should just suffer in silent hunger until someone else suggests food.*

- The other option is to take some convenience packaged goods with you in your bag so that, if for some mad reason, you end up staying with vampires who do not need human food for sustenance, you can eat these. **But that's not a meal, that's not what I want to eat for breakfast.** But look. Tomorrow, you will have breakfast again. And you can have something different. I mean, you *could* have "breakfast food" for lunch if that's what you are craving. Some days we wake up and we WANT something specific. Just because we can't get that thing doesn't mean we shouldn't eat: your body still needs energy to get through the day. Remember: there is always going to be another meal. There is always going to be another chance to eat. All food is good food because it nourishes your body.

- Eating in a routine is very useful for recovery and for normalising your hunger cues and for making your body feel safe. Eating a different food at a different location is *still* part of that routine for your body: as long as your body gets FOOD at relatively similar times, it isn't going to know the difference between the granola bars and fruit you ate in your best friend's guestroom to the toast and cereal you had at home. Being too rigid in your routine is going to let your eating disorder slip back in, you know this. **Don't let your eating disorder get in the way of your life:** to recover and thrive *properly* having those close, caring relationships and connections is SO MUCH MORE IMPORTANT than eating the exact same breakfast you have every day at the same spot out of the same bowl.

My Core Affirmations:
- If you don't eat before events, the whole day leading up to it will suck. You will be hungry, weak, lethargic and grumpy. Then, when you *get* to the event, you will be so focussed on food you can't even have a good time.

- If you continue to isolate yourself, or be controlled by your eating disorder at social events, eventually your friends are going to give up on you. **What you lose in weight will not be worth what you lose in life.**

- The "empty" calories in alcohol are not empty if they give you a fuller life.

- We NEED more energy when we are socialising anyway to be a high energy, fully engaged person and because we are experiencing more mental and physical exertion by being out and about.

- **I would rather be larger and out with friends, than smaller and sat at home alone. I would rather be in a larger body and living a larger life.**

19. REFRAMING: COMPARISON

ED THOUGHT: That influencer is gorgeous. She has a flat stomach, abs, *and* a round butt. If I do her programme, and eat like her, I'll look like that too.

Reframe:
- All bodies look different because of GENETICS. Genetics play a key role in determining how much body fat someone typically has, where they accumulate

their fat, and what their body composition looks like. YES you can change YOUR body somewhat using exercise, but you CANNOT change your body to gain muscle and lose fat in the same places as someone else. **Stop chasing a body that you physically cannot obtain.** Instead, think about your body. Do you carry your weight in your thighs and booty? Do you carry your weight in your shoulders and arms? What shape are you? Unfollow people on social media who regularly post bodies that you *know* you might *want to look like* but *you also know isn't a physical possibility for you.* Then, find people who DO look like you. People who look like you and celebrate their bodies for being healthy and happy. Follow them instead.

- The influencers who post videos on *how to get an hourglass figure* or *how to get a round booty and flat stomach* and *how to get eleven line abs*...**do you know what they looked like BEFORE they "started" their alleged exercise programme?** You'll notice that very few of them actually post their earlier photos. Why? Most of them **ALREADY LOOKED LIKE THE IMAGE THEY ARE TRYING TO SELL YOU.** *They already had an hourglass figure or a round booty or a very lean stomach area naturally.* Equally, many of them don't disclose the fact that BEFORE they started doing all of these ten minute workouts and pilates and whatnot, they came from a background of weightlifting for many years so HAD ALREADY BUILT A SUBSTANTIAL AMOUNT OF MUSCLE. **You are not starting from the same place as them - either in terms of your exercise history or your genetic makeup - so you cannot expect their alleged current routines to make your body look like theirs.**

- **Remember five years ago? Remember all those influencers you followed?** You watched their videos religiously: what I eat in a day, what I eat in a week, how I EAT WHAT I WANT and STAY LEAN, my workout split, my gym routine, how to GET BACK ON TRACK, my morning HEALTHY ROUTINE...Remember how you tried to copy them? You did everything they recommended, didn't you? And how did you feel? Tired. Weak. Lethargic. You didn't suddenly get lean and strong and toned and snatched. You didn't look like them and you didn't feel like them either. Or...maybe you did. Because in the last year, about 50% of those girls have come out and said: REMEMBER WHEN WE USED TO EAT AND EXERCISE LIKE THIS? **Well, we felt like trash the whole time.** Turns out we were stuck in disordered patterns of our own and we just didn't realise it. Turns out we weren't eating enough, and we were overexercising. Turns out living the way WE TOLD EVERYONE TO LIVE was actually REALLY BAD FOR US and we were unhappy and unwell. Oh and we stopped having periods, too. Who would have thought?

So, remind yourself: the fitness influencer industry is based on money and not on health. These influencers get stuck telling you all about their healthy lifestyle and how they manage to maintain their lean physique because MONEY TALKS. *They know they'll get far fewer sponsorships if they admit that surviving off protein products and living in the gym is actually making them feel like trash.* Remind yourself: if you do the things that influencer is telling you to do, there is a HIGH chance it will make you feel like trash because there is a HIGH chance that THEY feel like trash and, in a couple of years time, will be on a weight gain and food freedom journey of their own.

- **YOU DON'T LIKE WEIGHTLIFTING. YOU DON'T LIKE GOING TO THE GYM.** Life is too short to force yourself to do things that you don't want to do. *Their bodies look the way their bodies look because they DO THINGS with their bodies that you have NO INTEREST OR ENJOYMENT in doing.* You do not want to spend your weeks in a *workout schedule*. You do not want to wake up and *have to go to the gym* because *today is leg day and if you don't do it today your whole plan will be messed up.* So accept that. You do not want to do the thing that *could potentially* help your body look like theirs. What is more important to you? **Enjoying your free time, or maybe having a flat stomach?** Looking how your body naturally looks, or *forcing yourself to do things that make you miserable to try and force your body to look different*? When you are old, do you want to think about all the time you spent doing hobbies you love - team sports, climbing, yoga, hiking in nature - or do you want to remember the endless hours you spent hating every moment of being in a sweaty gym?

- **When people talk about you, what do you ACTUALLY want them to say? "Oh yeah, I know her, she's the one with a really hot body".** Would that make you happy? NO. I want people to say that I'm really KIND or FUNNY or SMART or be like, "oh yeah she's the one that does all that really cool rock climbing" and "yeah she's really cool because she wears quirky clothes and earrings". *I DO NOT WANT PEOPLE TO JUDGE MY WORTH ON WHAT MY BODY LOOKS LIKE so I NEED TO STOP JUDGING MY OWN WORTH ON THIS, TOO!*

ED THOUGHT: My friend has started doing keto. She says that it has made her feel the best that she's ever felt, that she loves it and that the weight is just MELTING off. She reckons she'll always eat like this now. Maybe I should try it?

Reframe:

- There is a new fad diet every five minutes. It just depends on whatever is "fashionable" at the moment: fasting, or low carb, or high fat, or protein, or mustard and cottage cheese. There's an incredibly, incredibly high chance that, in five years time, 99% of the sworn keto hardliners will now be doing a totally different fad diet based on some OTHER new research they've read. And chances are, this new fad diet will be THE ONE FOR THEM and it will also make them FEEL BETTER THAN THEY'VE EVER FELT.

- Do you *want* weight loss to be an achievement that you brag about? Or would you rather tell people about a promotion at work, or an article you wrote, or a bit of research you did? Would you rather tell people about a new skill you're working on, or a kind deed you did? **When people tell you that THEY lost weight, are you like TOTALLY SUPER IMPRESSED? Or do you quietly think…okay…cool…what a great use of your time…?** *Not.*

- It might be healthy for your friend to eat like that. It might make your friend feel good to live like that. But you are not your friend. And you need to remember: you have an eating disorder and so what is healthy and helpful for someone else is NOT going to be healthy or helpful for you. <u>Restriction, rules and control are your eating disorder's favourite foods. Don't feed it.</u> Just remind yourself: what is healthy for them is not healthy for me. Keto, or any other fad, will not make you feel good if it triggers your eating disorder because it's a one way road back the way you came.

  You might be tempted to tell yourself that it's been *ages* since you did anything disordered so *maybe you will be alright this time*. But…a fad diet IS disordered. Especially to someone who KNOWS they are susceptible to falling prey to obsessive thinking around controlling food and body. Ask yourself: is it WORTH it? **Are the *possible* benefits of this current fad WORTH the gamble that you could undo all of your hard work, and end up trapped back in that eating disorder hellscape once again?**

- *Is that the life you actually want?* A life where you have to carefully plan every meal based around specific requirements? A life where you struggle to eat out at restaurants? A life where you feel like you can't join in at birthday parties? A life where you turn into some kind of boring preacher, who finds that the most interesting topic of conversation available to them is the food they eat? A life where you can't go to the shop and see a new limited edition chocolate bar and pick it up? A life where you can't drink the seasonal hot drinks at coffee shops? A life where you have to pack a suitcase worth of food to lug around with you whenever you go anywhere? A life that is, by any other definition, entirely disordered and not free?

ED THOUGHT: My friend isn't eating breakfast. She says she isn't hungry. I'm hungry but I can't eat if nobody else is eating.

Reframe:
- **Different bodies need different things.** *Your body is hungry so it needs food. Your brain is at risk of disordered thinking so it needs food.* Your friend might not be hungry. Maybe your friend ate a lot more food than she usually does last night and her body is still digesting it. Maybe your friend's body has adjusted to a pattern of eating where she eats more energy throughout the day and doesn't have breakfast. That might be okay for your friend: remember, what is healthy for someone else is probably not healthy for you. **When you have a history of eating disorders, you KNOW that skipping meals is not something that you should be doing because it allows ED thoughts into your brain and feelings of not being safe into your body.**

- **Breakfast is an exceptional meal: why would you *want* to be the type of person who skips it?** Pancakes, porridge, toast, fruit and yoghurt, pastries, cereal…a big steaming mug of tea…a life lived as a breakfast eater is, in my opinion, far more glorious. Imagine being someone who doesn't eat until lunchtime! Just getting to shove a quick sandwich is around your work day when you *could* have your first meal looking out the window at the early morning sun, listening to the world wake up, eating yummy food. And breakfast dates…and breakfast in bed…GLORIOUS. Also, how on earth am I persuading myself to get out of bed on chilly winter mornings if not for some french toast?

- Remember: a fair few people skip meals for disordered reasons. **They have become so embroiled in diet culture that they have managed to convince themselves that it's normal and healthy to skip meals.** *They've probably down regulated their appetite too from systematically ignoring it or forcing themselves into a fasting regime.* If you told them that they *could* eat breakfast and lunch and dinner and snacks and NOT suddenly LOSE ALL CONTROL OVER THEMSELVES they would probably bite your hand off at the opportunity. What they don't realise, of course, is that THEY CAN DO THAT if they just LET GO OF RESTRICTION…and therein lies their issue. Just ask yourself: **do I want** to be someone who avoids meals deliberately, or do I want to be someone who eats regularly?

- **If anyone judges you for eating when nobody else is eating they are not the kind of people you want to have in your life.** If your best friend was staying at your house and started to eat some breakfast, would you judge her? Would you think she was greedy, and shouldn't be eating? Would you think she was some kind of freak for needing to eat breakfast? NO. So if you have friends that WOULD think those things about you and WOULD place a value judgement on you based on your body and its hunger levels...put them in the bin.

ED THOUGHT: I went out for lunch today and my grandma got a salad because she said she was "being good" and when I ordered chips she said "oh I wish I could be that naughty".

Reframe:
- **You cannot go to prison for eating chips unless you have stolen them or obtained them by holding someone at gunpoint.** Eating food - any kind of food - is not indicative of your BEHAVIOUR. Eating is not naughty behaviour unless you are naked and eating a candy bra off someone's body. Eating a salad is not good behaviour unless...you know what, I can't even think of an analogy. That's how silly this whole naughty and good thing is when it comes to food: not even the queen of analogies and metaphors can come up with one. Just think about it like this: in the UK, people often demonise oil. **Eating foods that are cooked in oil is often deemed as "naughty" and when people go out to eat in restaurants and their food has been cooked in oil, they go on and on about how tasty and naughty it is.** But in mediterranean countries, cooking food in oil is entirely commonplace (and linked to positive health outcomes, of course): this is not designated naughty behaviour at all, but rather the way in which everyone behaves. So, if eating one type of food was a *naughty* thing to do for the body, it would be universally naughty BUT it's not. Do you know why not? Because it's just a silly little rule that a certain culture has made up to demonise food and make people feel like they need to be focussing on controlling their body.

- **Do you want to be someone who goes out to a restaurant and orders a salad and never gets chips?** Do you want to live the rest of your life feeling like it's naughty to choose and eat a food that you enjoy? I don't. I do not want to be in my sixties, seventies, eighties and STILL denying myself the things that I want to eat. I do not want to survive off salads and sadness.

I have seen it play out in real life with many "GOOD" people in my life. I know several people who are in their fifties who spent their entire adult lives on cycles of diets and "good eating" and never allowed themselves to eat what they wanted. Now, they eat really small amounts of food because "if I eat more than this I gain weight" and "I can't eat naughty foods because just looking at them puts the pounds on". Why? Because they have only allowed themselves to eat small meals for many, many years and have eaten a lot of salad and not much else. Their bodies have got used to living on reduced amounts of food. **But I also know "NAUGHTY" people.** I have a friend in her fifties who I frequently go out for lunch with. Last time, she had a burrito and a brownie. The time before, she had a panini and chips. I've seen her eat a salad on occasion, when she was craving it. I've seen her eat vegetables. I've seen her eat cake. She doesn't struggle with her weight at all. She has a body that is strong and full of energy and allows her to do the activities she loves - cycling and swimming. She is FREE. And that's the person I want to be.

So when people say ANYTHING about being *good or naughty or not eating X or not needing to eat dinner after this big meal…*I tell myself: **<u>I feel SORRY for you. I feel SORRY for you that that is how you have to live your life</u>. I do not want to live like that. *I want to live a life where I am happy and free.* I do not want to spend the rest of my life worrying about what I can and can't eat. Poor you. Poor, poor you.** *eats a chip*.

<u>My Core Affirmations</u>
- **Stop chasing a body that is genetically impossible for you to obtain.** Different people carry their weight in different parts of their body. Different people gain muscle more easily in certain areas, and other people carry fat more easily. Your body will look like what your body is genetically geared to look like.

- **Remember: you have no idea what people have had to do, or continue to do, to build and maintain the body that you are jealous of.** There is a high chance that, to look like that, those people also have to feel like trash.

- You do not want to live a lifestyle that results in a typical "gym" body: you do not want to rigidly monitor your eating, you do not want to spend hours and hours a week in the gym, you do not enjoy lifting weights. **Focus on building a life you** will enjoy, rather than a body that will not bring you joy.** It is not worth the cost.

- People who live their lives avoiding yummy foods are not morally superior. Instead of being triggered by their comments, choose to focus on how you want to live your life. You want to eat the foods you enjoy. You want to be able to go out and pick whatever you want off a menu. **Feel sorry for the people that can't do that.** That's sad for them: it's not sad for you. You choose to be happy and free.

20. REFRAMING: RESTING

ED THOUGHT: I should be exercising. It is healthy to exercise. People who don't exercise are lazy, and they have let themselves go. The government website recommends that everyone should exercise. If I don't exercise, I'm going to become unhealthy, get heart disease and become obese…

Reframe:
- Listen. You are not "people" right now. You are *a person recovering from an eating disorder*. That means different rules apply to you.

- The Government advice on the NHS website is very generic, anyway, it is trying to make a blanket statement that applies to everyone. But everyone is different. A six foot tall woman may "need" to do more exercise than a five foot teenage boy in order to "maintain her health". Someone with one leg may need to do more movement than someone who is diabetic to "maintain their health". Someone who works in a restaurant or a nursery or a supermarket is probably ALREADY moving around enough to maintain their health to a degree. Someone who goes to bed very late will be moving more than someone who goes to bed straight after dinner. One person may run every day and be healthy, whereas another may lift weights a couple of times a week and be healthy. Markers of health cannot be reduced down to a set recommended amount of exercise: particularly as this doesn't take into account the vast complexity of the human body and its own unique buildup: people have different sized hearts and lungs and their organ function will be different, along with how quickly their body repairs and how much healing it needs. **Blanket recommendations for exercise amounts are senseless because human bodies are not the same. In the same way that we all need a different amount of food, we also all need a different amount of movement.** Obsessing over a recommended amount, therefore, is needless: that number you are focussed on is *statistically unlikely* to be the exact right amount of movement for you.

- So WHAT would be the right amount of movement? **The amount of movement that makes you feel strong and energised throughout your week.** The amount of movement that allows you to move in the way you want to move and **the amount of movement you enjoy with no feelings of guilt, compensation or *having* to do something**. The amount of movement that makes you feel healthy, as opposed to tired, worn out and hungry. So, then, when you're in eating disorder recovery…that amount of movement is AS LITTLE AS POSSIBLE. Because I'm willing to bet that you don't feel strong and energised yet. I'm willing to bet you still feel tired, worn out and hungry. And I'm willing to bet that you would feel guilty for not moving, that you would feel driven to exercise, and that you would definitely, *definitely,* in the back (or front if you're less in denial than I was) of your mind KNOW that you were thinking *hehehe exercise burns calories hehehe.*

- Your body needs every single little ounce of energy it can get right now to put towards healing the damage that you have done to it. **Your body is malnourished and in energy debt, and if you take some of the energy you put in and use it for exercise, you are stealing from the pot of energy that *could* be being used to heal and repair.** This just means that your body will take longer to heal, and you will be stuck "in recovery" for longer than you need. You may think it won't delay it *that much* but think about what actually happens when you exercise. You break down muscle fibres which then need to heal. So your body needs to heal from the exercise, and also continue healing from the effects of your eating disorder. What will your body choose to fix first? THE EASIEST THING. So it will fix the exercise damage first. This will put the eating disorder healing on hold. **This will mean that all those things you are struggling with - digestive issues, exhaustion, weakness, hormonal issues, grim skin and hair - will be put on hold.**

If you broke your leg, you would understand that you needed to put it in a cast, rest it and stop exercising until it was healed. If you started running on it, it wouldn't heal quickly and it wouldn't heal right either: you would probably end up with misaligned bones and pain and it would bother you for years after. But. If you rested for six weeks…you get the rest of your life with a fully healed leg. It's the same with your body. If you rest properly, you give it the chance to fully heal. If you keep pushing it whilst it is still damaged and weak, you risk prolonging the healing *and* ending up with longer term health ramifications as a result.

- Because you are still tired and weak from malnourishment, you are also not going to be able to engage in exercise at your full capacity. So what's the point? You are exercising to "be healthy" but you are not healthy because you are malnourished. You are exercising to "be healthy" but you can't do it properly because you are malnourished. This means that you won't get the same benefits from it as you would if you were nutritionally rehabilitated. **Your heart isn't going to get stronger from exercise when it is still weak from malnourishment. Your body isn't going to build strong, powerful muscles when they are still weak from malnourishment.** All you are going to do is put your body under more strain, which may in fact have the *opposite* effect on your health and make your heart and muscles WEAKER. If you want to be able to exercise at your full capacity, you need to be AT your full capacity first. Otherwise, you'll be giving half your energy to exercise and half your energy to healing and, therefore, not doing a good job at EITHER.

So NOT exercising is the HEALTHIEST THING you can be doing right now.

ED THOUGHT: I am exhausted all the time in recovery. I had MORE ENERGY when I was actively engaging in my eating disorder. I lie around doing nothing all the time. I'm lazy and unproductive.

Reframe:
- If your friend told you that they were exhausted and worn down, what would you tell them to do? Would you tell them to get up and start ticking things off a to-do list? Would you tell them they were lazy and unproductive, and that they needed to get a grip and get off the sofa? Or would you tell them to slow down, take a break and recharge? If someone you loved was in hospital because they were malnourished and needed to rehabilitate, would you call them lazy?

You are probably thinking *but that's not the same: they are tired for a legitimate reason, they are actually NOT WELL*. Newsflash. You are tired for a legitimate reason. You are malnourished. Your body is weak. You ARE unwell. You are fighting a mental illness which is exhausting enough on its own, with the added complication that the mental illness has weakened your body and your health.

If your friend was recovering from an eating disorder, would you tell them that resting was lazy and unproductive? Or would you fight tooth and nail to MAKE THEM STOP AND SLOW DOWN and TAKE THE TIME TO HEAL?

- When you start nourishing yourself again, your body is able to start healing. But what this means is that your body grabs hold of ALL THE ENERGY THAT YOU PUT IN as soon as it can because it doesn't quite trust you yet. **Your body has one priority: trying to heal the damage that has been caused ASAP because all your body wants is to SURVIVE.** Your body does not care about you going to work, or making it to Janet's engagement party, or cleaning the house from top to bottom, or your side hustle. **It's hardly going to allocate you enough energy to do those things when your digestive system doesn't work properly, your heartbeat is too weak and your leg muscles can't carry you further than a few hundred metres without aching.**

- If you insist on CARRYING ON WITH LIFE IN FULL whilst your body is trying to heal, you will be stealing energy from the healing process. You will not be committing your full energy to healing. But you also won't be able to commit your full energy to LIVING LIFE IN FULL because you *don't have that much energy available.* **So you will be splitting your energy between HEALING AND LIVING and therefore not doing very much of either.** What does that mean? You're stuck in limbo. Unable to heal fully and unable to live fully. Sooner or later, something has got to give. And it will. **What's likely to happen is this: you will give half your energy to healing and half to life. Because your eating disorder is one sneaky little goblin, it will see that you're only half-focussed on your recovery and it will find ways to wriggle back in.** Before you know it, you'll be back where you were before: half engaged in life and half engaged in your eating disorder and slowly, slowly, the half engaged in life will reduce down again and the half engaged in eating disorder will grow and BAM.

It's easier for your eating disorder thoughts to take control when you are still malnourished. The malnourished brain is more susceptible to silly little thoughts. So **by not allowing your body the maximum opportunity to heal, you are not allowing your mind the maximum opportunity to develop the resistance it would need to fight** those relapse urges.

Yes, it may be impossible for you to fully give up on work. We need money to live, that's the sad part of society. However, you can spend the time you are not at work resting. Lie on the sofa. Read. Binge watch TV. Do crosswords. Reorganise your music playlists. Write bad poetry. Sleep. The more time you spend resting, the easier it is going to be for your body to heal.

- Resting is NOT lazy. **It is actually productive: you are resting to allow your body and brain the time to heal so that, in the future, you can do all of the things that you want to do PROPERLY.** It is UNPRODUCTIVE to keep doing things badly and it is UNPRODUCTIVE to keep delaying and prolonging your healing. In the long run, taking time now to rest and heal will mean that you will be able to get back to doing the things you want to be doing sooner. **You are investing in your future self.** If you keep trying to be productive, you are not giving yourself the chance to heal properly. You are putting yourself at risk CONTINUALLY of relapse. The more healed you become, the further from your eating disorder you get. The safer you become. *And one day, you will be able to work full time, go out every evening, tick off endless to-dos and you'll be DREAMING of a lazy day on the sofa doing nothing!*

My Key Affirmations
- You would give a broken leg the time it needed to heal so give your malnourished body and brain the time that it needs to heal too.

- What is healthy for "most people" in terms of rest and movement does not apply to you. You are not "most people". You are recovering from an eating disorder and it is healthier for your body to be resting, repairing and rebuilding.

- Exercising and over-exerting yourself is NOT PRODUCTIVE. It sets your healing back, slows it down, and risks you developing longer term complications. It also risks you never actually recovering fully - mentally or physically.

- If I allow myself time to rest now, I will be creating a future where I can do all of the things I want to do PROPERLY and ENJOY them. Currently, trying to do all of the things I want to do is NOT ENJOYABLE because I cannot do them PROPERLY.

21. REFRAMING: MY BODY

ED THOUGHT: Everytime I try to eat like a normal person, my weight jumps up by a MASSIVE AMOUNT. I can't just eat normally because my weight just goes up so much faster than normal people. I have damaged my metabolism.

Reframe:
- Okay. Listen. When you *first* start eating again, you have gone from barely eating anything, getting rid of lots of what you ate and being *incredibly dehydrated*.

When you start eating again, your body retains a WHOLE LOT of water in order to start the healing process (that's the bloating!). It is also just a hydrated body. Also, you probably have RATHER A LOT OF FOOD still inside you. The food you just ate but also the food you've BEEN eating for the last few days. By that I mean, your digestive system won't be firing on all cylinders. Food will be chilling in your digestive system for a while. Constipation is very normal in recovery and you probably have a good few pounds of poop stocked up in there. **_Consider it this way: your lowest weight is the weight of your body when it is empty of food and poop, dehydrated and dying._ The jump in weight when you start eating again is a jump from that dying body to a body that is full of food, water, poop and healing.**

This is not me saying that you won't gain weight during recovery, or that weight gain is a bad thing. **This is just me saying that the weight gain won't continue to jump up like that *forever and ever and ever.*** I have spoken to SO MANY PEOPLE in recovery from eating disorders, and they have all said the same thing: a huge initial jump in weight that levelled off after the first few weeks and, as constipation and water retention reduced, the weight gain became more slow and steady as they restored.

- You might be thinking *okay that's them, though. I know my weight will keep jumping, it always does.* But, listen. **Have you ever kept going past the initial jump?** For how long? Or have you seen the jump, freaked out, and gone back to restricting almost immediately? But also…think about it like this…every time you went *back* to restriction again, did that extra scale weight stick around for as long as it SHOULD HAVE if it were real weight? Or was it gone in a few days? Gone because it wasn't all fat gain: it was hydration and healing fluid and poop and food.

- Metabolic damage is a myth. It's actually called METABOLIC ADAPTATION. And it happens, of course, because your body is incredibly smart and is doing the one job it knows it has: to try and keep you alive. **Your body doesn't know that you are DELIBERATELY malnourishing it: why would it know that?** Why would anyone *do* that? When you start dieting, typically your energy expenditure drops. You don't have the energy to move around as much. You may spend long periods of time on the sofa or lying in a darkened room. When you do go on walks or exercise (probably too much), you aren't able to do it as quickly or energetically as before. You are using less energy because you have less energy to use. Simultaneously, not eating enough also causes changes in your hormones which will prioritise fat storage when you do eventually eat. All of this is geared towards survival. For most of human history, food scarcity was an issue and people would go days without food. **The body therefore adapts so that it can survive this: when it is starving, metabolic rate slows (by shutting or slowing down those unnecessary bodily functions like reproductive hormones; bones, skin and hair health; and digestion), movement reduces to conserve energy, and, when you do eat, the body can gain fat more easily than expected.** *To survive, human bodies do the most sensible thing they can: slow down to save energy and, when they do get energy in, conserve it.*

This isn't metabolic damage. This is what metabolism is *meant* to do: stop you from starving to death. And the way to do that is to *reduce the energy you need to survive on* whilst stockpiling whatever it can whenever it can.

This sounds like a bad thing, okay, but it isn't. Because ADAPTATION is better than DAMAGE. **Because if your metabolism can adapt *down* to eating less, it can adapt back up again as you eat more.** As you start to eat again, your body will find itself with more energy. You will be able and willing to move around more. Your bodily functions that were paused or slowed will start up again, requiring more energy. Your body, eventually, will realise that there is a surplus of food now so it doesn't need to hang on to every little ounce of energy any more. You will *increase the amount of energy you need to live* and *stop stockpiling it.*

- It's rather unlikely, don't you think, that you are some kind of medical miracle? If you kept gaining weight at the same rate of the initial recovery weight gain, you would be one of the heaviest people on the planet in a matter of months. But what about all of the other people who recovered? They didn't turn into the heaviest people on the planet. In fact, after their initial period of rapid gain, for most people, the weight gain eventually plateaued. Their bodies finally felt safe again and the need to keep conserving energy and weight faded. So if you just happened to keep gaining and gaining and gaining forever, that would make you HIGHLY MEDICALLY UNUSUAL. Maybe you could sign up for medical research, and make a bunch of money. Recovery perks! **Or, maybe, just maybe…if you eat and keep eating past the initial terrifying gain, you'll see what the others saw too: that as long as you don't run back to restriction, and as long as you keep honouring your hunger and giving your body energy, eventually it will figure it out and find a balance.**

- But listen. Even if your weight DOES keep going up, even if you DO suddenly become the world's heaviest person, SO WHAT? The alternative is that you CONTINUE TO BE MISERABLE and CONTINUE TO RESTRICT and CONTINUE TO LIVE IN A NARROW, FOOD-OBSESSED HELLHOLE where you cycle between binge-restrict-compensate cycles FOR THE REST OF YOUR LIFE. Is that worth staying small? Is that worth not being larger? Is it worth spending *the rest of your life* caught between hell and gaining weight quickly and spiralling back to hell and gaining weight quickly?

ED THOUGHT: I miss my sick body. I don't like my new body. I don't like the way it looks, I don't like the way it feels and I don't like the way my clothes don't fit.

Reframe:
- DID you like your sick body, though? Did you like what it LOOKED LIKE? No, really, did you? Or did you look in the mirror, endlessly, all day, every day, and HATE what you saw? Picking apart the size of your thighs and your stomach. Pulling on clothes that felt tight in all the wrong places. Wrapping your fingers around your limbs only to be disappointed by the tightness of your grip. Tracing along your bones only to be annoyed that they weren't *sharp* enough. Looking at other people and thinking *they're smaller than me,* ALWAYS trying to BE SMALLER, ALWAYS feeling TOO BIG. Shrouding your body in huge clothes, hiding it from the world so they wouldn't see how *big* you still were. And your face? Your skin was dry and spotty and that sickly shade of malnourished grey, your eyes were glassy and sunken, your black bags had taken up permanent residence, your hair was falling out and greasy, and your smile looked more like a grimace because it was too much effort to force a real one. YOU DID NOT LIKE WHAT YOUR SICK BODY LOOKED LIKE. You never liked your body.

- DID you like how your sick body FELT? Did you like feeling like you couldn't walk up a hill? Did you like feeling like your limbs were dead weights, that could drop off at any moment? Being unable to carry your own shopping bags up the stairs without taking a break? Did you like feeling your heart pounding in your chest, did you like the constant palpitations? Did you like feeling dizzy when you stood up too fast? Did you like the constant ringing in your ears? The pounding headaches? The nausea? The constant hunger pains? The weakness? The constipation? Did you like feeling cold in the middle of summer? Did you like how it hurt to sit down? Did you like that you were incapable of socialising for any length of time? Did you like the way your brain stopped working properly? Did you like being incapable of focussing on anything for more than a few minutes? Did you like feeling irritable and grumpy with everyone around you? Did you like feeling anxious every time you even *smelt* food?

- You DO like how it FEELS to be in a healthy body. To get out of bed in the morning, and not feel like you're going to faint. To run after the bus and know you'll make it rather than feeling like you might keel over. To walk up a hill. To carry your shopping up the stairs. To be someone who is strong enough that your friends wouldn't think twice about asking you to help them move house. To sit on a wooden park bench and be comfortable. To feel warm again. To have a heart that beats normally. To have hunger cues that are well regulated, instead of being either intensive or entirely absent. To have a digestive system that works. To be able to work. To be able to read books. To be able to watch TV without the endless urge to get up and move around. To spend the weekend resting on the sofa if you need to, or hiking up a hill if you want to. To be present in your life. To *live*.

- And you DO LIKE the way your hair looks thicker and shinier now. You DO LIKE the way your skin appears to have cleared up, and the dryness has started to go, and sometimes that grey sheen has been replaced by a healthy pink glow. You DO LIKE the fact that you no longer have that saggy old person skin around your thighs and your arms. You DO LIKE that your eyes sparkle now, and that your smile makes other people smile, and that people no longer look at you in horror. You DO LIKE that you no longer look ten years older than you are.

- You might not LOVE the way your healthy body looks. But. You didn't LOVE the way your sick body looked either. So you may as well just accept that you exist in a body you may never love. **But you CAN love how your body FEELS. You CAN love what your body can DO.** That's your healthy body: your sick body feels like trash and is as useless as that lettuce you ate for breakfast.

- And so what if your clothes don't fit? Donate them to charity. Do your clothes still fit from when you were a baby? I bloody hope not. We outgrow clothes. That's what humans do. They change size. We aren't made of plastic. Most of us. Get a whole new wardrobe: charity shops are your best friend. **You can go from being shrouded in shame and baggy clothing to wearing whatever you damn well like: strawberry print leggings, pastel hoodies, crazy prints?** YES PLEASE. New clothes are a chance for you to show who you are. Those clothes that fit your sick body don't show who you are. <u>You are too much of a person to live in a small body so clothes that fit a body smaller than yours is meant to be are</u>

<u>clothes that are all wrong</u>. Also, what was the plan? Keep those exact clothes for the rest of your life? **Be a fifty year old wearing a size BABY crop top and a size BABY pair of denim shorts? You want to be a fifty year old wearing jazzy leggings and crocs, not tiny BABY SIZE clothes.**

ED THOUGHT: That person has a body that I want. I want to be able to exist in that body. Why can't I?

Reframe:

- You know that in order for YOUR BODY to be a similar size to THEIR BODY that you have to do unhealthy things. You have to mistreat your body, and feel like trash, and undereat. You become trapped in cycles of compensating, bingeing and restricting. So look at them and remind yourself: NOT MY HEALTHY BODY. NOT MY HEALTH BODY. NOT MY HEALTHY BODY. That might be THEIR healthy body: they may be maintaining that body by eating enough food, eating whatever they want, and moving as and when their body feels the need. But you KNOW that you CANNOT be that size and do those things. NOT MY HEALTHY BODY.

  For you to become that small, your life also has to become very small. Shrinking your body also shrinks your life.

- Besides which, you don't KNOW that those people you are looking at ARE in their healthy bodies. It's incredibly difficult for us to look at another person and determine their "physical health". It's IMPOSSIBLE for us to look at another person and determine their mental health. Those people you envy could very well be engaging in negative behaviours themselves. They could very well be undereating or overexercising or compensating. They could have incredibly poor mental health. **You cannot know, by looking at another person, that they are healthy.** They could be suffering to be in that body, just like you were. Either way, it doesn't matter: you *know* that being *that size* is NOT your healthy body.

ED THOUGHT: I want to lose weight. I feel better about myself at a lower weight. I don't want to gain weight.

Reframe:
- You don't feel better about yourself at a lower weight. The lower you go, the more impaired your cognitive function becomes and the less able you are to *look* at your body and *see it as it is*. **Body dysmorphia is a struggle anyway, let alone when you are so small and malnourished that your brain function has exited the chat.** At your lowest weight, you still felt huge. At your lowest weight, you still hated your body. At your lowest weight, you still wanted to be smaller. Losing weight again isn't going to make you feel better about yourself, then. It's just going to make you feel the same, if not worse, and ALSO make you feel worse physically and mentally because eating disorders make you feel like trash.
- **When you lose weight, it's not just weight you are losing.** Slowly at first, and then very rapidly, you begin to lose everything. Enjoyable time spent with friends and family. The ability to walk up stairs quickly. Any time spent with anyone. Freedom. Fun. Energy. Hair. Heart function. Proper digestive function. The ability to engage in your hobbies. Muscle strength and tone. Time. Brain function. Focus. Enjoying food. Friends. Healthy skin. Healthy nails. Opportunities. Ambition. The ability to work or study. Happiness. Hope. Sanity. Maybe one day your life. It's not just weight you lose. It's everything.
- **When you gain weight, it's not just weight you are gaining.** You are gaining back your life. The energy to do the things you want to do. Time spent laughing with friends, dancing all night, eating pizza and making memories. The ability to work again, and build a career, and have aspirations. To feel like you can make a difference. The idea of a future. Dreams and plans. Better friendships. New friendships. The capacity for love. Memories with your family that aren't marred by the dark cloud of the eating disorder. Your physical health: a stronger heart, a functioning digestive system, healthy hormones, healthy skin, healthy nails. Your glow. A smile that can light up a room again. Happiness. Hope. Sanity.
- You gained weight because you needed to. You ate. You nourished your body. *If you cannot eat and nourish your body enough to have the energy to freely live your life with sparkle and pizzazz, you are aiming for the wrong size body.* The body you should be aiming for is the body where you can eat and live freely. Anything else is not good enough. Anything else is too small. Too small a body for too small a life.

My Key Affirmations:

- You had to do unhealthy things to be in a smaller body. Your body was therefore never meant to be that size. Other people may be able to exist healthily in a smaller body than you. But that is NOT MY HEALTHY BODY and therefore I do not want it.

- When you are in a smaller body, your life is smaller. You want to live a FULL life full of energy and fun and sparkle: you cannot do that whilst forcing your body to shrink. **You are too much of a person to fit into a small, sick body.**

- You did not feel better about yourself when you lost weight. You still didn't like your body, you still wanted to be smaller, but you ALSO felt like trash, physically and mentally. *If you are going to dislike your body anyway, you may as well feel physically well and be able to engage in life.*
- You don't have to love how your body looks. But you CAN love how it feels. You CAN love what it can do.

- The more you continue to eat consistently and nourish your body, the more energy you will have and the more your metabolism will adapt again. It had adapted down because it was trying to help you survive. When it knows you are thriving, it will adapt back up again.

22. REFRAMING: SICK ENOUGH

ED THOUGHT: I am not sick enough to recover yet. There are people thinner than me, who eat less than me, who need to recover and deserve the help.

Reframe:
- **If the people who are thinner than you are "sick enough" to recover, why aren't they?** If they reached the magical, coveted *thin enough,* should they not be recovering? Are they not valid now? Are they not finally sick enough to get better? Are they not deserving of recovery? Are they not the most ready they have ever been? But that's the thing, isn't it? There IS no sick enough. Your eating disorder is NEVER going to let you be SICK ENOUGH. The more malnourished you become, the less your brain is able to function properly. With reduced brain function comes that total inability to see the situation for what it is. You will get sicker and sicker, whilst convincing yourself, always, that you are *not sick enough to recover.* There's a reason there are hoards of people walking around with eating disorders, every single one of them convinced that they need

to keep going for a little bit longer and get a little bit sicker in order to recover. **Have you *ever* met someone with an eating disorder who *does* think they are sick enough to recover?** There is no sick enough.

- You have been sick for YEARS. **You have been every weight under the sun. And did you feel any less sick when you were a higher weight? NO. You felt THE SAME at ALL WEIGHTS.** Physically you felt like trash: you were hungry and weak and tired, your heart was struggling, you couldn't walk without feeling breathless and dizzy, your skin was grey and dry and spotty, your hair was falling out, you lost your period. Mentally you felt like trash: you spent hours body checking, wasted your life counting numbers and looking up recipes and watching people eat online, you wanted to die, you isolated yourself. **All of those things happened long before you were underweight.**

- Your feeling of "sickness" doesn't change with your weight. You may think it does because you've heard the rhetoric that *being underweight is more dangerous because you can die* but you can quite literally die from the physical complications of an eating disorder and malnourishment at any weight. <u>In fact, it's probably *more dangerous* to *not* be underweight with an eating disorder because people don't realise the danger you are in</u>. When you are underweight, the danger is obvious to our silly little stereotyped society and people - friends, family, medical professionals - worry about you collapsing or your heart giving out so they watch you more closely. When you are not underweight, these risks are still there except this time people *don't* watch you closely and you're less likely to have medical intervention. So, if it helps, you are probably MORE SICK in terms of risk when you AREN'T underweight.

- Say that you COULD get sick enough. Say that one day you might wake up and think "yes, finally, I did it, I AM sick enough". What now? Are you going to recover? If so, you wasted *all of that time* getting sick enough because you are just going to recover anyway. You may as well have just started recovering BEFORE you got sicker, right? If you were always going to recover anyway? It's the same destination.

Imagine you were going on holiday to France, to relax and recharge from work related burnout. You could leave tomorrow. Alternatively, you could decide to wait until you *really, really need a holiday* and keep pushing through your burnout for another year. Then, you go to France. But NOW it's not going to be as fun and recharging of a trip as you thought, because you are so much more tired and worn down than you were a year ago. **You've ended up in the same** destination but it took longer and now you've got more work to do to heal. But you were always going to end up there. You were always going to need to take the holiday and heal your burnout. **But now it's going to take longer and now it's going to be harder.**

It's the same with your eating disorder. You are, one day, going to have to recover (or accept that you will live that way forever, or die). If you keep going with it until you are sicker, you are just going to be causing more damage to your health, risking longer term health complications and losing out on more and more of your life. And for what? **You could recover now. Or you could wait ten years until you are *sick enough* and then recover then. But you will still end up having to recover. The only difference is that the *sick enough* version of you will have lost ten years of their life, opportunities and memories in the process of delaying.** The *not sick enough version* that decided to recover will have ten years of life on you. <u>I did not think that I was sick enough ten years ago. I did not think I was sick enough five years ago. I did not think I was sick enough one month ago. But the fact is this: I have now woken up, ten years later, feeling the exact same way that I did before</u>. Hating my body, using behaviours, feeling physically and mentally like trash. **I am still the same level of sick: very sick. But I have also lost ten years of my life for no reason.**

- **Any human being who is sick enough to deprive themselves of nourishment, or binge, or purge, or stand in front of a mirror and hate themselves, is sick enough.** If you told someone else that you do any of those things, they are *hardly* going to think that you are a WELL INDIVIDUAL. Any human being who is unable to live their life freely because of their preoccupation with food and their body is sick enough. What is sick enough? Sick enough is when you are struggling. Sick enough is when there is something wrong that needs to get better. You wouldn't tell a child with a cold that they weren't sick enough because there was another child dying in hospital. **You would treat both children with the relevant medicine and care for their sickness**. It's the same with an eating disorder. The relevant care for the sickness. And an eating disorder is always a sickness. <u>Wanting to starve your body smaller is a sickness. Being unable to stop eating until you are physically and mentally in pain is a sickness. Making yourself exercise until you are ready to pass out is a sickness. Making yourself vomit is a sickness. Taking laxatives every day is a sickness. Isolating yourself and thinking about food and weight all day every day is a sickness.</u>

ED THOUGHT: I am not sick enough to recover because I am not underweight. I am not diagnosed as anorexic so I am not sick enough to recover. People won't take me seriously.

Reframe:
- The criteria for diagnosis of eating disorders is a series of tick lists that try to put people into boxes. But people don't fit in boxes. When I had a binge eating disorder, I also exhibited behaviours from the bulimia checklist. When I had bulimia, I also exhibited behaviours from the anorexia checklist. At every weight, and every diagnosis, I felt the exact same way about my body. I did the same behaviours. I felt the same. But, apparently, I had a different disorder each time. But, listen. **On the 28th January 2023, I had a diagnosis of bulimia nervosa. The next day, on the 29th January 2023, I was diagnosed with anorexia nervosa instead.** Nothing in my behaviours had changed. Nothing in the way I felt or acted had changed. I was doing the exact same things. Feeling the exact same way. Except now, because my weight had reached a certain BMI, I had somehow TURNED INTO AN ANOREXIC. I was still doing all of the things that had originally led to my diagnosis of bulimia. But now I was anorexic, apparently. And this is my point: chasing the anorexic label isn't going to change ANYTHING because the label means NOTHING. **If you can go from one eating disorder to another one overnight because of a change in weight, that just goes to show that these labels DO NOT DEFINE ANYTHING**. I was still the same. How could I have a different sickness? I DIDN'T. IT WAS THE SAME. IT WAS AN EATING DISORDER.

  From that moment on, I decided to ditch the labels all together. When I tell people, I tell them I have an eating disorder. When they ask me which one, I tell them: an eating disorder. If they press, I make it awkward. I go on my long rant about how my diagnosis changed overnight; I tell them how when I was morbidly obese I did the SAME THINGS I did when I was diagnosed as anorexic; I tell them that an eating disorder is an eating disorder regardless of weight. That tends to shut them up. But it's the truth. That label doesn't matter. Having that label doesn't change the fact that you have an eating disorder and that you have behaviours that need addressing. All the label does is put you in a box that you don't fit in. All the label does is keep you stuck. In reality, you probably have a myriad of behaviours that fit into several boxes and you could be any weight under the sun and still be the exact same. It's an eating disorder.

- The medical criteria of diagnosis are centred around saving money and services that have too much pressure on them. NOT on the validity of your sickness. **By**

defining anorexia based on a low weight threshold, the health service is able to refuse treatment to *most people who exhibit anorexic behaviours*. They do this to save money and to allocate the finite resources that they *do* have to those that they *perceive* to be the most at risk of dying. Key word: perceive. That's not necessarily the case AT ALL but it's so very complicated when it comes to the allocation of resources. Most people who work in ED services will admit that they think everyone with an eating disorder needs treatment but that they just don't have the resources available. **There is not enough time or money in the health services to go around. So they have to make choices. Those choices are not a testament to how sick anyone is, but a testament to how many resources are available at a given time.** This is evidenced by the fact that someone in one part of the country could be turned down or placed on a waitlist for a year for something that someone in a less overwhelmed service would receive treatment for immediately.

- If you are unable to access treatment because of overwhelmed services, that does not mean that you are not sick enough or deserving of recovery. **All it means is that our mental health services are broken.** If you reach out to eating disorder charities, there are many who can direct you to free support because the charities recognize that you are sick and that you need help regardless of the allocation of resources. It can be very tempting, though, to try and *get sick enough* to access the help. But listen: you don't know how long that will take. You don't know how long the waiting list is, or how much longer it might get, or how much you might impact your longer term health by trying to get sicker. You also don't know that the treatment will help you. Personally, NHS therapy was one of the most useless and ridiculous things I have engaged in and I regret wasting all of those years trying to get sick enough to access it. But, we return to the same point above, anyway: getting sicker just means wasting more time. Wasting more life. Wasting more opportunities. I wish, so much, that ten years ago I had done what I am doing now: reached out to charities, found online support groups, read recovery self-help manuals, sat down and *looked at my own issues myself* and stopped trying to get SICK ENOUGH for treatment. It may be that you still end up needing treatment one day. But if you do try to actively do what you can on your own, you may be able to prevent yourself from getting SO SICK that life becomes SO NARROW that you wake up in a decade and feel like you wasted it entirely. That's what happened to me.

ED THOUGHT: Everyone in the recovery community talks about that quote *nothing tastes as good as skinny feels* and then they show how skinny made them feel really bad. But I'm not skinny.

Reframe:
- Do you feel like trash right now? Oh, you do? Do you know why that is? IT'S NOT THE BEING SKINNY THAT FEELS LIKE TRASH. It's malnourishment. It's starving. It's bingeing. It's purging. It's compensation. It's over exercising. It's the stress you put on your body by not feeding it correctly, and not resting enough. It's the mental strain of an eating disorder: of the body checking and the self-hated and the obsessive thoughts and the need to shrink yourself.

- Everything tastes better than being skinny feels, okay? But everything tastes better than being "normal weight" and having an eating disorder feels too. Everything tastes better than being "obese" or "overweight" or "underweight" and having an eating disorder feels too. EATING tastes better than having an EATING DISORDER no MATTER WHAT SIZE YOU ARE. Whatever size your body is, having an eating disorder feels like trash.

- So what, ANYWAY? Will you keep going so that you CAN feel even MORE like trash than you currently do? Does that sound like a good thing, to you? Is it worth feeling *worse* than you already do? To prove that you are *skinny enough to feel like trash?* YOU KNOW YOU ALREADY FEEL LIKE TRASH.

- Remember: these trends that you see on social media where people show their sick, underweight bodies and their subsequent recovery into socially acceptable bodies still are, in part, people who are still struggling and therefore seeking validation. **Their eating disorder wants them to show the world that they were sick and that they were skinny enough to recover and THAT'S WHY IT'S OKAY FOR THEM TO EAT THAT CINNAMON BUN.** The quotes and the images of them going from underweight to a healthy weight and *eating yay* are all, in part, an attempt to convince themselves that it was *okay* for them to recover because they *were* underweight. And, it cannot be ignored that the algorithms of social media favour these kinds of stories. They sell. They have a shock factor. It doesn't mean that your story and your struggle is any less valid. It just means that you don't NEED to seek validation from others that you WERE SICK. Remember: it's not YOU that is being validated by social media trends. It's YOUR EATING DISORDER. And do you want to give that goblin any degree of satisfaction?

ED THOUGHT: I am recovering too quickly. Weight gain is making me feel invalid. Eating is making me feel invalid.

Reframe:
- Okay. Let's define invalid. Invalid means: *(especially of an argument, statement, or theory) not true because based on erroneous information or unsound reasoning.* Therefore, there is no way for YOU to be invalid, okay? There is no erroneous information here. You have an eating disorder because you have struggled with disordered behaviours around your body and food. This is true information. Recovering from it does not make it an *error* or change the *fact that you were sick.* If you break your arm, and then it heals, this does not then mean that you NEVER HAD A BROKEN ARM. It also doesn't mean that, sometimes, in the cold winter weather, your ARM WON'T TWINGE where you broke it. All wounds hurt sometimes, even when you think they've healed. Because they *were real. They were there. They were valid.*

- If we're talking about the unsound reasoning though…now what does *that* sound like? Not you. But YOUR EATING DISORDER. Your eating disorder bases ALL OF ITS THOUGHTS ON UNSOUND REASONING. Nothing that your eating disorder tells you makes ANY SENSE. So how about this: instead of thinking that YOU are invalid, how about you tell your EATING DISORDER THAT IT IS INVALID? Eating disorder you ARE invalid. You make NO SENSE. All of your information is ERRONEOUS. Everything you say is based on UNSOUND REASONING. That way, **recovering from an eating disorder is the MOST VALID thing you could be doing. Your healing is valid. Your battle is valid.**

- Who are you worried about thinking you are invalid, anyway? If there is anyone in your life who would see you gaining weight and know you were recovering from an eating disorder who would then tell you that you are *invalid* and *weren't sick enough to begin with*…THEY ARE NOT THE KIND OF PERSON YOU WANT IN YOUR LIFE. They need to go in the bin. **If anyone sees you as invalid because you are healing, they are the worst kind of person.** You don't need them. To be honest, *they're* pretty invalid as a friend!

- What does recovering *too quickly* even mean anyway? How much longer do you want to be sick for? How much longer do you want to suffer for? How many more moments do you want to be robbed from you? How many more opportunities do you want to miss? **The longer you hold on to your eating disorder so as to not recover "too quickly", the more of everything else you lose.** There is no "too quickly" when it comes to getting your life back. There is no "too quickly" when it comes to healing and leaving behind the darkest times of your life. There is *too slowly* though. If you go too slowly, you lose more. You increase the chances that you will have longer term complications: you could be doing lasting damage to your organs, bones and reproductive system so that, by the time you *are* ready to recover, your body just isn't. **And you'll find yourself recovering or recovered but into a life with lower quality of life - weak bones, failing organs, fertility issues - because you didn't want to recover "too quickly".** In the scale of the time you have left, do you not want to have as much free life as you can get? Do you want to wake up at 80 and draw a timeline of your life, and fill in most of it with time spent "sick" or "slowly recovering"? Or would you rather be able to fill in as little as possible of it with that, and as much as possible with "living"?

- Sure, other people may be recovering slower than you. You may see people on the internet still crying over a bowl of cereal two years into their recovery. You may see people ten years down the line still suffering. They are valid. But so are you. **Why would you want to be in their shoes? Why would you want to be crying over cereal again? Why would you want to be suffering in another decade?** Sure, they may feel valid in their sickness (but let's be honest, they probably don't: their disorder is probably also telling them they are not sick enough) but they also feel like trash. They are suffering. Their slow recovery is costing them. Time, opportunity and healing. You don't need to cost yourself the same.

- What WILL be valid? *You will, validly, be a survivor.* You will, validly, be a warrior. **You will, validly, be able to say: I overcame an eating disorder.** Nobody is going to turn around to you and stress test the validity of this. They aren't going to say: oh how long were you sick for? Were you as sick as the other people? Where did your sickness fall on the sickness scale? AND IF THEY DO? They aren't someone you want in your life. So you can put them in the bin. And you can have a speech prepared for how length of time, weight, behaviours etc are NO TESTAMENT to how sick someone is.

ED THOUGHT: I am not sick enough

Reframe:
- There is no scale of being sick enough. There is no badge to be won. **There are going to be people with eating disorders who are smaller than you, always. There are going to be people with eating disorders who are larger than you, always.** There are going to be people with eating disorders who have more

disordered thoughts than you, and people who have fewer disordered thoughts than you. There are going to be people who have lower resting heart rates than you, and people with higher ones. People whose organs are failing more than yours, and people whose organs are failing less. People who exercise more than you, and people who exercise less. People who have more fear foods than you, and people who have less. People who can eat more freely than you can, and people who cannot.

Someone who is smaller than you may have healthier organs than you. Which one of you is sicker? Someone who is larger than you might have a heart that is going to give up in the next week, but your heart has time left in it. Which one of you is sicker? Two people may have the same BMI: one hasn't eaten solid food in months and the other is exercising for four hours a day. Which one is sicker? What am I am trying to say is this: you cannot be *sick enough* when the sickness is *incomparable*. **Every single person is suffering in the same but totally different way.** You may appear "sicker" on some measures than other people, and "more well" on other measures. But you are still sick. <u>**Compared to non-disordered people, you are all wildly sick.**</u>

- Stand yourself next to someone who eats meals and snacks, rarely thinks about their body negatively and is happy, nourished and physically thriving. Who is sicker now? You. Now think about the person YOU want to be. ***Someone who who eats meals and snacks, rarely thinks about their body negatively and is happy, nourished and physically thriving.*** <u>**You are SICKER than the PERSON YOU WANT TO BE. That is SICK ENOUGH.**</u>

- I like to ask myself: how do I want people to talk about me as a person? Imagine there are two people who know you sitting in a cafe. One of them says: ***"Hey do you know this person?"*** What do you want their response to be? ***"Oh yeah, I know them. They're the really sick one. They're so good at being sick. They're sicker than everyone else I know."*** Will they think I'm fantastic because I was really good at being sick? Or would they pity me? And maybe, even a little bit, regard me with a degree of judgement? I don't want that to be the conversation people have about me. I want them to say ***"Oh yeah, I know them! They're so full of life! They light up the room when they walk in. They're honestly the NICEST person to be around. They make everyone feel so at ease and so welcome and so cared for. They GLOW."*** I do not want to chase sick enough anymore. <u>I want to chase *sparkly* enough.</u> I want to chase *happy* enough. I want to chase ALIVE *enough*.

My Key Affirmations:
- Your eating disorder is never going to let you think you are sick enough. The longer you are sick, the more malnourished your brain becomes and the less able you are to see logic. Less logic = more eating disorder = never sick enough.

- There is no scale of being sick enough. There is no badge or medal or trophy for being the sickest. If you are the sickest, you might just die.

- **You are SICKER than the PERSON YOU WANT TO BE. That is SICK ENOUGH.**

- The longer you stay sick in order to be valid, and in order to feel sick enough, the more life you lose. Your eating disorder is invalid. *You will, validly, be a survivor.* **You will, validly, be a warrior. You will, validly, be able to say: I overcame an eating disorder.**

- Anybody who knows that you had an eating disorder and considers that you were not sick enough is a person that you do not want in your life. Put them in the bin.

- I don't want people to talk about me and my one crowning accolade to be: OH YES THEY ARE THE SICKEST PERSON I KNOW. I want to be the MOST ALIVE person they know. The MOST SPARKLY person they know. Not the sickest.

23. REFRAMING MY LIFE

Even with all of those reframes, IT IS HARD. Even though I KNOW better, sometimes it can be hard to DO BETTER. It is EXHAUSTING to constantly wake up everyday and be inundated by those thoughts. It is TIRING to have to KEEP FIGHTING them ALL THE TIME. On bad days, it can feel like too much effort. It can feel like it would be easier, just for today, to give up a little bit. To listen to the thoughts, to let them wash over, to surrender. To decide that tomorrow, when you have rested, you will be able to fight the fight again.

But. What if tomorrow you feel the same? And the day after? You are going to be too tired to fight MOST days. Some days will be wonderful, and you'll be angry with the disorder and what it took from you, and you'll see the insanity of it all in CLEAR CUT

IMAGES. But most days won't be like this. And if you don't fight on the days that you need to fight, the days in which you *can* fight will slowly reduce. That's what happens.

It's like a weed. One day, you see one weed growing through the cracks and you are too tired to pull it up so you leave it there. The next day, there are two, three, but it's still not that bad, there's still loads of your lovely paved garden that ISN'T weedy. So you leave it. But then, one day, you go outside and your whole garden has been overrun by weeds and you have no idea how it happened. And now…you're far too tired to fight it now. It's taken control. The garden isn't yours anymore. So. When you see that ONE WEED, you need to pull it up. Not because it matters *right now* but because it WILL matter rather a lot in the future.

On those days where the weeds grow, pluck them. However hard it is, pluck them. And when you don't want to, when you feel like you can't, remember:

THIS IS FOR FUTURE ME.
THIS IS FOR THE FUTURE I WANT.

AND FOR THE ONE THAT I DON'T.

I AM DOING THE HARD THINGS WITH MY TODAYS SO THAT MY TOMORROWS CAN BE EASIER.

It can be quite hard to remember this at the moment, so I have found great value in really nailing down what I want my future to look like. Many of us say things like: "I want food freedom, I want to be normal, I want to be able to eat and move in the way that I want". But, at the time, when the goblin is loud, this doesn't sound *that* exciting.

It's too abstract, too vague. So I have sat and visualised how I want my life to look in extreme detail for a number of different moments. **These are the moments that my eating disorder has ruined for me. These are the moments that my eating disorder can still ruin for me.** I have thought about how I want my life to look and I have journalled it. I have reframed my life.

I encourage you to join me in this visualisation journey. And no, I'm not going to tell you to put on some instrumental music, light candles, sage the room, and focus on your breathing. Not that kind of visualisation. If you're into that, though, manifest away my darling. You do you. I'm a pragmatist though. I'm just gonna write it down. And the thing is, this won't happen all at once. You'll have a good idea of *some* of the things you want for the future. But some things will surprise you. Catch you off guard. **I, for example,**

didn't realise that I had an ideal vision for what my future TRIPS TO THE SUPERMARKET would look like until I caught myself anxiously comparing the energy content in JARS OF PICKLES. And you best bet, after that, I went home and I whacked out my journal and I planned what my future supermarket trips were going to look like.

Start with the obvious ones. And then whenever ANYTHING ELSE pops up, when you can, have a go at planning the future. Let's do this. Let's plan the lives we want. And we don't want eating disorder lives, trust me. Get out your pen. Write down what your life looks like *now* when it is controlled by your disorder: what does exercise look like? What do mornings look like? What do birthdays look like? Then, think about all the things you would change. Think about al the ways life would be better without the disorder. And then write down your *after*. What life are you aiming for *after* the disorder?

It's a before and after that *matters*. It's not a triggering *before* photo that makes you feel like you have to be really small to be valid with an *after* photo of you in a body that is still socially acceptable. **It's a *before* of a life that was really small. And it's an *after* of a life that is really large.**

Here are some of mine.

Exercise

Before:
When will I next go to the gym? Every day, obviously, but what time? Before work? After work? When will it be the least busy so that I definitely get to use the machines I want? Maybe I could go twice and train two different body parts. But I need to get my cardio in too. And my 10K steps. I'll run in the morning, then, and not sit down at work and then lift in the evening. I should buy some new workout clothes. If I have new workout clothes, maybe I will be more motivated and stop being so bloody lazy. I need to get some more protein products because I'm not gaining any muscle and I don't know why. They're so expensive. I don't really like them. But all the gym influencers eat them, and they look fab, and they seem to like them. Maybe they're an acquired taste and I just need to get used to them. It will be worth it, anyway, to look like them. Maybe I should try a new exercise programme? What workout split would be best? Maybe I should get a personal trainer? They're expensive but it would be an investment in myself, right? And they'll push me to stop being so lazy.

Everything revolves around exercise. I spend hours and hours on the Internet, googling exercises and workout splits and different diets for optimum performance. I read reviews of influencers workout programmes on social media. I spend so much money on new workout equipment and programmes and protein products, convinced that each new thing will suddenly change my body instantly. I spend hours doing exercise that I do not enjoy and do not want to be doing. I watch the clock, waiting for it to be over. I spend hours doing exercise that I am not adequately fuelled to even be able to do properly. **My body is not changing or getting stronger because it's overworked and underfuelled.** My mind hates every minute because I do not enjoy lifting. I am exhausted, worn down, aching, hungry and in pain. Always. I cancel plans so that I can go to the gym. I turn down invitations so that I can go to the gym. I lie to myself and tell myself that it's self-care. I don't need to socialise: I need to take care of my body and have some alone time. If I go out to eat with friends, or have a slip in self-control, I exercise more to burn it off. Cardio, of course, which I hate. But it's a necessary evil. Everyone knows cardio burns the most calories.

After:

Exercise exists in my life, but as something that fits around my life. I no longer live around my exercise schedule: there is no exercise schedule anymore. If someone invites me to dinner on a day where I sometimes exercise, I go to dinner. If I've had a long day at work, and just want pizza on the sofa, I just have pizza on the sofa. If I went away for the weekend and need time to just have an evening reset and do all my laundry, even if I didn't exercise in days, I won't exercise on Monday. If my friend invites me to go for a hike, and it's not raining, I'll go. I don't see this as part of any kind of exercise routine. It's just something I like to do, sometimes. If it's raining, though, I absolutely WILL NOT be caught outside walking. Instead, I'll be curled up on the sofa with a hot chocolate and a good book.

If there is a yoga class on and I'm feeling like my body wants a stretch, and I don't have too much else to do, I'll go. I love yoga: the way it makes me feel more present in my body; the way it gives me permission to change the poses or take a rest and slow down as my body asks for it; the way I feel my muscles relaxing and stretching and becoming stronger. I love the functional movement. I love the way it is about how my body FEELS and not how it LOOKS. I love how yoga class is full of people in all different bodies and all different abilities.

Sometimes, my body will tell me it wants to move. I feel the need to get up and use my muscles and so I will. But there's no structure to this. **If my body says move, I move. If my body says rest, I rest. I feel the best, physically, that I ever have.** My body is strong and capable - I can walk anywhere I need to, carry heavy shopping bags, touch my toes with ease, and sit without aches and pains. ***It doesn't look anything like a fit body, really, not an ab or rock solid bicep in sight, but it feels like one.*** And that's the important thing. Having visible abs isn't going to help me get fitter and stronger and more powerful. What will help me is being adequately fuelled, adequately rested and listening to my body.

I love exercise. I love my body for what it can do. And I love that I can wake up on a Sunday morning and stay in bed rather than rolling out into the cold air, pulling on a super tight matching set and forcing myself down to the gym. I love that I no longer feel exhausted and weak, and that my body no longer hurts everywhere from torn muscles and overwork. I love that I no longer miss out on my life because I feel the need to spend every second in a gym doing things I hate. Do I love my body? Not really, but I didn't before, either: and I don't think about it so much anymore. I used to think about it all the time when I was in the gym, looking at myself in the mirrors and comparing myself to all the people around me. Now, if I feel a niggle, I remind myself that I am so much stronger and healthier and happier and more free than I have ever been. And that's enough.

A Work Evening

Before:

The commute home from work is stressful every single day. I am tired, groggy and grumpy and other drivers infuriate me an insane amount. I feel shaky and irritable because I haven't eaten since 12pm, and the traffic is a nightmare. I feel tightly wound, like a spring that is about to pop up. Or a balloon that is seconds away from bursting. When I get in, I make dinner. It always takes a long time because it's always a recipe that uses a lot of whole ingredients and vegetables and I don't want to be using anything processed: sweet potato pizza, cauliflower pizza, vegetable stews and curries, cauliflower rice stir fry, ramen with konjac noodles. I sometimes wish I could just grab a ready meal but I know that would be bad for me. I usually spend about half an hour to an hour preparing dinner. **My eating always involves some complicated diet culture meal that is supposed to emulate something else but always falls short.** I pretend I like it. I hate myself for eating it anyway. I spend lots of time watching videos of other people eating, and searching up new recipes that I can make for lunch and dinner, exclusively using vegetables if possible. When I've eaten, I usually have to spend a good fifteen minutes cleaning up: eating clean requires SO MANY cooking utensils, it turns out.

I can never make spontaneous plans because they might interfere with my planned eating and exercise routine for the day. If friends text me to ask to go to a last minute dinner, or last minute yoga class, I say no: it would get in the way of my intricately planned out food and workout split schedule. I need more notice so that I can fit social events around the food and exercise plan. It's the only way to see progress: consistency and dedication. I go to the gym every night, even though I am always tired and sore. I am usually tired and crabby and unmotivated because of work, so I end up forcing my way through each workout, counting down the minutes until it is over and I can leave. I turn down plans if I already have them. Lie to myself and tell myself next time. I tell my friends it's because I am tired and had a long day and refuse to see the irony of the situation. When I get back, I usually spend half an hour or so preparing some complex recipe for lunch the next day. On a good day, that is. On a bad day, I binge and purge. Self-care is non-existent. I am often too tired to shower, wash my hair or even brush my teeth. I go to bed hungry.

After:

The commute home from work is annoying but I make it better with podcasts, biscuits and hot chocolate. I make the hot chocolate in my travel mug before I leave work - using the work hot chocolate and free water of COURSE. I keep biscuits in my glovebox: my traffic biscuits. I know that I'll be hungry before I get home, and biscuits make the perfect glove box snack. Easy to grab and eat; perfect to stabilise the blood sugar for safe driving; and FANTASTIC with hot chocolate. I almost enjoy it these days: now I'm no longer ravenously hungry, I find other drivers' annoyances merely amusing. I often think yeah fair enough mate, I've done that before too. The commute has become less of a race home to get food in me and more of a chance to unwind from the day before I get back.

I tend to have a loose idea of evening plans - I play netball once a week, go climbing on ladies night and whenever the urge strikes, and sometimes go to a class with a friend if I fancy it - but it all depends on how tired I am and how work was. Sometimes, a bad day makes me want to exercise to burn off some of the frustration but most of the time, it makes me want to curl up on the sofa with trashy teen TV. Sometimes, dinner is a nice, home cooked meal. Sometimes, it's a ready meal. Sometimes, it's a takeaway. It's never really planned out: I have a rough idea from whatever food I've got in the fridge but my body is pretty good at telling me what I fancy these days. If a friend texts to make last minute plans, or if I cannot be bothered to cook, I will chuck anything I was meant to eat into the freezer so that I can use it up later. I try to make plans often - the cinema, coffee with friends, a walk with my mum, DATES - but also will cancel them if I know I need a self-care evening. I try to meal prep lunches for the week at the weekend in one big batch so that I've got something ready to go and don't have to do it in the evening, but sometimes I get in from work and eat it for dinner. Then, I tend to do something easy: a meal deal, or a jam sandwich, or I'll grab and go from a cafe near work. I am often too tired to shower and wash my hair, so I tend to do it either when I get in, straight away, or in the morning. I always brush my teeth though. I have developed a routine: I have a playlist of appropriate length songs to brush my teeth to and we do a little boogie whilst we brush. A final bit of joy to end the day!

A Work Morning

Before:

I hate mornings. They suck. I have to wake up at 6am every day to fit in my morning routine. I am not a morning person so I always wake up to the blaring of my alarm: tired and groggy. How is it possible that I feel more tired than before I went to sleep? I always go straight to the bathroom and pee, and then weigh myself. Every morning without fail. **Usually I am disappointed: if it's gone up; if it's stayed the same; if it's not gone down enough. I start the day feeling bad about myself.** But what option is there? I can't weigh myself at night as I will be full of food and liquid so it won't be accurate.

I roll my yoga mat out on the floor. I like to start the day with a 20 minute core workout: I used to intend to do my core workouts at the end of my normal workout but I would never have the motivation left at that point to actually do it. Instead, I do it in the morning: they say start the day as you mean to go on. That way, even if something happens that means I don't do my workout later, at least I've trained my core. I hate it though. I push through the 20 minutes, wondering if anyone in the whole world actually enjoys working out their core. When I'm done I take a couple of progress photos in the mirror because they say that's the best way to track changes, not weight because it fluctuates too much. When my core is trained, I put the yoga mat away and pull on jogging bottoms and a baggy t-shirt. I grab my headphones, put them on and head out the door. Walking in the morning is good for your circadian rhythms or something. I do it mostly because I know I'll be sitting down for most of the morning, first driving and then at work, and I know that my body needs to move. **Can't become one of these people that uses their desk job as an excuse for letting themselves go.** I walk in the rain. I walk in the snow. I don't eat breakfast before any of this because a) fasted exercise burns more fat and b) the longer I delay breakfast, the later I'll get hungry for lunch.

I always have 20 minutes when I get back to the flat before I need to leave. I'm so tired all I want to do is crawl back into bed but…work. Ugh. Gazing in the mirror, I realise I look very pale and have dark circles - I need to get some better sleep quality. I throw some foundation and blush over my face in a bid to look more alive and get dressed. I glug two cups of tea and scarf down a bowl of porridge with strawberries and sugar-free syrup, weighed to the last oat, grab my meal-prepped cauliflower rice or soup or stew for lunch, and head out the door. I'm only ten minutes into the commute before my stomach starts rumbling again. Goddamn the bottomless pit, why is nothing ever enough?

After:
I wake up slightly before my alarm which is set to 7.30am. I get a full seven hours of sleep these days, which for me seems like something of a miracle. **I was convinced that I was just an insomniac and that sleep was something I was bad out: it turned out that sleep is disrupted by hunger and malnourishment, and that forcing myself awake at 6am (as well as drinking 3l of caffeine to get through the day) was disrupting my sleep rhythms.** I lie in bed, waiting for the alarm to go off. No need to get up before I need to. I stretch and yawn, check my phone. Nothing exciting. My stomach rumbles so I sit up and pull my fluffy bed socks on. I turn the alarm off so it doesn't start blaring at me and pad into the kitchen. I yawn. I gaze into the cupboards. What do I want? Pancakes? Toast? Porridge? I make whatever sounds good.

I sit down to eat my breakfast with a crossword book. I'm like an old lady, but nothing is more enjoyable to me in the morning than waking my brain up with a yummy meal and a crossword. Nerd. But when you spent years with a brain that didn't work half right, operating off sheer adrenaline and insanity, the novelty of being able to use your brain again doesn't wear off easily.

Work mornings are slower now: I wake up gently, eat breakfast straight away, shower if I need to. Sometimes I do some stretching if my body feels tight. If it's sunny, I might go for a 20 minute stroll to get some fresh air. Other mornings, I'll just lay about on the sofa browsing the internet until it's time to go. No regimented routine. Work mornings should be as gentle as possible to prepare for the hectic rush of the day. **My mornings aren't regimented or routined: I go with the flow. They're almost nice. I'm almost a morning person now. Almost.**

A Trip To The Cinema

Before:

Life looks like a whole lot of anxiety both before, during and after. The cinema is always a struggle for me because of the time spent sitting down. Rather than seeing it as time to relax, I see it as being lazy. I worry about the impact it will have on my body. I spend the morning before I go to the cinema walking. I'm going to be sitting down for hours in the evening, so I need to make sure that I get my daily movement in before that. It's also good to be out in the fresh air when you're going to be cooped up inside for hours. I know these are all just disordered justifications. I know I don't want to be walking for three hours. I hate walking. It's boring. I know there are hundreds of other things I would rather be doing. But. I want to go to the cinema. So I need to make sure that the activities won't make me gain weight. This is what balance is I tell myself. This is what people say online. This is my 80%. Dinner and the cinema is my 20%.

People often want to get food before or after the cinema: it becomes a whole EVENT, dinner and a movie. If there is food involved, I eat as little as possible beforehand as there is no way of predicting the actual calories AND I'll be sitting down and not burning energy straight after eating. **I hate the popcorn at the cinema. I hate how good it smells, and how good it tastes, and how much I want to eat it.** I hate how high in calories and salt and sugar it is. I hate that it's not good for you. I hate that it will make me fat. I hate that the people I am with can eat it, and try to make me eat it, every time we go. People always get popcorn to share. And then I spend the next two hours unable to focus on the film because they are sat right next to me, with the popcorn, and it smells so good and they keeps offering it to me, so I take some and pretend to eat it and then spit it out and throw it on the floor and the whole thing just feels so messed up and icky and horrible and I hate myself because I should just be able to eat the popcorn, and burn it off later, but I can't make myself do it. It's like being in hell. The smell of the popcorn. The buttery salty texture in my fingers. The taste explosion when I put it in my mouth. My stomach thinks it's coming. Salivating. Then I take it out.

I am never really able to watch the film properly as I am always stressed about the popcorn, and the sitting still, and the desire to get up and move, and the feeling of dinner sitting in my stomach. My brain is unable to focus on things for any length of time either as I'm always so tired and scatty and hungry, so I never really enjoy the films. It's hard to enjoy something when you don't understand what's going on, keep missing whole chunks, and are in popcorn purgatory. I almost resent my family or friends for putting me through it. And I also resent them for being able to enjoy it. **And, ultimately, I resent my body. If it were able to be normal, and just have control and eat like a normal person without it turning into bingeing and ballooning in weight, I would be able to enjoy it too.**

After the film, I go home and search the internet for what on earth happened so that when people ask me about it at work I can tell them. I could hardly say: no idea because I spent so long throwing popcorn on the floor and wandering to the toilet that I entirely missed the plot.

After:

I look forwards to going to the cinema in the days leading up to it now. Sometimes I watch the trailers on YouTube to really get in the mood. Life doesn't look any different before I go to the cinema. I go about my normal day: if it's a work day, I go to work. Eat breakfast, lunch, snacks and dinner. If it's a weekend day, I go about my plans: reading, resting, brunch or yoga with friends, maybe some rock climbing or a dance class. Eat breakfast, lunch, snack and dinner. Sometimes, we go for dinner before the cinema.I tend to go to the shop just down the road from the cinema and buy some drinks to take in because the £4 for a cup of lemonade is extortion. I also think the popcorn is extortionate too but it's worth it: you cannot get the pure joy from bagged popcorn as you get from the freshly popped cinema stuff. The sweet, salty, buttery crunchy JOY. I usually get a large popcorn to share, or a medium one of my own. There's usually someone there who says they don't want any and don't get any of their own because it's "naughty" or "they're not hungry" and they always end up trying to eat some of mine. **I am not mean enough to deprive a diet culture victim of a popcorn hit so I share, always. It's almost like healing the past me, who threw her popcorn on the floor.**

I watch the whole film without going to the toilet five or six times these days. It makes it much easier to understand what is actually going on when you don't keep leaving and missing critical details. It makes it much easier to understand a film when you are watching it, and thinking about it, rather than spinning around in your head about MOVEMENT and POPCORN CALORIES and FEELING LAZY. And the general cognitive decline that just makes it harder to use your brain properly anyway. I love going to work after watching a film and doing a debrief with the other cinema goers. There are some real film nerds at work - I'm not one of them - and so it can be really funny to give them my "uneducated" opinions and watch them froth at the mouth. It's funny because I don't watch films at home - I always say they're too long and I don't like sitting for that long which is true. But there's something about the cinema EXPERIENCE that just appeals to me. Maybe it's because we always used to go as a treat, or a birthday party, when we were kids. It has that exciting nostalgic vibe. And popcorn. It has popcorn. And, halfway through, when you've finished your smuggled drinks…ice blasts.

My Love Life

Before:

I don't have a love life. I need to be thinner before I can be loved: nobody is going to love me in this bigger body. Everyone knows that only thin people are attractive and, these days, in the tough old world of dating apps, there is too much choice for a bigger person to get many matches. There are so many skinny people on them that there is no point in me going on those until I'm small enough to compete. I know this is true, too, because I *did* go on a few dates with this one guy and we ended up going home together one night. I thought we had a great night but then he ghosted me: the only thing that changed was that he had finally seen my naked body. I was clearly so disgusting that I put him off. It's not really fair of me to keep dating when I'm still in a body that would put people off even texting me back or making up some lame excuse for why it wasn't going to work.

I did try to date, a while back. I went on a bunch of dates with a few different people and really tried to make it work for a good few months. But it wasn't helping me lose weight: normally, they suggested going out for drinks for the first date. If it got past the first date, it would then be food. How are you supposed to lose weight when you are having WASTED LIQUID CALORIES in alcohol? And when you're going out for dinner several times a week? It's a shame, really, but dating isn't compatible with weight loss. **I also wasn't ENJOYING the dates because I was stressed about the weight gain possibilities.** And when I had a disappointing date (which, let's be real, was most of them) it then all felt like THE BIGGEST WASTE OF CALORIES ANYWAY. I had broken from my gym routine, wasted a day of progress, ingested things that weren't good for my body and FOR WHAT? To go home and cry about how I was going to be alone forever AGAIN. Nothing good was coming out of trying to have a love life.

I just needed to put it all on hold until a) I was in a better body and b) I had lost the weight and gained more self-control over my eating so that a few drinks and dinner would not derail all of my progress and therefore be a waste of time when the dates didn't go anywhere.

After:
I don't have a love life. Actually, that's not true. I'm not in a relationship: yet. But that's because I KNOW what I want out of a relationship now. I have been on lots of dates with lots of lovely people, and I have figured out what I am looking for in a partner and a relationship. And that's beautiful. **I am aware that the size of my body has NOTHING to do with how attractive I am. I exist in a bigger body than I did the last time I was dating and get just as much attention, if not more.** But also I am aware that if

someone would only want to be with me because I am skinny then they are NOT the kind of person I want to be with. *I do not look at my date's body size when I am considering if I want to see them again: I think about if we had chemistry, if they made me laugh, if they were funny, if we had similar interests, and if they treated me well.* And those are the things I want my dates to choose to see me again based on.

I am able to be present on the dates now, too. I am not tired, hungry, cold and irritable so I am giving these people far more of a chance that I ever did before. **It makes me feel bad, really, the number of poor people that I dismissed as not right for me or bad dates when, in reality, it was probably ME just being too disengaged with them to really get to know them.** Not to mention the number of people that turned ME down, likely because *I was so dull, boring and glassy eyed that they felt like spending more time with me would be like squeezing blood from a stone.*

And…sometimes I get a free dinner out of it! I ALWAYS try to split the bill but if the other person insists…who am I to say no? It's wild to me that I used to resent people buying me dinner. Now, as an adult who is spending TOO MUCH MONEY ON HER FOOD BILL, it's incredibly welcome.

Dates that don't go well are now no longer "failures" as I now no longer fixate on the fact that I consumed calories when I didn't need to. **Because I need calories to live and I need calories from nice food and alcohol to live a full and fun life.** Instead, I now see every date I go on as an opportunity to learn something new and chat to people I wouldn't normally get to chat to. I have, after all, always BEEN a people person. Just, deep in my ED, I forgot who I was. I saw dates as nothing more than TRYING TO FIND THE PERFECT PERSON and if I didn't find them then it was a WASTE OF EXERCISE TIME AND CALORIES. How silly. Last week, I went on a date with a lovely man who explained the Wall Street Crash to me. I've never understood it, but now I do. I'm sure, if I had gone on that date a year ago, I still wouldn't understand it: my brain was too malnourished and would have been trying to calculate the calories in the extra rocket that they had added on top of the pizza.

And I also know that if I end up going home with someone, and they don't call me back, it could be for many reasons: maybe they were only ever after that one thing; maybe they heard from their ex; maybe we were incompatible in bed; maybe they got crushed to death by a meteor; or maybe they didn't find me attractive. **If they didn't find me attractive, it's not because there is an issue with my body. It's just because different people are attracted to different things.** And I would never want to be with someone who wasn't attracted to me anyway, so that's okay. If I end up going home with someone, and they don't call me back, that's okay. Their loss. Why would they not want a gal full of sparkle and pizzazz?! If I am too much for someone, I invite them to go and find someone who is less.

A Sunday

Before:

Every Sunday, I wake up to my 6am alarm. I don't lie in, ever, because that messes with your sleep schedule. Having a sleep schedule is very important for weight loss. If you don't get enough sleep, your body holds on to weight. And, if you lie in, that's unproductive. The weekends are the only time you get WHOLE DAYS to be productive. I wake up at 6am. I get out of bed straight away and usually have a couple of cups of tea to get some caffeine in and still my stomach. Then, I do my laundry and hoover and clean the flat. After that, I go for a walk. It's important to get my steps in on Sundays because I go to my mum's house for dinner so I need to make sure I mitigate most of the damage of the Sunday roast. I usually walk for two hours. It's a lovely time to walk because everyone else is still in bed and so there are no other annoying pedestrians and cars on the road. I can go as quickly as I like.

I get home from my walk and have a pre-workout snack: usually a bowl of low fat, high protein yoghurt for protein and some fruit for the carbs. Then, I head to the gym. Sundays are good days for the gym as I have more time so I usually do full body: half an hour on legs, half an hour on upper body, half an hour on abs, and have an hour on glutes. Midway through, I stop for an energy drink. Sweaty and sore, I head to the supermarket and do my food shop for the week. That's an extra few thousand steps as I walk up and down every aisle.

Then, I usually spend a couple of hours watching videos and researching new healthy eating plans and WHAT I EAT IN A WEEK videos. I know it's not a good or productive use of my time to lay on the sofa aimlessly browsing the internet but I can't make myself stop. I've always got this idea in my head that if I don't keep my finger on the pulse, I might miss some key piece of information about health and fitness. I might miss the miracle weight loss solution.

Finally, I drive to my mum's house. We have a family roast together every Sunday. Other people might think it was a wholesome activity but I find it very stressful. If she cooked the roast in a health conscious way, it would be fine but she doesn't. She covers the potatoes in oil. She fills the mash with butter. SHE EVEN COVERS THE VEGETABLES IN OIL. The gravy is the high sodium kind. Nightmare. And, there's always dessert: chocolate cake, rocky road, or brownie. As if we hadn't just eaten enough food already! I hate it, too, because she gets all angry and stressed and says that I'm not eating enough if I don't finish my plate or say that I don't want dessert. So I end up having to eat it all anyway, and I hate it. It's the opposite of intuitive eating: I have to force myself to eat past the point of being stuffed to placate her. It's awful. I hate every bite. I try to console myself that it's okay because I haven't eaten much all day in preparation but that doesn't make it much easier. I'm sure the way she cooks it means that it's more than anyone's full daily allowance of calories, anyway.

The evening then goes one of two ways, depending on my willpower. The food sits in my stomach, refusing to digest. I am heavy, bloated and look pregnant. Some weeks, I go for a run. It's uncomfortable and gross and I'm slow and sluggish, but at least it feels better than sitting there with the food like a rock in my stomach. Then, I take some laxatives. And Monday morning, I make sure to eat a little less than other days, just to make sure everything is accounted for. Other weeks, I just need to get the food out of me there and then. So I do. And then, because I've purged, I decide I might as well do it again. And I end up ordering hundreds of pounds of food from local takeaways, or going to the local corner shop and buying everything I can lay my hands on. I eat for hours. Then I get rid. **Either way, all Sundays end the same: me, tired, exhausted, gross and full of shame. Full of shame for not being able to say no to eating all of that roast dinner. Full of shame for the lack of willpower that meant I had to run and take laxatives, or had to purge to get rid of the excess food.** Pathetic.

After:

I think Sundays might be my favourite day of the week. They are just so peaceful because nobody really expects you to DO anything. They are FREE and FUN days. I've started doing my food shop on a Friday evening, and my laundry and cleaning periodically through the week, so that I can spend my whole weekends NOT doing ANYTHING OTHER THAN WHAT I WANT. I tend to have a small lie in on Sundays, if my body asks for it. Mostly, I wake up at 7.30am every day because my body has found a natural schedule and I wake up before my alarm. It's amazing how regular my sleep is now, and how much better it is: I no longer have to force myself awake, I no longer wake up more tired than before, groggy and grumpy and angry. Some weeks, though, if it's been busy or stressful or work, or if I've gone out more, or moved more, the weekends are a perfect opportunity to get those extra hours in. It figures that if you move more, or stress more, or do more, your body would need more rest to repair those things. In that case, having a lie in isn't lazy or unproductive: in fact, it's very productive as it means your body can get itself back to its healthiest version rather than going into a new week still tired and drained.

As I don't have to get to work, I will usually lie in bed for half an hour or so, scrolling on my phone. **People say you shouldn't do that, but I don't care: it's relaxing and I enjoy it. I'm over forcing myself to live a life that I don't enjoy. If I want to scroll for half an hour on Sunday morning, wrapped up in my duvet, then I will!** When I peel myself out of bed, I make a breakfast that takes more time as I have more time: French Toast or pancakes! Every other week or so, I head out for breakfast with my step dad or my grandparents and I usually get some form of vegetarian cooked breakfast. Sundays don't really follow a pattern anymore: some weeks, I go for a breakfast; some weeks I go for a stroll in the park with friends; some weeks I go to the library and replace my books; some weeks I wake up hungover and spend the day in bed; some weeks I have outings planned to fun places.

I still go to my mum's house for a roast most Sundays. I look forward to it all week, really: I love a roast dinner but am far too lazy to make all the components myself! And, I love seeing my family. It's no longer stressful: now it's SO BLOODY WHOLESOME. Me and my sister lie on the sofa chatting and catching up whilst the smell of gravy and roasting potatoes drifts through into the living room. If the weather is good, we all go for a little family stroll through the countryside. If it's bad, we watch old reruns of Come Dine With Me and Four In The Bed. I never used to enjoy these pre-dinner activities because I was STARVING and just focussed on WHEN WILL DINNER BE READY. Now, though, I love them because I've eaten enough throughout the day to have the energy to engage and join in. When dinner comes, it's delicious. I eat what I want - which is usually all of it - and if I am too full to finish, nobody comments anymore. There's no need to worry about me now. **My family no longer scrutinises everything I eat. They are no longer convinced my heart is going to give out at any moment. The barely veiled tension is gone.** I eat and love dessert. And the food doesn't sit around painfully in my stomach for hours. Because I've been eating regularly throughout the day, and the week, my digestive system sets to work properly now. It knows what to do now. It knows that it can digest the food, because more will always be coming. It knows it needs to digest the food because I won't be doing anything to get rid of it.

I hang around at my mum's house after dinner, too. I used to shoot off to exercise or purge. But now, I lie around in the living room, doing crosswords with my mum and sister, or watching TV again. Eventually, I peel myself away and go home. Sometimes, I do a bit of yoga before bed and then make sure I've got my work clothes and bag ready. Then, I snuggle up in bed with a good book and a hot chocolate. Bliss.

Going On Holiday
Before:

I spend the weeks in the lead up to going on a holiday feeling incredibly frazzled. I don't feel excited, either: I feel dread. For many reasons. First, the obvious: everyone gains weight on holiday. There's just SO MUCH FOOD and there's never any way of knowing how many calories you are consuming. People just sit around eating, like it's an activity. Being on holiday also seems to give people this free pass to eat even when they aren't hungry, which is just so weird. Sounds disordered to me. And then you can't go to the gym as much, if it all. People start making comments if you go to the gym on holiday, like you should just stop looking after yourself just because you're away for a few days? I hate it. Then, there's the CLOTHES. The universal assumption that you should wear a bikini at the beach. Especially these days: everyone is shouting EVERY BODY IS A BIKINI BODY from the rooftops and so if you don't wear one, people assume you hate your body and are vain. And other clothes too: in hot countries, you have to wear less. **The last thing I want is people seeing my body: the rolls of my stomach, my huge upper arms, my chunky thighs.** I spend hours browsing the Internet looking for clothes. This doesn't help much as all of the models are stick thin and gorgeous and so the clothes look better on them than they do on me when they arrive, and they just trigger me all the more. In the hours where I'm not shopping, I'm exercising. I always increase my workout routine and throw in a few beach body and bikini ready workouts. They're easy enough to add in as they're usually only about 10 to 20 minutes long so I do a few a day.

The holiday itself is always the opposite of relaxing. I get up early, hours before everyone else, to get my steps in before the day begins. I do core workouts on the hard floor of the hotel bathroom. Every time we go out to eat, I am stressed. First, everyone takes so long deciding where they want to go. Then, when we eventually get somewhere, there's loads of faffing and chatting and reading the menu for HOURS. I hate sitting down for such a long time: it's lazy and unnecessary and I want to get up and MOVE, get some steps in to at least burn off SOME of the food. I try to eat the lowest calories options but even the salads come drenched in oils and covered in nuts and seeds. People comment, of course, go on, have the chips, you're on holiday! I want to scream at them: DO YOU NOT KNOW HOW EASILY I GAIN WEIGHT? IT'S EASY FOR YOU TO SAY BUT IF I EAT FRIES EVERY DAY FOR A WEEK, I'LL GAIN A STONE! Wherever possible, I do try to skip meals. I don't eat breakfast: I say I feel nauseous in the morning. **Instead, I sit drinking my tea and envying my friends or family as they eat flaky pastries and juicy, fresh fruit or perfectly cooked eggs and sourdough with melted butter pooling on top…**There's also not many good options for lean protein so I'm worried about muscle preservation. I've got a bunch of protein bars with me but I'm reluctant to eat them as that would be adding calories in when that's the last thing I need to be doing.

The day to day activities aren't enjoyable to me because I'm tired, lethargic and grumpy from eating so much unhealthy and heavy food. I can't focus on anything. Getting dressed each morning is horrible. I stand in front of the hotel mirror, looking at my exposed body, hating every part of it. During the day, I insist on taking most of the photos. I don't need photographic evidence of my chunky body on holiday. When we go to the beach, I spend the whole time hiding under a towel.

The best part about the holiday is going home. I tell myself it's because I'm a homebody and I love my routine. I'm not sure if any of that is true, but I do know that I hate going on holiday. I never weigh myself when I get home. It's the only time I resist the urge. Instead, as soon as I get in my flat, I take some laxatives, unpack my clothes and go straight to the gym. I weigh myself the next morning, assess the damage and formulate a plan to drop the weight again.

After:

I spend the weeks in the lead up to going on a holiday feeling a little frazzled. There's so much to do! I like to research the place I am going to and make sure that I've booked and planned all of the fun activities that I want to do. **I like to read up on the best local restaurants to go to, and the best places to go for cocktails, and the best places to get dessert.** Then there's clothes shopping: I don't want to buy a whole new wardrobe for holiday as that's wasteful and how I look is the LEAST important part but my wardrobe is NOT a hot weather one. I live in England, okay! Charity shops are my best friend; and borrowing clothes off friends. This is a new concept for me: I would never have said yes to sharing clothes before because I was so convinced that I was so much bigger than everyone else. But now I see my body more realistically. Anyway, my friends are ANGELS and we let each other just try stuff on to see if it fits. **And if it doesn't fit...it doesn't fit. It doesn't mean anything other than that the piece of clothing is not the right size.** As I surround myself with good people, nobody comments or judges anyone else on their ability to fit into an item of clothing because that's stupid anyway. I don't do any extra exercise or movement in preparation for holidays as I've realised now that those "get bikini ready in three weeks" programmes are a con anyway. It's not possible to change your body that fast and, if it is, IT ISN'T HEALTHY. I've come to value my health far more than the size of my body. Anyway, I was never in any holiday photos anyway when I had my "holiday body" so what was the POINT? Plus, I remind myself: if I spend the time in the lead up to the holiday EXHAUSTING MYSELF, I'll be too tired when I finally get there to have a good time and do everything that I want.

Holidays are beautiful now. I lie in, enjoying the comfort of the squishy hotel bed and wishing I had a queen sized bed at home. I start the day slowly, with fresh juice from the hotel bar, or hot chocolate on the balcony, or tea in the gardens overlooking the sea. I don't skip meals, or choose the lowest calorie option on the menu. Instead, I choose what I want. Some days, I want fries. Other days, I do want the salad - especially if it's really warm. But usually with a side of fresh sourdough. I try local delicacies. Foods I've never heard of before, let alone eaten. I discover new favourites. And things I will never put in my mouth ever again. I eat dessert and I drink cocktails.

During the day, I do fun things: exploring, hiking, swimming, going to the beach, going on adventure trails, sightseeing and, sometimes, just laying around in the sun with a good book. I do lots of walking, too, around the local area and on the trips: but I have no idea HOW much because I'm no longer tracking it to the step. I almost get a tan from lying on the beach. Almost. The factor 50 gets in the way a bit but it's necessary. I'm in ALL the photos now: I insist on it. I did NOT spend all that time before the holiday planning outfits and thrifting and borrowing clothes to NOT show social media how cute I look. **Sometimes, I look at the photos and think things like my arms look big or I wish I could be smaller but then I remind myself: I would rather have bigger arms and a bigger body than a small life. I would rather have big arms and BIG FUN on holiday than little, weak arms and <u>spend a whole holiday waiting to go home and starve again.</u>**

The best part about the holiday is…being on holiday. Spending time with my family or friends. Making new memories. Trying new foods. Doing new things. Laughing. Feeling the sun on my skin. Feeling free. Relaxing. Being on the go. Exploring. Seeing new things. Recharging. I enjoy going home, too, and doing all my laundry and eating a trusty bowl of porridge and finding routine again. I enjoy all parts of my life. The holiday and the homecoming. Neither one of them means restriction and suffering anymore. Both are freedom. Both are happy and safe.

I don't weigh myself when I get home. I don't have a scale. And it's inconsequential.

Christmas

Before:

I used to love Christmas, but not anymore. The whole month of December becomes a health-conscious person's worst nightmare. Every time you go into the staff room at work, there are biscuits and cakes and chocolates and sweets. People are inviting you out to dinner and drinks practically every night. Friends are inviting you to Friendmas.

People give you gifts: boxes of chocolate and bottles of wine. Everyone talks about how they're going to eat whatever they want for now and then go on a diet in January. And there's some kind of weird expectation that you wear hideous Christmas jumpers, big, baggy sacks that don't flatter anyone. **December has been ruining my progress for about five years.** Every time it comes around, I tell myself that this year will be different. I will resist all of the sweet foods and I will say no to MOST of the dinners and drinks and when I do go I will make sensible choices. I tell myself that Christmas is JUST ONE DAY so there is NO NEED to completely fall off the diet and exercise wagon for an entire month. I try my best. I avoid the staffroom. I choose salads and lean proteins at restaurants. Tell everyone I'm on medication that means I can't drink. I increase my gym routine to twice a day to counteract the extra socialising. I throw away or regift any food or alcohol gifts that people give to me. But it never works. I always crumble. **I find myself standing in the staffroom, shovelling in a whole box of gingerbread.** I come home from my dinner of salad and order the Christmas Curry from my local takeaway and eat all four portions. I cave and have "just one wine" which turns into six and a whole greasy pizza. In the car on the way home from work, I find myself mindlessly unwrapping gifted chocolates and shoving them in. I hate myself for it. No self control. No regard for my health. I am pathetic. I counteract these binges in the only ways I know how: purging, laxatives and exercise. It's miserable but there's no other option.

The holiday itself is just as bad as the run up. I used to go and stay with my family for about a week around Christmas time, but now I try to keep it to two nights: Christmas Eve and Christmas Day. That way, I can get back to my diet and exercise routine and mitigate any damage as quickly as possible. Before I go over there, I go to the gym and go on a few really long walks, just to make sure that I'm in as big of a deficit as possible. On Christmas Eve, my family and I have a tradition where we watch a movie and eat snacks. I spend the whole thing anxiously trying to pretend I'm eating the same amount of popcorn and chocolate and crisps as everyone else without triggering my own urges to just SHOVE IT ALL IN. I say no to the hot chocolate everyone is drinking, citing the fact that it will stop me from sleeping. When everyone else is in bed, I do a quick 30 minutes core workout, following a YouTube video on my phone.

Christmas Day is the worst. It starts with breakfast: croissants and hot chocolate and toast with butter. Then we do stockings and there's this expectation that everyone just starts eating the chocolate right away even though we JUST ate breakfast and CANNOT POSSIBLY BE HUNGRY. Next, presents. I try my best to look happy and grateful when I open the chocolate and sweets. By this point, I'm getting antsy: I hate being cooped up inside and it's been hours. My mum goes into the kitchen and begins the task of cooking the roast. I offer to help her in a bid to try and make there be less oil in the dinner, but she says no: she always does. My siblings are in the living room, playing video games. I ask them if they want to come for a walk and they look at me like I'm insane: we go for a walk AFTER Christmas Lunch they say. **They invite me to join them. I say no. I go for a walk alone.** I walk past loads of families, all bundled up in coats and scarves and mittens, smiling and laughing and chatting. *I feel a twinge. I should be with my family. But I can't make myself go back.*

Christmas Lunch is always put in the middle of the table and we get to serve ourselves. I make sure to give myself mostly vegetables - but even then I know this isn't healthy as they're all drenched in oil and butter. I allow myself a spoonful of mashed potato and a stuffing ball. No pigs in blankets for me because I'm currently vegetarian. They smell so good though. We eat. Everyone is pulling crackers and talking about life and drinking Prosecco or gin and lemonade. Everyone is so happy and loud and full of life. **I feel like I'm watching an advert on TV: like I'm watching a family have fun, but I'm not part of it. I'm tired. I feel like I'm underwater, like my hearing is dull and muted, like I can't be heard properly.** Like I can't hear properly. Like I'm not really there. I focus on putting the vegetables in my mouth. Chew. Swallow. I try not to feel my stomach squishing into folds as I sit. I try to ignore the clammy feeling of my thighs sticking together. I try to ignore the uncomfortable fullness building in my stomach from eating so much food at once.

After lunch, we help clean up. There's still heaps of leftover stuffing and potatoes and pigs in blankets and I have to stop myself mindlessly eating them as I walk past them. They make my mouth water. Then, we go for our walk. I don't enjoy this walk. My family are walking too slowly, they may as well be crawling. **There's no way they're burning off ANY dinner at the pace they're going at. I walk in front to build up a bit of speed.** Everytime I turn around, they're trailing and I have to stop and wait for them to catch up. I can feel the food in my stomach, heavy and fattening. Why did there have to be so much oil? When we get home, Mum brings out the chocolate log. Nobody is hungry but IT'S CHRISTMAS so we HAVE TO HAVE DESSERT. I force it down. I can barely taste it. I feel sweaty and swollen and big.

I go to the bathroom for a while. Then, I spend the rest of the day feeling ashamed. Who does that on Christmas day? My mother spent a lot of money and time and effort and planning to produce a delicious Christmas roast that I couldn't even have the decency to enjoy or keep down. I look at myself in the mirror. <u>**Red face, streaming eyes, glassy, sweaty, clammy, spotty skin, thinning hair. I don't recognise myself. At that moment, none of this feels worth it.**</u> I hate myself. I can hear my family downstairs, still laughing and chatting and being happy. None of them care that they just ate a roast dinner and cake. None of them are in the bathroom doing depraved and disgusting things. Still, I tell myself. It's nearly over. Soon Christmas will be over and life will be normal again.

When I get home on Boxing Day to my cold, empty flat, I feel empty. I put my gym clothes on and head to the gym. I'll weigh myself in the morning.

After:

I love Christmas. I love it so much. The fact that there is a WHOLE MONTH dedicated to family and friends and fun and SPARKLY LIGHTS and PRESENTS and JOY! The dream. I am one of these people that wears Christmas jumpers for the whole of December: I've got the most wonderful collection. And the beautiful thing? People look at me and they say "oh I love that jumper" or "you look so cheerful" or they SMILE at the silly jumper. They don't look at me and say "you look fat in that jumper, it's not very flattering". And if anyone DID say that, I would tell them they weren't my kind of person! Imagine. Luckily I'm not friends with anyone who would look at a Christmas jumper on someone's body and think anything other than HOW HAPPY.

December is busy for me now, but in a different way. I'm not busy trying to avoid food and people whilst attending to a rigid gym schedule. **I'm busy going to all of the parties and meals and Friendmas events. I'm busy buying presents and hand making cards and trying to learn how to bake. I'm busy experimenting with new Christmassy recipes: cranberry and chocolate orange porridge; stuffing and pigs in blankets pasta bake; gingerbread muffins. I'm busy going to cafes and trying the new seasonal drinks rather than standing outside, gazing at the pictures like some sad ghost who cannot drink liquid.** I'm so busy that I'm probably doing the number of steps my former self would have approved of, but the difference is that now I don't know, and now I don't care. And now, I get home after a busy day of party hopping and Christmas shopping and lay on the sofa to watch Elf, rather than going to the gym and forcing my tired, hungry body to do things it doesn't want to do. The staffroom is no longer a place of fear. Instead, I creep down there like some overgrown mouse to check out the goods. And the funny thing is, now that I allow myself to eat whatever I want, whenever I want, I find that I do not want to devour everything that is in there every single day. One day, I may fancy one of the gingerbread men. The next day, a handful of chocolates. On Wednesday, if there are mince pies, I definitely will NOT be partaking in those. <u>There is no need, anymore, for me to eat nothing or everything. I can just eat what I want.</u>

When people give me gifts of chocolate and cake and food and alcohol, IT'S MINE NOW. I am grateful. It makes me feel a bit icky that I used to RESENT people for giving me things. They were using food to show me love and appreciation, and I was taking it and tossing it in the bin. Now I can accept their love. And I can eat those truffles. I do regift the fruity chocolates, though. Nobody has any business putting fruit puree in chocolate. No thank you.

I go and stay with my family for a few days. That means I can go and visit friends, and my grandparents, and also spend some time actually chilling. Life is so GO GO GO and Christmastime is the perfect opportunity to bundle up on the sofa with a film and a hot chocolate. On Christmas Eve, we watch movies. I drink hot chocolate, eat popcorn, crisps and sweets. I laugh with my family. On Christmas Day, I eat pastries and fruit for breakfast. I eat my chocolate coins straight from my stocking. Shriek with joy when my mum gives me this new lemon meringue flavoured chocolate I've been looking for in shops for AGES. Give and receive gifts. My mum goes off to cook the roast and it smells DELICIOUS. My siblings and I play MarioKart. We're doing a tournament. I lose. I always lose. **My sister says: are you going for a walk? We laugh. We can laugh about it now. It's the PAST. It's OVER.** We eat Christmas lunch. I have everything. And then I have seconds: but only mashed potato, sprouts, stuffing and gravy. A killer combination. My mum says she will save the rest to make Bubble and Squeak on Boxing Day. We used to do that when we were kids but I haven't had it in years because I would always go home as soon as possible after Christmas was over. But bubble and squeak, fried eggs and ketchup…I can't wait. I'm drinking pink gin. We all get a bit giggly.

I go to the bathroom. I look in the mirror. My stomach is full, and bloated. I look a little pregnant. I touch the stretched skin and feel a familiar twist. Then I look at my face. **My skin is pink and flushed. My eyes are sparkling. My skin is clear, smooth, shining: it is distinctly NOT grey. I don't have dark circles or burst blood vessels. My hair is long and thick, not a bald patch in sight. I've walked up the stairs without getting out of breath. I can see the muscles of my arms and shoulders. I am strong. I am healthy. I am happy.** I pull my jumper back down. Go to the toilet. Go downstairs. Eat my chocolate log. The moment has passed. Healthy is better. The days pass in a blur of happiness: I feel full and content. Full of food, and happiness, and love, and laughter. I weigh more than I ever have. Well, I assume I do because I wear bigger clothes now: I don't weigh myself. I know I am bigger. But I'm happier than I've ever been.

Food Shop

Before:

I don't need to make a shopping list. I know everything that I need to buy off by heart now. Vegetables. Fruit. Spinach. Zero fat yoghurt. Rice cakes. Almond milk. Egg whites. Low carb wraps. Oats. Miracle Noodles. Diet Cola. Diet Lemonade. Diet Energy Drink. Pickles. Sugar Free jelly. Tinned soup. I get a basket. It all fits in a basket. You would think that it would take me NO TIME AT ALL to do my shopping but that's not the case. I find myself wandering up and down every aisle. It's extra steps, I suppose. But I look at everything. I peruse new products, reading the back carefully to check ingredients and calorie content in case there's a new miracle food that I can add to my rotation. It's painful to look at all the food whilst my stomach is rumbling and gnawing at itself. I watch people putting bread and cakes and chocolate and crisps into their trolleys like it's a normal, everyday thing. Some days, I am jealous of them. I wish I could do that. Other days, I am judgemental. Look at them, HOW unhealthy. I always feel self-conscious when I'm doing the shop. People must look at me in my big body, in my gym kit, trying to buy healthy food and think yeah alright love of COURSE you eat salads…NOT.

The other option, of course, is the out of control shop. The binge shop. I won't typically be wearing gym kit then: usually, I look a bit wild, hair messy, jogging bottoms, stomach probably already bulging a bit as I have likely already started. I get a trolley. Always. Again, there is no list but I get different things depending on how I'm feeling. Sometimes it'll be ingredients to make family sized pasta bakes. Other times, pizzas and garlic bread. Sandwich making things. Bags and bags of chips. Always, there will be quick things too: pork pies, sausage rolls, crumpets and butter, crisps, chocolate, biscuits, breadsticks, cereal, sweets, meal deal sandwiches, cold pasta pots, cakes, trifles, croissants, cinnamon swirls, cookie dough, ice-cream. Anything I can lay my greedy little hands on. And lots and lots of diet cola or flavoured fizzy water. I am SURE that people MUST KNOW what I am doing. **Why else would a chubby young woman be in the supermarket at nighttime, buying a TROLLEY FULL of foods like that?** I switch up the supermarkets often to avoid any kind of pattern being spotted, and try to use places with self-scan. But I'm sure that anyone who works regularly in any of them knows who I am. *I bet they watch me on CCTV. I bet they talk about me. Oh, back again. What's it going to be this time? Did you know, she was only here yesterday buying rice cakes and greek yoghurt, and now she's doing that?*

Either way, food shopping sucks. I hate it. I hate people watching me buy food. I hate buying food. I hate that I need to buy food. I hate that I want to buy food. I hate that I want to buy food that I can't buy. I hate that my lack of self control often FORCES me to buy food that will only go to waste.

And I hate getting in the car with my weekly shopping, starving hungry, and not being able to eat ANY of it because it all needs preparing or cooking first. You're probably thinking I could eat an apple. But no. It would need to be weighed first.

After:

Shopping takes me ages. I love a food shop these days. Wandering up and down the aisles, looking for new things and trying to figure out what I fancy. I usually have an idea of one of two meals that I could have so pick up things for those. I also have my core staples of things I love: All Bran cereal, seeded bread for toast and sandwiches, pickles, sauerkraut, tofu, veggie sausages, SWEET POTATOES, lemon yoghurt, SALMON, prawns. Ketchup. Kimchi. I always buy at least one packet of biscuits, depending on what is on offer, and some chocolate. I spend too long in these aisles, looking at all the new things, figuring out what I WANT. New things, but always my old favourites too: Nice biscuits, malted milks, lemon drizzle cake bars. Oat milk, because that's the milk I like even though it's not the lowest energy one. **The irony is, people probably look at my trolley NOW and think I'm more healthy than when I had a basket full of rice cakes and lettuce. And they would be CORRECT. I thought I was being so healthy, but you can spot an eating disordered shopping basket from a mile away. That, and the grey, lifeless human attached to it.**

I used to struggle with the cost of the shopping, at first. My normal food shop before (the weekly one, not the binge ones!) was half my food shop after. At first, it made me wobble. It made me think I was eating far too much if my food bill had doubled. **But then I reminded myself that it wasn't that I was eating too much now: it was that I had been eating no way near enough before.** I also reminded myself that I was saving money in other ways: *not having an expensive gym membership, not buying endless supplements just to keep me alive, not buying expensive protein bars and powders and new gym equipment and workout programmes every week, not buying dodgy pills off the Internet*. And, the kicker, of course, not spending hundreds of pounds on binge foods **when my malnourishment finally got too much for my brain and body and drove me to the other extreme**. To be honest, in the longer run, I was probably saving money.

I walk past the old foods I used to buy and feel sad for that girl. The girl who didn't like rice cakes but ate them anyway. The girl who hadn't eaten a whole egg in years. The girl who was spending £3.50 on carb-free wraps instead of £1 on the normal ones. But sometimes, I walk past the diet cereal and the high fibre low calories snack cakes and my brain shouts GRIM. I don't want that anymore. I know they won't taste nice. I know they won't keep me full. I know they're just capitalism trying to profit off people's insecurities. It's wonderfully liberating to feel that way; to be able to walk past the cereal and pick up a box of normal granola, to be able to ignore those snack cakes and buy biscuits, or mini cheesecakes or…whatever it is I fancy on that day.

And the best part? Now that I buy packaged goods again, if I'm hungry when I get in the car…I eat! **No more driving home hungry (dangerous, stupid, reckless). No more ravenous hunger whilst I unpack the bags. Just…a cake bar in a car park.**

Wedding

Before:

It is one of my best friend's weddings. I have spent the month in the run up to it on a tighter than usual diet, and trying to get an extra 5000 steps in a day. I don't need to lose weight for the wedding as obviously we already have our dresses but I need to make ABSOLUTELY SURE that I don't GAIN anything. If I GAIN, that's a disaster as the dress won't fit. If the dress is a little too loose, that's okay as it has a tie and it can be pinned. I now fully understand why so many brides go on an EXTREME diet before their wedding: the pressure I feel to fit into the dress is INTENSE and I'm just a bridesmaid. Then there's the fact that there will be PHOTOS of course, so I have to look as thin as possible. Imagine looking at the photos if I'm bursting at the seams of my dress: me next to the bride (who is skinnier than me) and the bridesmaids (who are skinnier than me)…like a MONSTER ON THE HILL. **I would ruin the photos because nobody would be looking at the bride, but rather her beached whale friend.** The dress is also sleeveless which means my arms will be out. My upper arms in particular. I spend a lot of time in front of the mirror, moving and lifting and holding my arms in certain ways to see how I can make them look the least fat for the photos. I have purchased compression shorts to pull my stomach in. Three pairs.

The night before the wedding comes. We all stay in a cottage. We watch cheesy movies about weddings, and there is champagne and popcorn and pizza. I avoid eating most of it: I say I ate a lot before I came. I drink some champagne, but pour bits into plant pots when nobody's looking. Everyone else gets merry and happy. They laugh at the films, but I don't think they're particularly funny. **It's another one of these events where I'm there but I don't feel like I'm there. I feel like I'm watching other people have fun and I'm trapped behind a glass door. A prison of my own making.** I get so tired I can't hold my eyes open. Even though everyone is still going, I apologise and take myself off to bed. I can hear them, laughing and joking for hours, but I didn't have the energy to stay sitting upright anymore. I don't really have the energy to feel sad, either. I drift in and out of a fitful sleep.

The day of the wedding is here. There's a buffet breakfast which is good because I load my plate up with fresh fruit: watermelon, strawberries, blueberries, oranges. There's also Prosecco. It's a special day, so I'm definitely going to drink. Fruit and Prosecco. Classic eating disorder breakfast. We all get ready together. We do each other's makeup. The bride looks GLORIOUS. Her waist is so tiny in her dress I feel a stab of envy. How is it fair that she spent all night eating popcorn and pizza, and has eaten TWO CROISSANTS this morning and still looks thinner than me? I pull myself back. Nice thoughts. Nice thoughts. The other bridesmaids look gorgeous in their dresses. I don't. It clings to my stomach uncomfortably. I hate it. I gaze at myself in the mirror and want to cry. But I don't have time for that.

The day passes in a blur. I drink lots of Prosecco to make myself feel better, and to make myself feel less anxious and stressed about how many people will be LOOKING at us when we walk down the aisle and LOOKING AT ME when I make my speech. Funnily enough, the drunker I become, the less hungry I am. The wedding ceremony goes well. I have hazy memories of it. Then we do photos. Then the food. I don't remember what the food is because I barely touch it: I'm not hungry. Too full of bubbles. I make my speech and it goes well: people laugh and clap, anyway. **The bride and groom cut the cake. I say I am too full to have any right now but I will have some later. Later never comes**. The night is going well. Until it isn't. For some reason, it ends with me sitting outside the venue, hysterically crying. I'm just sobbing. And then, I'm on the dance floor, still sobbing. And then I'm lying in the field behind the venue, sobbing. I have hazy memories of people coming to comfort me, asking what's wrong, and me not being able to say. I'm sick a few times. My friend laughs about it: says it's the bridesmaid's JOB to get really drunk. She doesn't seem fussed. She still looks gorgeous: **I'm covered in tears, streaky makeup and the smell of vomit. Not quite the glamorous image you see on the weight loss adverts. Not quite the aesthetic photos of thinspo on the Internet.**

I wake up the next day full of shame. I have multiple texts from people at the wedding, asking if I was okay. I feel a twist like a knife in my stomach. **Now, when they think about my friend's wedding, as well as remembering her dress and the love and the fun…they're going to remember the crazy friend who got really drunk, cried everywhere and vomited on her dress.** Now, I've tarnished the memories of the wedding with my mess. I text my friend to say congratulations and apologise again. It takes hours before she responds. She says it's fine but I'm wondering if she's thinking the same thing. I stand on the scales. I've gained far too much weight overnight. All the alcohol, probably. The gain sticks with me for two whole weeks and I have to cut even lower to make it go away.

A month later, the photos come. **I have ruined them. I look wooden. My arms stick out at funny angles. I'm not smiling in any of them.** I look pained: a combination of the compression shorts I'm wearing, hunger pains and holding my breath to suck in my stomach. My skin is grey. My eyes are glazed over. I don't order any of them. I don't want to see them ever again.

After:

It is one of my best friend's weddings. I did nothing to prepare for the wedding. I didn't need to. My body has stayed relatively the same size for the last few years. **Ever since I let go of my eating disorder and stopped swinging wildly between restricting and bingeing and overexercising and laying in bed for days, my body has found and settled at the size it wants to be.** The size it feels best at. The size where it isn't hungry and cold and grumpy and weak. It is a bigger body than the body I last went to a wedding in: but it's a body that doesn't make people ask, "are you okay?" It's a body that is READY to dance the night away. Anyway, I know the dress will fit because I have continued to live my life the way I always do now: listening to my hunger cues, eating what I want, exercising when I want and not doing anything extreme. And, anyway, if the dress is a little tight on the day…just more chance to show off my curves, right?

The night before the wedding, there is a rehearsal dinner. Friends and family of the bride and groom gather in a cute little pub in the village where the wedding is happening. There is a buffet of pizza and bottles of wine scattered around. I eat pizza, drink wine, and mingle. We don't drink too much - we have somewhere to be in the morning, after all, but enough to feel a little bit jolly. We head back to the bridal suite and lie around on the big sofas, reminiscing about school and how far we have all come. I have come far now. **In the last couple of years, I've made lots of progress with my career that I was unable to make when I was ill. It's refreshing, now, to be able to join in with these conversations: to laugh about how we were in school, and how our teachers would be AMAZED to see us now.** Before, those conversations filled me with shame. In the years since I left school, *I had accomplished very little other than shrinking and growing my body in a continuous cycle whilst life waited on the sidelines.* Now, I have accomplished a lot. **My body has grown along with my life but that's okay.** It means I can lie on a sofa, the night before a wedding, full of pizza and wine, and say wow I've come so far. We go to bed far too late, but the bride wasn't going to sleep well anyway.

In the morning, we eat croissants and drink hot chocolate and Prosecco. We all get ready together. We do each other's makeup. We all look GLORIOUS. The bride looks BEAUTIFUL: the dress she has chosen is so perfect for her personality and she looks like a forest fairy. The bridesmaid dresses are a deep navy that look glorious against everyone's skin tone. I send my mum a photo of me in my dress because I love it. She responds with a heart eye emoji.

The day passes in a blur. In the lead up to the ceremony, we snack on crisps and canapes: a glorious combination. The wedding ceremony goes well. I cry a little. It's very beautiful and I am very grateful to be alive and to have friends who invite me to their weddings. **It sounds silly but it isn't: to be living, to be loving, is a beautiful thing after so long feeling cold and alone and like I was living on the outside looking in.** My friends stuck with me through those icy years, the years where I was a robot in a human body, and I am grateful. Then we do photos. It's fun. We pull silly faces and pretend to be candid when the photographer tells us to, which is so silly. Then the food. A gorgeous roast dinner. Chocolate tart. I spill gravy and cream on my dress. Standard. The speeches are made. I cry again. I'm so full of emotions these days. Big ones. Nice ones. Good ones.

The bride and groom cut the cake. I eat the cake. It's DELICIOUS: lemon flavoured, would you believe? My favourite. My friend has good taste. I spend the night on the dance floor. We made the playlist ourselves in the week before the wedding: it's a compilation of all of the songs we have ever listened to at house parties over the last ten years. I dance. And I dance. And I dance. I'm aware that I've become quite sweaty. A fleeting thought enters my head oh good, I must be burning so many calories. I almost laugh. That means I'll probably be hungry tomorrow and that's fine because I'll EAT MORE. **The thoughts are still there. But they don't mean the same thing anymore. They don't mean anything.** The evening food is fish and chips but I miss it because I'm too busy dancing, and also wildly drunk. When I get back to the hotel room, I order takeaway pizza with a couple of friends and we sit, drunk in our pyjamas, eating cheese pizza. We leave a couple of pieces outside the bride and groom's room, knock and run away giggling. High on life. Pizza and Prosecco and PIZZAZZ. I feel alive.

I do not feel alive the next day.

I don't weigh myself. That's irrelevant information. I know, logically, I might weigh more: lots of alcohol and salt was consumed last night. But that's not real weight. **Not that it matters anyway: I would happily pay a few pounds for the amount of fun we had.**

A month later, the photos come. I dig out a photo I printed out from a wedding I attended a year ago. I am in the background, my bones sticking out, my skin grey. I look sad and tired. My arms are folded across my body, hiding it. My hair is thin and you can visibly see the bald patches. I put it next to the photos from the wedding. **It's impossible to identify the two people as the same.** In the new photos, I am glowing. My skin is pink and flushed, my eyes are sparkling, my face is shining. I am beaming. We all are. It was a day of joy and happiness and I was THERE. And I look THERE. My hair is thick and shiny. Even though I had three hours of sleep the night before, I look FULL OF ENERGY. **My body is bigger. My arms are larger but they are no longer cradling my body in an attempt to hide it: they are thrown in the air in excitement, they are wrapped around my best friend, they are holding the groom up in a funny photo.** My dress is bigger but it fits me better: it doesn't hang off my frame like a child in her mother's dress. It clings to my hips and my boobs, it makes me look kind of hot.

I did it. I went to a wedding. I drank alcohol, ate food, and danced. I joined in. I had fun. I was present. And nothing bad happened. I didn't lose control. Nobody hated me because my dress was a size bigger than a year ago. Nobody said anything to me OTHER than how lovely the dress was and how nice my hair was and how gorgeous we all looked. **Nothing bad happened. But lots of good did.**

Birthday

Before:

I used to love my birthday. I don't anymore. Go figure. As you get older, birthdays are less exciting. Instead, they become excuses to eat. Everyone wants to go out for a meal, or grab drinks. My mum wants to make a cake. Every year. **The lead up to my birthday becomes like the lead up to any big event: increasing my exercise routine and eating a little bit less so that when I am forced by social pressure to eat more than I want, the impact isn't as bad.** My friends tried to arrange drinks but I told a lot of lies and pretended I was busy on all of the proposed days. We left it as we'll sort something out afterwards which is a promise I intend to NEVER call in.

On the day of my birthday, I spend hours trying on all of my clothes. **I am trying to find something that makes me look as small as possible, but that won't show my**

bulging stomach after I've eaten. There will be photos and I need to look small and nice. Well. Not even small. I would settle for just not fat at this point. I try on everything. My room becomes a mess around me as I discard everything. My body is gross. I hate looking at it this much: every item of clothing I take off to try a new one on is another forced opportunity to see my white pasty fat rolls, my pale skin coated in stretch mark scars and imperfections. I have nothing to wear. I end up going into town and spending hours in clothes shops. That's a bad idea too because the lighting in there is harsher than in my room and the shadows make my pot belly and jiggly thighs all the more obvious. I eventually find something that will do. I rush home and get changed. My hair is then refusing to cooperate. I have so many random baby hairs and the rest of my hair is horribly thin. As I brush out the knots, it comes out in clumps. I ignore it. In the end, I have to settle for sweeping it back into a bun. I'm looking very tired so I slather some makeup on. I'm starving by this point as I haven't eaten all day, but that's totally fine. I'll eat enough for a whole day later, I'm sure.

I head over to my mum's house. She's hosting a family dinner this year and my siblings and grandparents are coming over. We are having a takeaway curry. I have perused the menu many times over the past week and googled the approximate calories in each thing to figure out what the lowest calorie option will be. People give me presents and I open them, but I barely have the energy to fake enthusiasm when I open chocolate and sweets and a jumper that is definitely not going to be flattering. My grandparents have given me a clothes voucher which is nice, I guess, but it sends me down a bit of a mental spiral about what size clothes I should buy. My current size which is TOO BIG? Or a small size, as inspiration and motivation? They're all chattering in the background and I am trying to smile and nod at the right times to show I'm listening but the new dress is clinging to my arms a bit too tightly and the chocolate from my mum is SCREAMING my name and I feel dizzy and weak and lethargic.

Then disaster strikes. We go to the Indian takeaway to pick up the order and it's SHUT. I knew what I was having. I had planned out my meal. And now what? NOW WHAT?

"It's okay," my sister says. "Let's go get pizza!"

PIZZA? HOW IS THAT OKAY? HOW IS THAT OKAY?

Everyone is staring at me now. **It's your birthday, love, what do you want to do? OH I DON'T KNOW, STARVE?** NOT GET FAT? NOT EAT PIZZA? NOT EAT THIS STUPID, HIGH CALORIE FOOD? I WANT TO EAT VEGETABLES AND SALADS AND WHOLE FOODS BUT NONE OF YOU WANT THAT.

"Pizza, yeah," I say. I force a smile on my face. I want to cry. I gaze out the window and squeeze my eyes shut. Do. Not. Cry. That would really give me away. My mum has been saying for a while now that she thinks I'm taking things too far, but it's because she doesn't understand what a healthy life actually looks like. Nobody does these days. They think everyone should live like them: eating all the processed food and never exercising and gaining weight and saying it's just your metabolism slowing down as you age.

When we go in, I order the vegetable pizza on the gluten free base with no cheese. I'm vegan at the moment so that's fortunate. Is there no vegan cheese? Grandma asks. I want you to enjoy your pizza! I tell her that vegan cheese is gross (valid) and that I never really liked cheese anyway. My mum looks like she disagrees but doesn't say anything. I point out that I'm going to lather my pizza in ketchup anyway. Are you gluten free? Grandad asks. I explain that I've been having some digestive issues (valid) and that eating gluten free appears to be helping (no idea, I don't eat bread other than in enforced situations so can't gather data on this).

We take the pizza home. The car smells DELICIOUS but I know full well it's not my pizza that smells good. It's the pepperoni on my sister's and the cheese on everyone else's. I dip my dry, bland pizza in half a bottle of ketchup to make it taste nicer. I'm angry that I am wasting so many calories on something that ISN'T nice and that I DIDN'T want. **I'm angry that everyone else is able to eat PIZZA on MY BIRTHDAY and ENJOY IT.** Why is it just me that can't control my weight? Why is everyone else able to eat pizza and not BALLOON and not hate themselves?

Then the cake comes out. A big chocolate cake with fresh cream and strawberries. People are pointing cameras at me and I try to sit up as straight as possible so that my stomach doesn't look big and bulbous and rolling. I blow out the candle. It's tradition in our family that the birthday person cuts themselves the first slice of cake and there's always this expectation that it needs to be HUGE. My mum goes into the kitchen to make a pot of tea and I cut the cake. I put the giant slice on my plate. Everyone else cuts their pieces too, a similar size to mine. The tea comes. We eat the cake. It's delicious. I was only going to eat half of what I had cut and then say I was full but I can't stop. I eat it all. You can have some more? Mum says. She's beaming. She loves it when people love her baking. Go on, Grandma says. It's your birthday. And people with your metabolism can eat whatever they want! I want to scream at her. But it's too late. The cake is in my head. I feel like I'm starving even though I can't possibly be. My stomach is FULL but nothing appears to be filling it. I cut another slice of cake. Wolf it down. I've eaten about a quarter of the cake. My ears are ringing.

"Shall we take a family photo?" Grandma proposes.

"What, now?" I ask.

WHY NOW? WHY DIDN'T WE DO IT BEFORE WE ATE? WHY? WHY? I don't want to. I really don't want to. But I can see my mum looking at me like Grandma will die one day and we want family photos. So I agree. We set the phone up on a self-timer and everyone gathers in the middle. They want me to stand in the middle. Of course. I try to hide my body with my arms. We take a few photos. When I look at them later, I look like a prisoner on day release. I look like I'm being held hostage. Everyone around me is smiling. And I'm in the middle, my arms awkwardly wrapped around my body, my posture crooked and bent and yucky as I try to shrink in on myself. I hate it.

I go home. I stare at my bulging, bloated and swollen body in the mirror. I am surrounded by the clothes I never put away. I go to the dustbin and throw away the chocolate and sweets and jumper. I throw up. I go back to the mirror. I weigh myself. I cry. Happy birthday, whale. The next morning, I wake up earlier than usual and go to the gym.

After:

I wake up on my birthday and spring out of bed. I'm a birthday LOVER. Not just birthdays, really, I just love EVENTS. Any excuse to get people together and CELEBRATE. Christmas, New Year, Easter, birthdays…I love them all! I've already done lots of birthday celebrations this week: breakfast with my grandparents (I had French toast, they paid, delightful); cocktails with the girls from work (the next morning was not delightful); and coffee and cake (lemon drizzle for me) with my besties. I get dressed casually in shorts and a t-shirt because I'm going climbing with my friends after breakfast.

I meet my stepdad for breakfast. I have a hot chocolate with cream and marshmallows, and sourdough toast with smoked salmon and scrambled eggs. I feel very bougie. I love salmon. I can't believe I spent years not eating it on the premise that it was too high in fat. It's SO GOOD for you. Now I realise that just because foods are high fat and high energy doesn't mean they are bad for you. Since I started eating salmon and yoghurt and avocado and oil, I have skin that glows and hair that isn't balding and a body that doesn't ache. My step dad and I talk about plans for the future: my career plans, the PhD I'm starting in a couple of months. He tells me he's proud of me. **I'm proud of myself too. It's hard to believe I am here, two months away from starting a PhD,** eating salmon and sourdough toast, when, a year ago, I was too scared to eat a banana and my brain was too mushy to even do a Sudoku.

After breakfast, I head off climbing. I meet a few of my climbing friends at the centre and they've got some balloons and party hats. We climb in the hats. **I'm getting stronger every day and I LOVE IT. There's nothing more satisfying than using your body when you're fully fuelled; feeling the yummy food you are giving you the energy and power to do something really cool.** One of my friends has made little birthday cupcakes with little iced climbing holds on them. I eat a couple with a cup of tea whilst we lounge around on the sofas afterwards. We grab lunch at the climbing centre because they do these really good GIANT pizza slices so I get one with veggies and extra pineapple. Obviously.

Then I rush home and have a quick shower to get all the climbing chalk off me. My sister texts me a picture of her outfit. I pick a dress that is similar so we look cute in the photos and put it in. My hair is still damp so I improvise and plait it rather than wearing it down and dripping all over the place. I am meeting my family at a restaurant - a Japanese place that me and my sister LOVE. My mum has never tried Japanese food before and so we are excited to widen her culinary experience. It's one of these places where you get lots of small plates and share them, and the food just comes when it's ready. We order EVERYTHING: dynamite cauliflower, bao buns, gyoza, agedashi tofu, kimchi, tempura prawns, tempura vegetables, pumpkin croquettes, sushi rolls… *I have no idea how much I actually eat. And that's fine. I eat what I want. It's delicious*. My mum loves it but she can't use chopsticks. We try to show her but it just doesn't work and we are all laughing and I feel so warm and happy inside. To go to a restaurant for dinner, after eating meals all day, to feel happy and fuelled and confident and to spend time being PRESENT with my family rather than STRESSED about how much I was eating…It's something so normal but it feels so big. So beautiful.

We order desserts. I get apple gyoza because I've never tried sweet gyoza before and I'm intrigued. I love them. I pop to the toilet once we've finished and me and my sister take some mirror selfies. Of course. We come back. The waiter comes round the corner with a brownie with a sparkler in it and everyone starts singing. Excellent. Of course. Everyone's got their cameras out and they're pointed at me. It's embarrassing and cringey but also I LOVE IT. I blow out the sparkler. **And even though this was unplanned and even though I've already had dessert my first thought is actually: FREE CAKE. EXCELLENT.** I share it with my sister. I make a mental note to leave a good trip adviser review.

I go home. I look at myself in the mirror: ***I have a tiny food baby, but nothing major. Now that I'm used to eating normal amounts of food, I don't swell up in the same way that I used to before.*** I pat my satisfied stomach and change into my pyjamas. I'm tired so I put the cake in the fridge, grab my book and clamber into bed. Happy birthday to me.

Restaurant

Before:

Going out to eat is a constant source of stress. Firstly, restaurant food is ALWAYS excessively high in calories. It's always cooked in oil. Then it always has so many unnecessary extras like mayonnaise and cheese. The portions are always HUGE, way bigger than any normal person should have. And other people are always watching you eat and making judgements: if I eat too much, or too little, or too unhealthily, or too healthily. People judge what you eat, and you, and your body size when you eat in front of them.

I try to avoid eating out wherever I can and would NEVER be the kind of person to just pop into a restaurant for dinner if I was alone. Most of the time, I pretend that I'm double booked or something. But if there's something I really can't avoid - like a close friend or family member's birthday, for example - I have a set protocol that helps me avoid TOO much weight gain. I look at the menu online before I go anywhere. If the place has calories listed on the menu, that makes things easier: I select the lowest calorie option. I log it on my app straight away, so I know that that is what I'm having. **If calories are on the menu, I don't spend too much time looking at the other options: there's no point in dreaming about the things that I would eat if I could.** When calories aren't on the menu, that presents more of a problem. I have to read the whole menu carefully, several times. I plug in various different options into online calculators to try and figure out which option would be the lowest calorie. It's risky, though, because of things like added oil and butter and cream and cheese, and not knowing what quantities of each ingredient may have been used. I always overestimate to be safe.

I make sure to eat as little as possible throughout the rest of the day to make sure that I don't gain too much weight from the event itself. I fill up on hot drinks and water. **Before I leave, I spend a good thirty minutes trying on different outfits to assess which**

will make me look the least bloated when I eat. Eating out at restaurants always makes me bloat instantly - because of the salt content, probably. I try to walk to the restaurant wherever possible - usually if it's less than an hour away, that seems like fair game.

I never enjoy eating out. I'm always RAVENOUSLY hungry by the time I get there, and everyone wants to sit around and make silly small talk for the first fifteen minutes. I sit there, ravenous, wanting to order but nobody else is ever ready to, amongst the *how's work going* and *how was your holiday* and *it's been a really wet summer, hasn't it?* I sit there, silent, too hungry to join in. Then, the kerfuffle with the menus comes. Everyone looks at them for hours. *I could have this or this or this* someone says. *I don't know if I want this or that* someone else says. *Do you think this or this is going to be nicer?* **It's ANNOYING**. Why haven't they decided what they want already? Why didn't they look BEFOREHAND? We are there to eat, not chat. The restaurant fills with the smell and sound of other people enjoying their food. I want to kill someone. Everyone has decided what they want now, but the waiter is nowhere to be found, of course. We wait. And wait. We finally order and then the food takes HOURS to arrive. Everyone is chatting but the conversation is rushing over me. I am too hungry to focus and the smell of food is driving me insane.

Food finally arrives. Everyone else's looks nicer than mine, of course. They've ordered whatever they want - pizza or burgers or pasta or something covered in cheese - but I've just got the salad, or the burger with no bread and salad instead of fries, or the nourish grain bowl. It's nice enough but it's not what anyone would choose for their last meal. Still, I remind myself: it's not my last meal. That's the point. It's a healthy meal to keep me healthy. So I don't have a last meal anytime soon - unlike some of this lot, clogging up their arteries with bread and cheese. I wolf my food down. I finish first. Everyone else is taking their merry time. I barely even taste the food because I've eaten it that quickly.

I can feel myself being bloated almost immediately. My clothes feel tighter. I try to join in with the conversation but **I'm too confused by this point as everyone has done all the catching up without me, when I was too hungry to listen.** I resent them - although it's my own fault, really - if they had just ordered quicker, everything would have been fine.

Then, they start talking about DESSERT. I want to go home by this point. I'm exhausted from all of the social interaction and if I leave now, I can get to the gym at a reasonable time. I say no to dessert. *I'm not really a sweet toothed person* I say with a shrug. A couple of people say the same. But we still have to sit and wait whilst everyone else gets dessert. And then they try to offer you "little bits" of theirs. How's that meant to work? How would I calorie count that?!

Finally, I get to escape. I walk home. Get changed into my gym clothes. Look at my bloated stomach in the mirror. Hate myself. Go the gym. Someone always texts me afterwards: *are you okay? You seemed upset.* I text back: *thank for noticing. Just a lot on at work at the moment. Sorry for being a grump!* I could hardly tell the truth, could I? Actually, I'm fine, you lot just took too long ordering and I was hungry or fine, thanks, but annoyed that I just derailed my diet for a dinner that wasn't even that nice.

I wake up the next day and I don't eat breakfast. I don't need to - I've still got enough energy from the giant meal to keep me going. If a friend texts me to invite me out again for the next couple of weeks at least, I have excuses ready. I weigh myself. I hate myself.

After:

I love going out to restaurants now. For several reasons: **I get to eat food that is far nicer than anything I can make; I get to try new things; there is no washing up; and I get to spend time with my friends and family.** I now know that the REASON why restaurants use so much extra oil and added extras is to make the food taste GOOD. That's why it tastes nicer than my own cooking. I try to make my cooking taste nice with those things, but I'm no chef and half the time you never have whatever fancy oil or spice it is in your kitchen.

Sometimes, I look at the menu before I go somewhere - but just to get a flavour for what's on offer. *I never choose what I'm having in advance because there's no point: I won't know what I fancy until I'm there.* I'm always really guided by what other people are eating when I walk in, anyway - if I see something that looks and smells banging, I'm instantly attracted like a moth to the flame.

I usually wear loose trousers or a flowy dress to dinner so that my stomach has room to comfortably expand when I eat, but I no longer stress about what I look like. **If my stomach does bloat from eating, nobody is going to think anything of it, right?** *They'll have quite literally seen me eat my meal so know that that's what's going on.* Chances are, they'll have a little food baby too! **Besides which, anyone who would judge me based on my expanding stomach as I eat is NOT someone that I would want to be eating with anyway!** Anyway...the bloating when I eat out is no way near as noticeable as it used to be. I had convinced myself that it was caused by the restaurant food itself, specifically, but I now know what it was: a combination of eating salt when I LITERALLY NEVER HAD ANY and the fact that I hadn't eaten anything all day, then wolfed down a meal along with litres of liquid. **The extreme bloating was being caused by my poor, slow and overloaded digestive system rather than the food.** Ironically, it was the lack of food causing the very thing I was blaming on food.

Now, I tend to drive to restaurants. Gone are the days where I turn up sweaty and grumpy and tired and a little freaked out from the man who may or may not have been following me down the questionable alleyway. Don't get me wrong, if it's summer and light and sunny and I'm not tired or anything, I'll walk. But if it's dark, or late, or rainy…no step count is worth that!

I sit down. I join in with the small talk and the conversation, and offer my own contributions to the conversation. I am hungry, but not ravenous. I've eaten throughout the day: the normal amount of food that I would eat anyway. **Because…dinner in a restaurant is still just dinner. It's just food. Eaten somewhere else.** I chat. I look at the menu. I join in with the oh should I have this or that conversation. **I snack on the table bread.** I choose what sounds good to me: no veganism, no imaginary dairy intolerance, no lowest energy option. I just choose what I want. If it doesn't have chips with it, I usually get a side of chips. I can't help myself. I love them too much. Chips and ketchup, on the side of anything. Poke bowl? Chips. Salmon and quinoa? Chips. French Toast? Chips. Chips? CHIPS. I decide what I want. We laugh about how long the waiter is taking to come. We chat more. We order.

The food comes. I eat it at a normal speed because I'm not so hungry I might spontaneously combust. I have food envy, but not much. People let me try theirs, anyway. And I let them try mine. **People never used to ask for bites of my food when it was the kale salad.** Sometimes, I eat all of the meal. Sometimes, I get full and stop. I get a box to take it home. Sometimes, if I'm still hungry or really fancy something, I'll get dessert.If other people get desserts and I don't, and they offer, I try some of theirs. Sometimes I share a dessert. Sometimes, if I'm stuffed, or the menu isn't very inspiring, I won't. There are no rules anymore. It's just flexible. It's just whatever I want, whenever I want. Often, I get home and a few hours later will either finish the leftovers or grab myself another snack. **Because the body gets hungry every few hours, no matter the location of the last meal.** I don't go to the gym after. I can't imagine anything that would make my body feel worse than forcing it to work out at the end of the day when my stomach is full of good food.

The next day looks like any other next day. I get up and I have breakfast. Sometimes, the leftovers. Sometimes porridge. Sometimes yoghurt and cereal. Sometimes toast. It's just whatever I want, whenever I want. I don't weigh myself.

If a friend texts and invites me out for dinner that evening, I pause. Is that a smart financial decision? **I look at my budget.**

Do you notice something about all of the befores? **They are all SO BORING.** They are all, also, the same. Exercise before. Exercise after. Worry about food. Under or over eat. Binge. Get rid. Isolate myself. Loneliness. Boredom. Pointlessness.

MY BEFORE:

So much thinking. Thinking about food. What I want to eat. What I won't eat. What I should eat. Watching videos of other people eating. Researching low calorie recipes. Trying to eat as much food for as few calories as possible. Hungry all of the time. Or not hungry at all. Worried about being too hungry or not hungry enough.

Thinking about exercise. When I would fit it in. Making sure I got a set number of steps. Researching workout programmes. Following influencers on social media, trying to copy their routines. Trying to change my body with specific exercise routines. Hating the exercise. Feeling weak and tired whilst doing it.

Thinking about my body. Agonising over what clothes to wear to hide my body *and* make it look as small as possible at the same time. Looking at the parts of it I hated. Researching how to get rid of those parts. Researching how to tighten loose skin. Clothes shopping for hours. Wasting money on clothes I would never wear. Crying in changing rooms. Crying in the bathroom. Crying on the bedroom floor. Taking endless photographs of my body at unnatural angles. Deleting photos. Taking more. Weighing myself several times a day. **Hating every number I saw: too heavy, no weight loss, weight gain, not a big enough loss, not a fast enough loss.** My weight fluctuating wildly: up ten pounds, down ten pounds. My body stretching and shrinking in a bizarre and uncomfortable way. Stretch marks and loose skin being made worse by the constant whiplash my body faced.

Avoiding people. People who might ask questions. People who might try to make me eat. Not enjoying being around people. Too short tempered and grumpy to engage with them. Finding everyone annoying and frustrating. Dreading social events. Cancelling most of them. Letting people down. **Being a bad friend.** A bad family member. **All events coloured by the lead up and the aftermath: starving before and after, increasing exercise before and after, planning outfits and restrictions and rules well in advance.** Attending events and not being able to join in properly. Too tired. Too grumpy. Too weak. Feeling like an outsider looking in. Wanting to go home and go to the gym. Or curl up in bed and cease to exist.

Hair falling out. Dry skin. Spots. Grey, tired looking face. Puffy, swollen cheeks. No smile. No sparkle in my eyes. Low blood sugar. Shaky and weak. Low blood pressure. Dizzy all the time. Palpitations. **And the sheer exhaustion.** Feeling like my limbs were too heavy to move. Feeling like it would take too much out of me to even climb a set of stairs. Aching bones. Freezing cold. No energy to do anything.

Falling behind at work. No mental space or energy to do anything *other* than eat, or try not to eat. Evenings spent staring blankly at walls or lying in bed. Or in the gym.

Tired. Bored. Sad. Trapped.

The most ironic part? Still seeing my body as gross. Never liking what I looked like. Weight loss stalled long ago. My body in self-preservation mode. On the go slow. *The cruellest part of an eating disorder is the moment you find yourself starving but stagnating:* you cannot eat less because you will die, but you cannot eat more because your body has shut down so much that anything at all makes the scale shoot up.

<u>**Hating life. Hating myself.**</u>

I wouldn't be too surprised if my BEFORE sounds a lot like your NOW. **It was my NOW for many years.** There was a very real time where I believed that it was going to be my FOREVER. Some things differed over the years, of course, but the core components were still there. It's easy to boil down a life with an eating disorder to the same grey, boring description. It's easy to boil it down to what it is: a waste of a life. An eating disorder is, at its core, so desperately pointless that it's painful. And I know, of course, that you have to reach this conclusion for yourself. It would be ridiculously hypocritical of me to say to you: STOP NOW WHILST YOU CAN. Because I didn't. I kept doing it, over and over, year after year after year. I can't make you stop now, in the same way that I wouldn't make myself stop. But I can invite you to do the same things that I did that *finally* made the difference to me. **What does your after look like? What does your life look like without the disorder?**

MY AFTER:

Eating when I am hungry. Eating what I enjoy. **A balance that I never thought I would find: I crave everything and so I eat everything.** Chocolate, vegetables, cake, yoghurt, porridge, stir fry, pasta, biscuits, salad, salmon, eggs, avocado toast, chips, hot chocolate, bread, rice, sandwiches, protein bars…everything. Some days, I eat three chocolate bars. Then, I won't eat another one for a week because I'm all sugared out. Sometimes, I eat one every day. Sometimes I go months without one. I eat vegetables most days. Some days I don't. I eat fruit every day because I LOVE it. I drink hot chocolate every day.

I exercise as and when I want to. No schedule. Lots of rest. **But I am starting to feel strong. Flexible. Functional. I am starting to feel like I may be an elderly person who can climb up a hill and carry her shopping home, rather than one crippled by osteoporosis.** I feel like I might just about be able to throw an attacker off and run away for more than ten seconds. I love exercise now. Because I've chosen movement that I love. I love feeling powerful. I no longer feel tired and weak. I have muscles, too. They look…nice? I think. I try not to think about how I feel about what my body looks like because it doesn't matter. *It's how it feels that matters.*

But I don't hate how I look anymore because I simply don't think about it that much. I glance in the mirror to make sure my outfit looks okay and that my hair doesn't look too crazy, and that's about it. I no longer gaze at the parts of me I hate. I no longer take endless photos of myself in my underwear. Sometimes I see myself in photos or in a shop window and think I look good. My skin is clear and shining. My hair is thick and healthy. My eyes sparkle. I smile so big my dimples show. Someone who has known me for years says *I didn't know you had dimples, they're so cute.* I feel cute.

Some days, I do still feel bad. I think I've eaten too much. I worry I will gain weight. But then I remember: if I do gain weight, that's better than going back to where I came from. **I would rather be larger and in a larger life, than smaller and in the prison of a tiny, starving life.** I know I would. *Because I am bigger now than I was then. And I am happier now than I was then.* Getting bigger did not make me unhappier. It made getting dressed in the mornings a little harder, sometimes. But it made *everything else* easier. And so if I get bigger again, that's okay. Bigger is better than backwards.

It doesn't happen, though. My body has reached a safe and healthy point where it trusts me. Because I know I will eat what I want when I want it, I do not have urges to binge very much anymore. When I do, I know it's because I must be restricting something and so I eat whatever it is that I want. And the urges go away. My body doesn't push me to eat more than I need anymore. I don't force down platefuls of food I don't even want because I'm planning to starve for the next few days. I just listen to my body. And my body tells me when it needs more and when it needs less and so my weight stays stable. Or at least, I imagine it does. My clothes fit the same. I haven't weighed myself in years.

I don't love my body. I'm indifferent to it. But you know what I do love? My life.

MY NOW:

I'm not at the after, yet. I live somewhere in between. Some days look like the after. Some days look like the before. Most days are somewhere in between. But the more I eat, and the more I fight, the closer we get to the after days. There are more sunny moments. More sunny days. Even if I don't act on the before, it's all still there. The feelings. The thoughts. But they help me now. Because I know what I don't want. I know how miserable that life is. And so I focus on the after. I focus on where I want to be. The days where I feel like living in the before, and I don't…those are the days where I get stronger.

Everyday, I choose to reframe. Everyday, I choose to remind myself of the reasons why I need to eat each food group. Of the reasons why I need to eat regularly. Of the reasons why a disordered life is never worth the price. Of the reasons why I shouldn't obsessively exercise. **And deep down, it all comes down to the same thing. Every thought I get towards my body, or food, or exercise I ask myself: IS THAT THE LIFE I WANT TO LIVE?**

And when the answer is no, which it always is, I do something different. I am creating the life I want to live. One second at a time. One choice after another. Over and over.

This is why I failed so many times. I gave up at every thought. Every disordered thought convinced me that I wasn't ready yet. And one more week turned into one more month into one more year. And another decade.

Listen. I reframe my thoughts every day. I go through the stages laid out in these pages multiple times a day. And no, it's not easy. Yes, it is effort. Yes, it is hard. Yes, it sucks. But noway NEAR as much as all of the stuff that came before it.

24. THE (LITTLE) THINGS THAT MADE ALL THE DIFFERENCE

And now, before I bow out, and go back to living in my nice little NEVER-ENDING ERA, here are some tips and tricks that I carry with me that I have found the most helpful in my continued recovery. These are questions I get asked quite a lot, and I feel like the answers could be of some potential help. These are, once again, entirely unprofessional opinions. This is not medical advice, or mental health advice, or anything other than my own specific and personal experience. None of it is factual: other than for me. If it works for you, groovy, golden. If it doesn't, try something else. Keep trying something else until you find the thing that sticks.

MANAGING CALORIES

Many people advocate for avoiding calories in recovery, and in life. But I do not subscribe to that school of thought: **I think that avoiding calories gives them a power that they don't need to have.** We could spend the rest of our lives scribbling the calories off packets and only eating at restaurants where the calories aren't on the menu. We could shut our eyes and look the other way, block our ears when people talk about things being high calorie or low calorie, bury our heads in calorie-free sand. But that's almost as disordered as obsessing over calories.

Instead, I have chosen to embrace them for what they are: information. The calorie content of the food is simply another piece of information about the food. Treat it like you would with the rest of the information about the product: it's got eggs, it's got butter, it's got 400 calories, it's suitable for vegetarians, and it's in a green packet.

When I see calories, or people mention calories, or I *think* about calories, I utilise my top tips:

1. **See calories for what they are. They are energy**. If a food is high in calories, it is high in energy. If a food is low in calories, it is low in energy. If I eat lots of low energy food, I will become a low energy person again and I do not want that. I don't use the word calories anymore. Using it less has removed the power from it. Energy. Energy. Energy.

2. I remind myself that the number is NOT going to be accurate anyway. There is no way on earth that this restaurant is making the cheesy pasta the EXACT same way with the EXACT same amount of pasta, cheese, cream and stock every single time. NO WAY. They don't have time for that. The calorie content on foods is an *estimation*. So it's NOT CORRECT ANYWAY. Therefore, what is the point in stressing and being upset over a number that isn't even accurate anyway?

3. I look at the menu. I look at the energy content of the options. I find the lowest energy option and I don't choose it. Why? To teach my brain that I do not need to eat the lowest energy option. If I *do* want the lowest energy thing on the menu (unlikely), I get something else with it: I want that energy! I want the pizzazz! I want that sparkle!

When other people speak about calories and say things like *oh this is so high in calories* I think *oh that's so high in energy.* When they select the salad or the flatbread instead of the fries and say they're *being good* I think *you're being low energy and that's not how I want to live MY life.* When I do my food shop and see the calories on the packaging I think *let's make sure I choose foods that will make meals that will give me enough energy to thrive.* When someone says *that cinnamon bun has 423 calories in it* I think *that's highly unlikely it has exactly 423 energy in it, but it does look good so I might eat it with a cup of tea.*

TELLING PEOPLE

When it comes to telling people about your eating disorder, my top tip is this: TELL PEOPLE ABOUT YOUR EATING DISORDER.

I didn't tell anyone for years. Not telling anyone meant that my disorder was able to keep hiding in the shadows. Everytime I went to the toilet after eating, it wasn't suspicious. Me being vegan wasn't suspicious. Me not eating because I ate before I came wasn't suspicious. Me bringing my own snacks and food for allergy reasons wasn't suspicious. Me going to the gym twice a day because I JUST LOVED EXERCISE SO MUCH wasn't suspicious.

1. Tell people. The more people you tell, the less safe your disorder feels. The more people who know, the less able you will feel to actively engage in behaviours.

But the telling can be hard. The telling *is* hard. Why? Because there is still stigma and shame attached to eating disorders. Because people don't really understand. Because people will say silly things like *but you're not fat* and *why don't you just eat* and *it's all about finding balance.* This is therefore the next important point:

2. When you tell people, be prepared that they WILL NOT UNDERSTAND easily. Eating disorders are complicated mental illnesses which, by nature, will be very hard for anyone who has not experienced them to understand. If people ask silly questions or say silly things, remind yourself: they do not understand because they have not experienced it.

With that in mind, I decided that I was going to HELP people understand.

3. Help people understand by *explaining* properly. Do not just say "I have an eating disorder" and expect them to just understand. Tell them what this means. Tell them what it means to you. Tell them what it doesn't mean. Print out information from charities and research. Show it to them. Tell them what not to say. Tell them how they can help, and how they can't. **We should live in a world where there is enough exposure and education and understanding of mental health conditions that we do not need to do this.** But we don't. Yet. So to best help our families and friends to help us: let's help them. Let's explain.

I find that people struggle to understand or take in information easily when they are shocked. So I knew that if I just ANNOUNCED my eating disorder to my friends and family, there would be a high chance that they would be too surprised or shocked to respond appropriately. I wanted to avoid this. I didn't want them to be in a position where they accidentally said something insensitive or triggering to me simply because they were blindsided. So instead of telling them, I wrote letters. I have included my letter at the end, for you to see, in case it may help you.

I gave them the letter when I was going to be away from them for a few hours or days. I told them that it contained some big news and that I wanted them to read it and take time to process it, but that it was something I wanted and trusted them to know. I told them to ask any questions they had in any way they felt comfortable. And then I ran away, and anxiously tried to avoid checking my phone.

You may be worried. You may think *but what if I tell them and they make fun of me? What if I tell them and they don't understand? What if I tell them and they don't want to see me anymore?* **If you tell someone you have a mental health condition and they make fun of you, you don't want or need that person in your life. Put them in the bin. If you tell someone about your mental health condition and they don't understand and they don't make any effort to understand or expand their knowledge, you don't want or need that person in your life. Put them in the bin. If you tell someone about your mental health condition and they don't want to see you anymore, you don't want to SEE them anymore either.** Just think of it like this: if one of your friends told *you* in a letter that they had a mental health condition, would you laugh at them? Would you refuse to understand? Would you tell them you didn't want to be friends anymore? Or would you do your very best to understand, to support them, and to be there for them? If other people do not treat you the way you deserve to be treated, they have shown you who they are and that's a good thing because you get to get rid of them.

I am lucky enough that I have some brilliant and wonderful people in my life. Nobody acted weirdly towards me at all. They all read the letter. They all listened to the letter. And my eating disorder felt a little less safe. It felt a little more seen.

It also had a side effect I never could have expected: it helped OTHER people feel more seen too. Friends. Family. Coming out of the woodwork. Telling me they had been there too. In their own hellscape. Or were still there.

WHEN PEOPLE ARE TRIGGERS

One of the hardest things when you have a brain that is susceptible to disordered thoughts is OTHER PEOPLE. And by that I mean…the things that other people say and do. Unfortunately, we can't get away from it. People talk about food and diets and exercise and controlling their bodies and being unhappy with their diet and appearance ALL THE TIME. *It is an unfortunate byproduct of living in a society that is infected with diet culture at every imaginable level.*

1. **Surround yourself with good people.** This is not to say that people who talk about food, diet and body image are *bad people.* They are not. They are victims too. When I say good people I mean this: surround yourself with people who understand that they should not talk about these topics around you. Surround yourself with people who will *actively try to stop* talking about these topics around you. Surround yourself with people who will *listen* when you tell them that something is difficult for you. Be patient with it: diet culture is a HABIT. It is INGRAINED. They may say things, sometimes, that are silly. But we are learning together. Let them know, gently, that it didn't help. A friendly text message the next day. Another letter. An email. A phone call. Non-confrontational. I normally let them know *not in person.* Just because it feels less awkward and less like I'm putting them on the spot. It gives them a chance to think about what I am saying without feeling attacked or like they need to come up with the right thing to say in response RIGHT NOW. Most people in your life will not be trying to hurt you. Give them grace.

    Unless it becomes apparent that they aren't trying. Then the grace is gone. In recovery, I have loosened my grip on certain friendships. There was no BIG FIGHT or DRAMA or anything. I just slowly stopped reaching out as much.

Because those people listened when I told them I had an eating disorder; listened when I told them that diet and food talk was triggering to me; listened when I told them how unwell I had been and how it was a mental illness that I may always be battling...and *still* chose to talk diet and food and body around me. So I loosened my grip. Instead, I filled my time with other friends. The ones who listened. The ones who chose to try.

2. **Develop a bank of non-confrontational phrases** that you can say when other people *do* mention triggering topics.

    - *I have struggled with an eating disorder. I would appreciate it if you would avoid talking about food, weight or exercise around me.*
    - *I am working on my relationship with food and body image at the moment and it would be good for me if we could avoid talking about those things.*
    - *I know you are talking about food in relation to yourself, but I find all diet talk quite difficult. Could we avoid the topic altogether please?*

There is no need to say sorry. You shouldn't have to apologise for setting healthy boundaries. Anyone worth their salt will not get offended by these boundaries. In fact, it may just spark them to consider their words and actions around other people more.

3. **Take active steps to not be triggered by people you can't avoid**. Sometimes, the people around us are not people that we can choose so easily. We can choose our friends, and leave friends behind who persistently ignore our boundaries. But family members? That's trickier. It is quite likely you have family members who are also victims of diet culture. A grandma who has dieted her whole life. A mother who is always on a fad diet plan. A father who thinks that keto is the WAY. Older family members may be more set in their ways and more resistant to change because they have lived like this for so long. They may also struggle to understand that eating disorders are *mental illnesses* because there was a distinct lack of education or conversation about mental illness when they were growing up. So be prepared that the understanding may NOT come and the option to AVOID IT ALTOGETHER may not be there.

Lob them a copy of this book, first. It might help. But in these circumstances, I found that once I had *tried* to educate them and *tried* to explain it to them and it was still not working, I had to take some key steps to safeguard myself. I set some clear boundaries.

- If any of these people commented on MY body, exercise or food choices in ANY way (negative or positive), I would leave.
- Once it became apparent that the problem wasn't going to resolve, I would NOT attend events or see these individuals when EATING was involved. I would meet them for a walk in the park, or for a cup of coffee, or I would chat to them on the phone. But I would not go for dinner with them.
- Whenever I saw them and they *did* make comments about food, diet or body image (related to themselves or to me or to others), I developed a little mantra to chant to myself in my head. **Well that's how you want to live your life. That's not how I want to live my life.** Over and over again. **That's not how I want to live my life. What a sad little life!**

BODY IMAGE

Body image is one of the hardest topics for me to give advice on because I still struggle with my body image. **Most days, I do not like my body. But then again, I never have.** There is a lot of pressure in today's society to sit in one of three camps: either to be a gym rat with a perfectly sculpted body and love your body because it is gorgeous; to be on a diet or plan to actively change your body so that you CAN love it; or be an advocate for BODY POSITIVITY and love your body NO MATTER WHAT and find yourself gorgeous NO MATTER WHAT.

Listen. It's okay if you don't sit in any of those camps. It's okay if you do not like your body. It's okay if you do not like how you look. The thing is…when we place any kind of focus on how we look, that's TOO MUCH. I found that, instead of trying to love my body, it was easier to just…stop thinking about it as something to look at based on size and shape.

1. **I stopped looking at myself all the time. This involved a two pronged plan of action: I stopped trying to dress a certain way (so that the mirror became less "essential") and I decided to track and deliberately reduce the number of times I looked at myself.**

    Previously, I had always tried to pick clothes and outfits that would make me look as small as possible. In order to do this, I ***had*** to spend a long time trying on clothes and observing how they looked at lots of different angles. I decided that I wasn't going to do this anymore. Instead, I was going to wear *whatever I wanted*. For me, that turned out to be brightly coloured and ostentatiously patterned leggings; big pastel hoodies; funny jumpers; quirky earrings; and dungarees. Some of these clothes made me look bigger. Some made me look smaller. *Nobody ever came up to me, though, and said: you look bigger in those dungarees than you did in your leggings.* **If they had, they really would NOT have been someone I ever chose to see again!** Instead, people started to say: I love that top, it's so cool; I love your fashion sense; you always look so cosy and comfy; where did you get that jumper from? People never asked me that when I was dressing to look small: probably because, no matter what I wore, I looked *wildly uncomfortable* in my tight clothing with my stomach sucked in 24/7.

Having decided to stop trying to dress to look small helped with this: when I tried on clothes, I was just doing it to see if they were comfortable. I didn't, therefore, need to spend a long time looking in the mirror every time I got dressed. **One of the most useful things I did was make sure that there were no mirrors in my house where I could look at my whole body at once.** I propped my long mirror on the floor in the corner where I could only see myself if I was sitting down. This meant I could check patterns and colours together, and do my hair and jewellery, but being sat down meant that I wasn't spending any time fixating on my abdominal area and how it looked.

It can be hard to go from being someone who looks at their body a hundred times an hour to someone who never does. *It sounds really silly but I decided that I would wean myself off it, like an addict.* I reasoned that it was just a *habit* and that I could break the habit by reducing the amount I did it. I told myself that I could look at my body 20 times an hour. That sounds like a lot but, trust me, compared to where it started, it was not. I decided to track it on my phone, using a habit tracker app. Everytime I did it, I had to tick a box. I found that I started to delay the checks every hour because I ran out very quickly at first. This meant that I was going for longer and longer stretches of time without looking at myself. THe longer I went without looking, the less I felt the urge to do it. The inconvenience of counting and logging also got on my nerves and made me want to do it less.

It also made me *realise* how much time I had *wasted* just…looking at myself. I had never actively considered it before and when I did…it was a massive motivator to stop. **I don't want to be someone who spends fifteen minutes of every hour looking in the mirror.** Think of all the friends I could text in that time. All the cups of tea I could have. All the chapters in the books I *never have time to read* that I could read. All the unwashed dishes I could wash. The unhoovered floors I could hoover.

2. **I spent dedicated time changing my social media exposure.** Yes, we should reduce our screen time. Yes, we should stop looking at other people's lives on social media. Yes, we should remember that social media is fake. But, let's be real. I'm addicted to my phone. I use it more than I should. It's something I am working on but whilst I *do* work on it, I needed to create a safe space. I went through my social media and I saved all photos and memories that were important to me. Then, I deleted the accounts and made new ones.

That might sound extreme but I didn't want to have to sit through hours and hours and hours of finding all of the toxic accounts I had followed when I was unwell. I didn't want to look at them all over again and try and decide which were safe and which weren't. It was easier to have a clean slate. If you are particularly attached to your feeds, or have far too many photos to go back and save, you could ask someone you love to go through and unfollow any troubling accounts for you. Or, you could set aside an hour every day to do it gradually. But you need to *commit* to it. It needs to be an *activity:* the SOCIAL MEDIA CLEANSE. **And I mean everything: the gym accounts; the quasi recovery accounts; the "healthy lifestyle" accounts; the high protein foodie accounts, the thin and pretty girls who claim they eat intuitively but make all of their baked goods from oat flour.** *Then, I followed my friends, my family, and influencers who lived the kind of life that I wanted to live.* That is: **influencers who moved their bodies in line with what felt good; and who ate what they wanted, when they wanted; and who dressed similarly to me; and who had similar hobbies and interests to me**. If any of them started to waver and mentioned going on a "reset" or saying they felt they needed to "get healthier" I would simply unfollow them. In doing this, I was able to curate a feed full of different people of all different shapes, sizes and appearances. Because that is what happens when you live the life you want: you settle into a body that looks like *your* body and not like anyone else's.

It was remarkable how much *less* I thought about my body and what I looked like when I wasn't constantly bombarding my brain with images of people in small or toned bodies and pictures of "healthy" or diet food. Well. Maybe not so remarkable. Maybe quite obvious. Either way, it was glorious.

3. **I actively decided to value my body for what it could do, how it felt and the life it allowed me to live.** It has to be an active decision, at first. You have to remind yourself, over and over and over. Don't be hard on yourself. You spent

years being told that your body's appearance was the most important thing about it. *You spent years thinking that if you were smaller, you were better.*

But remind yourself of what your body *couldn't do* when you were starving it. Remind yourself of how your body *felt* when you were not nourishing it properly. Remind yourself of the life you *lived - or didn't -* when you were trying to live in a smaller body. Now what can you do? Whatever you want. You can carry your shopping up the stairs easily, you can hike up a hill with friends, you can get out of bed without feeling faint. You can run if you want to. Or lie in bed all day. You can do a handstand. Now how do you feel? Strong. Energetic. Not freezing cold. Not achey. Like your bones might *not* be disintegrating. Powerful. Alive. Happier. What life can you lead? One where you go to work and do well. You see family and friends and actually have fun. You can go on spontaneous trips. Date. Focus. Have fun. Laugh. Cry. Live.

It sounds impossible but the further I walked down this path, the better things got. **My desire to look at myself all the time reduced as I stopped trying to be smaller and started trying to live.** Being surrounded on social media by people who were happy and thriving in bodies of all sizes; dressing how I wanted to dress; actively choosing not to spend hours gazing into a mirror; focussing on my body as something OTHER than an object to look at…slowly, but surely, I stopped *caring*. If I stopped to think about it, I *did* still dislike my body. I do still dislike my body. But I don't think about it anymore. Because I'm too busy liking my life. And I don't *think* about it as much because I am no longer surrounded by those images of smaller people, and I'm no longer looking at myself as I try to look smaller, and I'm no longer placing value on being smaller.

EXTREME HUNGER

Hunger. For people with eating disorders, hunger is ALREADY the worst thing in the world. I am sure that most of us have, at some point, wished that we would just *never get hungry*. Envied the people who would claim that they just went all day and forgot to eat. FORGOT??? How? During my eating disorder, I did *everything* within my power to suppress my appetite. I tried it all. Volume eating. Drinking endless fluids. Appetite suppressant pills. Eating tiny amounts regularly, trying OMAD instead, intermittent fasting. You name it. I tried it. And I was still hungry. But I learnt to ignore it. My body adjusted to it. It became a dull ache rather than a screaming siren. Just part of me. Something that was always there.

So then when I committed to recovery and started to eat more...and the hunger started...it INSTANTLY made me want to relapse. **In fact, hunger made me relapse more times than I can count over the ten years of my illness.** I would get RAVENOUS. And eat everything in sight. And then I would panic about weight gain. And restrict. Or compensate. I would tell myself: the *less* you eat, the *less* hungry you are. The *less* you eat, the *more manageable the hunger is*. But ask yourself why that is. It's not a good thing. Your body has literally realised that you are just going to IGNORE the hunger signals so it doesn't bother sending them anymore. That's not good. You're starving yourself and malnourishing yourself and mistreating yourself and your body is so used to it that it just...stops.

But when you commit to recovery and start to eat and eat and eat, your body starts to wake up again. It starts to see that, sometimes, when it sends a hunger signal...you listen. And so the hunger...it doesn't just HIT...it CRASHES INTO YOU WITH THE FORCE OF A TANK. How do you avoid the urges to relapse when this extreme hunger hits? How do you stop it from derailing you?

It's actually simple. You eat.

Ha. Solved it. Cured your eating disorder. No. But really. This is going to be the hardest thing. This is going to take everything you have in you. But you need to do it right. You need to eat.

Here is how I did it.

1. **Understand it.** As I always say: knowledge is power. So RESEARCH extreme hunger. There are two camps: those who believe in extreme hunger and those who don't. I don't think it really matters either way: the main point is that you get REALLY REALLY HUNGRY when you are in eating disorder recovery. **It doesn't matter if this is "extreme hunger" or NOT. It's hunger either way. And it has a logical explanation.**

    Let's logic this one out. Your body needs a certain amount of energy to get through the day. This is the minimum amount of energy you need to live, survive and thrive. You have, however, been depriving your body of some of this energy for a while. You OWE your body a certain amount of energy, right? **But it's not that simple: you don't just owe it the amount that you deprived it of.** Because over time, your body has become malnourished and weak as a result of not having the energy it needs. It has been eating itself. Your organs have been getting weaker, your muscles have been wasting, your heart has been struggling.

Your body and brain has been trying to do everything you are asking it to do with *less* energy than it needs to do that.

You owe your body the energy that you didn't give it AND interest. The interest is necessary to help you HEAL THE DAMAGE THAT HAS BEEN CAUSED. If you just eat *a little bit more* to *repay the debt,* you aren't going to get anywhere. You need to eat enough to repay what you owe AND to fix the damage. But how do you know how much damage has been caused? You don't. So how do you know how much you need to eat to heal it? You don't. Your body does, though. And that's why the hunger comes. Your body is telling you: more. I am still healing. I need more energy to heal.

It can feel extreme, but it isn't. It's actually an entirely logical response. Your body has been starving, and it has suffered. And now it sees that food is available again which means that it can begin to heal. It is, in fact, perfectly reasonable that your body would therefore say YES. FEED ME. NOURISH ME SO I CAN HEAL NOW. Do you know what *is* extreme? Starving yourself. Undernourishment. Over Exercising. Your eating disorder. Eating disorders are extreme. Your body asking for the food it needs to heal and repair from an eating disorder is NOT extreme.

You might wonder why you can't just do it slowly. Why can't you just eat a little bit more, here and there, slowly? Because your body doesn't trust you. Again, reasonable.

Imagine you have a friend and you have been borrowing money off your friend every week. Not a big amount, really: just a few pounds a week. But over the years, it has added up. You owe your friend thousands and thousands of pounds. Your friendship is in ruins, too, because the amount of money you owe has made the trust begin to break down. Your friend is tired of you. They don't trust you. And then, you win the lottery. Suddenly, there is money everywhere. You are RICH. So much money. You can spend what you like. You can do what you like. Your friend calls you up and they ask for their money back. But they don't want it back in weekly payments, a few pounds a week, like you borrowed it. No. Of course they don't. They don't trust you: they have seen how bad you are with money. They do not trust that you will have that money for very long. So they want you to give them ALL of the money back RIGHT NOW just in case it goes away again.

That's what's going on with your body and your hunger. **Your body doesn't trust that the food is always going to be there, because you have spent years showing it that food will be there…and then it will be taken away again.** You have taught your body that food is NOT readily available. So when there IS food around, your body wants it ALL right now so that it can try and do as much healing as possible before the food goes away again.

So…eat. When you are hungry, eat. Your body will use the extra energy to heal. And as it does, and as you become closer and closer to being healed, the hunger will become less intense. Your body will ask you for what it needs. As it needs less energy to heal, it will ask for less food.

It can be hard not to panic. But remind yourself: you owe your body a lot of energy. *It needs energy to get through the day, energy to repay what you deprived it of, and energy to fix the damage you caused.* That's a lot, right? That's why you're so hungry! It's not extreme at all. It's rather normal.

2. **Make sure you are actually eating enough.** You might think you are. A very common thing I have seen online, and in myself, was that the extreme hunger wouldn't hit until the EVENING. It would be okay during the day. I would float along, eating my meals and snacks with a *normal* level of hunger. **Then, in the evening, it would be INSATIABLE.** I would become a monster. I would be shaky and irritable and SO HUNGRY that I could have eaten an entire box of stale crackers if that was all that was there. I will not comment on how I know this information. I would eat and eat and eat, so quickly that it felt like nothing was even touching the sides.

Every evening.

And then I asked myself: *why* does this only happen at night? I tried a little experiment. I decided to eat more earlier in the day. Instead of just having cereal and toast for breakfast, I started to have porridge with nut butter, fruit and yoghurt. Or pancakes. Or eggs and toast and fruit and yoghurt. Instead of just having a cereal bar for a snack, I started to have a smoothie or a sandwich or toast and nut butter and fruit. Instead of just having a sandwich for lunch, I started to have a sandwich and a chocolate bar and a bag of crisps. Or a cooked meal.

Slowly, the more I ate during the day, the less and less frequent my evening ravenous hunger became. I realised that it was probably that I just wasn't getting ENOUGH throughout the day for everything. Sure, I was giving myself enough food to get through the day and maybe do a *little bit* of healing but, <u>by the evening, my body was realising that it still had LOADS of healing left to do and panicking.</u> Why? **Because it wasn't sure, of course, that there would be enough food around the next day**. By eating more earlier in the day, it meant that my body was getting enough energy to live AND heal during the day, rather than having to wait until the end of the day when it was already tired and worn out.

The second important thing is making sure that you are actually eating enough of the *right* stuff. This might apply to you if you are CONFUSED about why you are getting extreme hunger because you are ALREADY EATING LOTS. **You may know that you are eating above and beyond your meal plan, or energy goals. You may know that you are eating far above whatever "energy limit" your body needs. So why are you still hungry, if you are eating enough?** But are you eating enough of WHAT YOU NEED? Remember: there are three macronutrients for a reason. Your body needs each one for DIFFERENT things. So if you are eating 7 million carbohydrates, or 7 million proteins, but 0 fats…your body will still ask you for food. Because it's still missing the thing it needs.

Imagine you are babysitting a child. You give the child some paint and send it off to be quiet in a corner. The child comes over and asks you for some red and blue paint. You give the child some red paint. They go away and do some painting. They come back and ask for blue paint. You give them more red paint. They go away. But then they come back. They keep coming back. They need BLUE paint for the sky. Giving them more red paint won't help. Giving them green paint won't help. The child is going to keep coming back, getting louder and more frustrated and more insistent, until you give them the COLOUR they need.

Early in recovery, many of us get better at eating protein. We can rationalise that the most easily. Carbohydrates tend to come next. And then many of us get stuck on *fat*. Even with all the logic in the world, we know that it is the most energy dense and we are SO WORRIED that fat will make us fat. But. In the evenings, when your cravings start, what do you tend to be reaching for? Eggs and chicken? Sweet potatoes and quinoa? Or…chocolate? Biscuits? Peanut butter? Listen to what your body asks for you when you feel "extreme" hunger. **Is it asking you for things from a food group that you are potentially not eating enough from?** Remind yourself of the reasons why your body needs each thing. It may, for example, be asking you for more fat because it needs more fat to help you absorb certain vitamins. It may be asking you for more fat because it needs more fat for hormonal balance. Listen to it.

Or, better yet, pre-empt the need to listen to it in the evening by eating a balanced diet throughout the day. Eat your proteins, carbohydrates and fats *throughout* the day. At the end of the day, then, your body will not need to panic and think *I haven't got enough fat for XYZ process yet* and DEMAND IT in that extreme way that freaks you out so much.

As soon as I started eating MORE throughout the day - more food and more of each food group - I found that the extreme hunger cravings reduced and all but vanished.

3. **Remind yourself of the life you want to live.** This is important because it relates to the last sentence above. I found that the extreme hunger cravings ***all but vanished.*** All but. Sometimes, they were back. Why? Sometimes, I had wobbly days. I woke up and skipped breakfast. Or, I decided that I didn't need to snack between meals and should just have three meals. Or, I felt hungry but knew I was eating in an hour, so ignored it. Sometimes, it was accidental. Sometimes, I was just busier than normal and didn't have time to eat. But. Whenever I didn't eat enough food during the day, the extreme hunger would come BACK. And if I ignored it, it would be there the NEXT DAY TOO.

Ask yourself: do you want to live a life where you are in a constant cycle of not eating enough and then being PLAGUED by INTENSE HUNGER? Or do you want to live a life where your body trusts you, and has enough of an energy reserve, that you feel NORMAL LEVELS of hunger and you don't need to overthink it anymore? <u>Do you want to spend all of your time worrying about being hungry? And swinging between dulling down and triggering the hunger over and over again? Or do you want to…be free? Do you want to eat enough food and feel normal, manageable amounts of hunger?</u>

I ask myself this every time I get an urge to relapse. I remind myself that if I relapse, the extreme hunger won't get better. Sure, I may be able to shut it up for a while. But think logically. **Relapse is just causing MORE damage to my body. Relapse is just INCREASING THE AMOUNT OF ENERGY I OWE. Relapse is just ensuring that my extreme hunger will come back again, and making it likely that it will come back WORSE because I will have more damage and more debt to repay.**

It's rough and difficult and horrible when you're there. But surely the promise of a life where extreme hunger is no longer a constant threat on the horizon is worth getting through it?

DIGESTIVE ISSUES

Hand in hand with extreme hunger in terms of TRIGGERING THINGS THAT HAPPEN IN RECOVERY, we've got DIGESTIVE ISSUES. **Now. This is important: SEE A DOCTOR. It doesn't have to be an eating disorders doctor. Just your GP. You don't need to get too specific if you don't want to. But. Your digestive system is unique to you. There could be something going on with it that *isn't* related to your eating disorder and if you only follow random advice from people who are DISTINCTLY NOT MEDICAL PROFESSIONALS you could risk something else not being picked up.**

That being said. In recovery, you are likely to convince yourself that you are intolerant to everything: gluten, lactose, fat. Food. Why? *Your body is going to act like it is intolerant to everything.* Why? Because it has forgotten what to do with food. For too long, you have not given your body enough food. Or you have given it too much at once. Or you have given it the same things over and over again and deprived it of variety. Or you have used laxatives or compensation to get rid of the food. In short, your body no longer knows how to efficiently and effectively digest regular food. So when you first start eating again, you ARE going to be uncomfortable. Sorry. You ARE going to bloat.

1. **Understand what is going on.** As usual, KNOWLEDGE IS POWER. If we understand *why* the digestive issues and bloating are happening, we can fight the eating disorder urges that tell us WE DIDN'T HAVE THESE PROBLEMS WHEN WE WERE ENGAGING IN OUR EATING DISORDER.

   First. The food is sat there. Not digesting. It's not digesting because your body isn't sure what you want it to do with the food. You've spent a long time *not* wanting it to digest food. So now you want it to, it's understandably confused. It got used to you never putting anything in, or getting rid of the food yourself. It just needs a bit of time, therefore, to realise that you want it to digest things more quickly now. Your digestive system slows down when you are not eating enough. **This is actually a clever survival mechanism: digestion takes a LOT of energy and when you aren't getting much energy, your body slows down anything that isn't vital for IMMEDIATE SURVIVAL (like breathing and your**

heart beating). It also wants the food to stay in your stomach for as long as possible because it thinks that there is an absence of food. It doesn't know when food will next be available as it isn't used to food being there regularly. So, if it holds on to what it *does* have for as long as possible, that's going to help survival too. *The solution to this is uncomfortable: you need to keep eating, even with the undigested food.*

As you put more in, your body will realise that it is okay to digest what is already in there. And the more you start to eat, regularly, consistently and often, your body will start to realise that food *is* readily available again and it can digest and use the energy NOW rather than hanging on to it. That should help ease the bloating from the undigested food and the constipation. **Your body is also likely only used to digesting a few safe foods.** This will mean that when you start eating a wider range of food, it will need some time to figure out how to digest these and to develop the digestive enzymes it needs for this. The only way it can do this, though, is if you *keep* going through the discomfort. If you stop, your body will never learn to adjust.

Next, there is likely to be a hell of a lot of water retention around your stomach area. You are likely to look very bloated, and your skin may be stretched and tight. This is a good thing. When you sprain your ankle, what happens? It swells up instantly. Why? Water retention. **Water helps with healing as it allows all of the bad stuff to move OUT as old, damaged cells are removed and replaced with new, healthy ones.** Your digestive system has undergone a lot of damage. It needs to heal. So the water retention is a vehicle for this healing: the water is a good thing as it means your digestive system can start to heal. The solution to this is uncomfortable: you need to keep eating, even with the full, bloated, tight feeling. Because the FOOD is the key to the healing. You need to get those nutrients in, so that your body can use the energy to heal. If you are not eating enough, your body won't be able to use energy for healing: remember, it is just trying to survive as efficiently as possible. **It will use energy on LIVING first (breathing, heart beating, walking around, movement) and HEALING next: so you need to make sure you are eating enough. You're eating for two, baby!**

2. **Make sure you are actually eating enough.** This is the exact same piece of advice that I gave for extreme hunger as well, right down to the very basic premise: eat larger meals regularly throughout the day and ensure that you are eating enough of each of the food groups.

Again, saving up your calories until the evening and eating a massive meal is not going to help you here. **For one thing your water retention isn't going to go away because your body HASN'T spent the whole day healing.** It's been using the energy from the small amounts of food you have been giving it to live and get through the day. So, by the evening, it hasn't done much healing and that may be why you're still JUST AS BLOATED as you were at the beginning. <u>If you were spreading your calories out throughout the day and eating a good amount at each meal, your body would have enough energy to LIVE and to HEAL and therefore the edema has more chance of dissipating sooner.</u>

Next. **When you save your food up until the end of the day, you overload your digestive system.** It has got used to digesting small amounts through the day, so it probably isn't operating at full steam ahead, right? And then you suddenly decide to DUMP a whole load of food in…and let's be honest, most of it is probably HIGH FIBRE HARD TO DIGEST VEGETABLES…what happens? The food sits there uncomfortably because your body has no idea what to do with it. *And so, you spend every evening bloated and puffy: bloated from your undigested food, puffy from the water retention that isn't going away because you still aren't giving your body a fair shot at healing.*

Imagine you have lit a fire. It's nearly burnt out at the start of the day, and you keep adding coal to it, two tiny pieces at a time. It's enough to keep the embers glowing but not enough to get the fire going. Still, you keep going: a couple of small pieces of coal at a time. Then, at the end of the day, you realise you need *more energy* to get the fire going so you get a WHOLE LOAD OF COAL and DUMP IT ON THE FIRE. But the fire has got used to idling along all day, slowly burning the coal and conserving its energy. It doesn't have enough energy in it NOW to BURN ALL THAT COAL and so it…goes out. It's overloaded. It cannot burn the coal. That's what happens to your digestive system, right? You have been slowly dripping energy in all day, so it has been going slowly, then you suddenly SHOVE A BUNCH IN and it's not ready and raring to process it so for a while it just…doesn't.

Solve the problem by eating bigger meals throughout the day. Then <u>your digestive system is awake and ready to go</u>, your <u>body is regularly extracting enough nutrients from your food to begin the healing process</u> and, whilst you will still have water retention and bloating at the end of the day as this is *normal*, it will likely be far reduced in comparison.

Each of the food groups is vital too. Early on in recovery, when your digestive system is sluggish and slow, **you need to be giving it quicker digesting foods.** Vegetables are incredibly high in fibre: eating a mixing bowl of vegetables is not going to help you. Instead, reduce these and eat more simple carbohydrates as these digest quicker: bread, pasta, rice, biscuits, cake. These foods will get you the energy you need to heal your digestive system QUICKLY because they will digest MORE QUICKLY. *That means that if you want to get back to eating mounds of vegetables again, you'll be able to do this quicker as your digestion will pick up quicker.* You may well find that you don't *want* that though, and that you want to eat a BALANCE OF EVERYTHING: and that's healing. Fats are also vital for helping certain vitamins to be absorbed - fat soluble ones. Eating a mixture of carbohydrates, fats and proteins will therefore help your digestive system wake back up and learn how to digest all of the things it needs to digest once again so that you can thrive and be a healthy little bean.

3. **Make yourself comfortable.** It's going to happen, okay? The digestive issues are going to suck. You will bloat. You will be uncomfortably full. Your eating disorder will take this as evidence that recovery doesn't work and try and persuade you to go back to it. But remember: relapsing will not solve your digestive issues. Relapsing will just PAUSE them whilst simultaneously creating more damage so that when you do try to recover again, it will be worse and take even longer. SO: accept that you need to go through it and make yourself as comfortable as you can during the process.

    My steps for this included:

    a. Comfortable clothes. I started to wear men's jogging bottoms and hoodies as they were loose, baggy and covered my cute bloated belly up nicely.
    b. I didn't look in the mirror. What was the point looking at my bloated stomach? I *knew* why it was bloated. I *knew* my stomach wasn't going to look like that forever. I *knew* it was part of recovery. So why look at it if it would just upset me? So I stopped.
    c. Peppermint tea. Hot tea in general, but peppermint tea works some magic.
    d. Hot water bottles or an electric blanket wrapped around my achy bloated stomach.
    e. Gentle (VERY GENTLE, SO GENTLE YOU DO NOT BREAK A SWEAT OR EVEN TREMBLE ONCE) stretching: cat/cow, child's pose and downward dog helped a lot.
    f. Probiotics *recommended by a dietician* and NOT PURCHASED OFF SOME RANDOM WEBSITE ONLINE USING AN INFLUENCER'S CODE
    g. Eating gut friendly fermented foods such as sauerkraut, kimchi and kefir.

All of the above tips are very helpful but it doesn't matter if you don't do ANY of them. The one thing that is key and the one thing you MUST do if you want to fix your digestive is **EAT REGULARLY.** The hardest thing for someone recovering from an eating disorder, of course, but the stunningly simple truth: regular consumption of nourishing food is what your body needs to heal.

I had been unwell for over ten years. I had done things to my digestive system that felt largely unforgivable. Everytime I tried to recover, food sat in my stomach for days. I bloated like a whale. I was swollen and in pain. I believed every time this happened that I was unable to fix my digestive system. I believed that I had ruined it forever. And so I decided that recovery was not worth it for me. And so I relapsed. The last time was different. I had reached my tipping point. And that meant I no longer cared. Sure, I may have ruined my digestive system. Sure I may be bloated and full of undigested food FOREVER. But at least I was full. At least I had food. At least I was beginning to have energy. <u>I rationalised that I would rather live a life where I was bloated and uncomfortable from eating than one where I was weak, dying, isolated, sad and uncomfortable from *not eating*.</u> So I committed. I ate regularly. I ate similar amounts throughout the day and stopped saving up all my food until the end of the day. I reduced my vegetable consumption and increased my simple carbohydrates.

It took months. Months. Nearly a year. But slowly, slowly, my body began to bounce back. Bodies are resilient. T***hey want to survive.*** OF COURSE IT TOOK AGES for my body to start to heal. I had spent YEARS destroying it. I had spent YEARS not allowing it to digest food properly. But still. It started to fight back. And six months into recovery, I still had some bloating sometimes but the water retention was gone. The bloating was so reduced that, to the naked eye, you wouldn't see it: I no longer looked six months pregnant with whale twins. Instead, I looked like someone whose body was able to digest food in a normal way.

SECTION FOUR: YOUR BENDING MENDING AND NEVER-ENDING ERA

Now you've read the book, I hope that I have convinced you of one thing: recovery was not easy for me. It was not easy at all. It was incredibly hard and involved FAR TOO MUCH thinking and reframing and trying over and over again. It was something that I worked at every single second of every single day. It is something that I still work on every single day, but now there are seconds where I live in between.

I know one thing for sure, though: it took me this long to get here before because I never did the things in this book. If I could go back and tell myself, a decade ago, that I would waste ten years of my life, I would do all of the things in this book IMMEDIATELY.

You might choose not to believe me. You might think it's different for you. But if you don't decide to recover NOW or NEXT WEEK or NEXT MONTH…you'll still be here in a decade too. You need to decide. You need to decide that you are going to do all of this hard and horrible and impossible stuff. You need to decide every day that you are going to do it. You need to do it all, over and over and over and over and over.

So here we are: this is your bending era and your never-ending era.

See you on the other side.

I'll leave you with my final thought. My mantra: *I want to be a high energy person living a high energy life full of pizzazz and sparkle. I want that for you, too.*

Bog off, eating disorder.

Printed in Great Britain
by Amazon